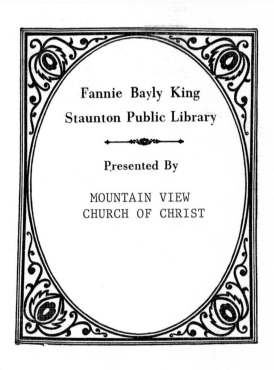

A COMMENTARY

ON THE

New Testament Epistles

BY

DAVID LIPSCOMB

EDITED, WITH ADDITIONAL NOTES,

BY

J. W. SHEPHERD

VOLUME II

First Corinthians

GOSPEL ADVOCATE COMPANY
Nashville, Tenn.
1984

Complete Set ISBN 0-89225-000-3
This Volume ISBN 0-89225-007-0

PREFACE

The hearty reception given to the Commentary on the Epistle to the Romans is very encouraging, and it is hoped that this volume will receive a like reception. That the instruction given in this series of commentaries is needed is apparent to all who are informed of the conditions now facing the Lord's work in every place; for in them is set forth in no uncertain terms the principles which gave David Lipscomb such a wide influence in his battle against every form of error, during the half century of his editorial work.

In this volume there is no change from that on Romans. The same general plan is followed throughout.

Each volume is complete within itself. When the same subject is discussed in different epistles it is treated as though it was not mentioned elsewhere. This will be quite an advantage to those using the book, and I think will be appreciated.

Just here I must acknowledge the very valuable assistance rendered by the congregation at Lincoln Park, Detroit, Michigan, which furnished us an apartment in which to live and supplied us with the necessaries of life for about four years, while I was engaged in preparing these volumes. It is true that I assisted them in various ways in the Lord's work, but their desire was to have part in the work in which I was engaged. For their valuable assistance I am truly thankful, for had it not been for their interest in the work I could not have made the progress I have.

Here I also acknowledge the part Mrs. Shepherd has done in the work. During all the years while this work has been occupying my mind she has had, in a large measure, the burden to bear. She has lived a lonely life, because I have been so busily engaged that I could not be with her much. But for the sake of the good the work will be in the Lord's service, she willingly made the sacrifice. For her patience, faithfulness, and loving devotion to the Lord's work I am deeply grateful, for without her willing cooperation, together with that of the Lincoln Park church, I could not have accomplished this work.

It is hoped that the volume on Second Corinthians and Galatians will be ready for the press within a short time.

This book will do good only in proportion to the number of readers and the disposition to receive correction, instruction, consolation, and encouragement from one of God's noblest servants; and I send it forth with an earnest prayer that it may tend to the promotion of pure and undefiled religion, help extend the knowledge of God, and be instrumental in aiding the glorious work of converting and edifying all who seek a habitation in "the city which hath the foundations, whose builder and maker is God."

J. W. SHEPHERD.

Nashville, Tennessee, November 20, 1934.

CONTENTS

SECTION THREE

SECTION FOUR

SECTION FIVE

SECTION SIX

SECTION SEVEN

SECTION EIGHT

INTRODUCTION

I. CORINTH

Corinth was built upon the narrow neck of land called the isthmus or "neck of Corinth," that connects the Peloponnesus with the mainland. This gave it the command of the land traffic from north to south, whilst from the two ports on the Ionian and Aegean seas, Cenchreae and Lechaeum, much of the traffic between Asia and the west was brought to its harbors and portage because of the convenience of the water route afforded by the Saronic Gulf on the east of the isthmus and the Gulf of Corinth on the west. The way across the isthmus shortened the route to the west many miles and obviated the perilous voyage around the southern coast of Greece, the terror of the seamen of those days. Arriving at either port, the large vessels transhipped their cargoes across the isthmus for further transport. A road about five miles long was built across the isthmus on which small vessels were often hauled. The value of this shortened trade route is evident from the fact that plans were made in Paul's day to cut a canal through the isthmus. Nero actually began to dig one, but found the undertaking so difficult and expensive that he abandoned it. In A.D. 1893 the work was completed and the two gulfs are now united.

In respect to military strength, Corinth from nature had almost unequaled advantages; and, of these its builders wisely availed themselves. They built it about a mile and a half south of the isthmus, on a rocky eminence about two hundred feet above the sea level. Behind the city stood the magnificent rock known as the citadel of Corinth, and called "Acrocorinthus," about 2,000 feet high. To the west there ran from the city to the Gulf of Corinth a double wall, a mile and a half long, terminating at Lechaeum; while on the east the city was connected with the seaport town of Cenchreae (Rom. 16: 1), on the Saronic Gulf, by a road eight miles in length. Thus fitted as Corinth was to take a distinguished place among the cities of Greece, alike for military and political influence, its rulers early saw by developing its commercial resources it

might easily rise to the wealthiest and most powerful of the
Grecian cities—a distinction of which, indeed, it had given
early promise, about a thousand years before Christ, and
reached some centuries later. Its fortunes, however, fluc-
tuated greatly in the succeeding centuries; and when its liberties were crushed by Philip of Macedon, B.C. 338, Corinth
became subject to the Macedonian kings, who took care to
keep it always strongly garrisoned. The galling yoke was
broken B.C. 196, when Corinth was reunited to the Achean
League; but though nominally free, it became really subject
to its Roman liberators. And when the league was so unwise
as to go to war with Rome, and even to maltreat the Roman
ambassadors at Corinth, the Achean troops were easily de-
feated; and the Romans under Mummius their commander,
B.C. 146, revenged the insult with great barbarity—killing all
the males, selling into slavery the women and children, strip-
ping the city of its immense wealth, and carrying off its innu-
merable works of art. Having done this, the conquerors laid
the city in ashes.

After lying in ruins exactly 100 years, Julius Caesar, B.C.
46, in pursuance of a scheme to create an empire in the prov-
inces that might balance the power of Rome, rebuilt and peopled it with a Roman colony, to be peopled, in the first in-
stance, by his own veterans and freedmen. By them the city
was rebuilt, and grew to be a city of six hundred thousand inhabitants. Greek merchants poured into it to make it their
home, while Jews were attracted to it from its advantages for
business and its proximity to their native land. In fact,
though it was constituted into a Roman colony, it became the
capital of the Roman province of Achaia, and was governed
by a proconsul residing at Corinth. (Acts 18: 12.) The Romans themselves were outnumbered by their Greek and Jewish fellow citizens.

Corinth now became more wealthy than ever, its temples
and civic buildings glittered as of old, and the same luxury
and vice, for which it had become so infamous, reappeared
and flourished in all their ancient vigor. Even religion gave
sanction to immorality by its cult of sexual indulgence.

Strabo tells us that in the temple of Venus there were more than a thousand harlots, the slaves of the temple, who, in honor of the goddess, prostrated themselves to all comers for hire, and through these the city was crowded, and became wealthy. Such was Corinth, when, in the year A.D. 52, Paul entered it; and what a sight it must have presented to his eyes! He wrote his epistle to the Romans from Corinth, and it was from her life that he got the description of heathenism which is found in Rom. 1: 21-32. Drunkenness was common and dishonesty notorious.

It would be unfair, however, to leave the impression that business and profligacy were the only characteristics of the city. There were intellectual interests both in art and in philosophy. Her citizens were proud of their mental acuteness; so much so that in their conceit they criticized all men and questioned anything and everything. They loved disputation, but their intellectual activity resulted in nothing of much value. The knowledge of the schools took but little hold upon the earnest realities of life. They dabbled in philosophy. The knowledge that puffeth up was the consequence. Indeed, "the artificiality and flowing rhetoric of the sophists were quite satisfying."

Its population was increased and its character somewhat formed from another circumstance. In the neighborhood of the city the Isthmian games, which attracted so much attention, and which drew so many strangers from different parts of the world, were celebrated. To these games, Paul frequently refers when pressing Christian energy and activity.

II. ORIGIN OF THE CORINTHIAN CHURCH

That the church at Corinth was founded by Paul is abundantly evident. He came to Corinth from Athens on his second missionary journey. He entered the city alone, a total stranger, and penniless. The little means he had brought with him from Macedonia were exhausted, and his attention was turned first to the supply of his daily bread. Possibly by a combination of circumstances he secured most desirable lodgings, and means of livelihood, with "a certain Jew named Aquila, a man of Pontus by race, lately come from Italy, with his wife Priscilla, because Claudius had commanded all the Jews to depart from Rome: and he came unto them; and because he was of the same trade, he abode with them, and they wrought; for by their trade they were tentmakers." (Acts 18: 2, 3.) To be thus under the necessity of laboring as a tentmaker, when his heart was set on evangelizing this proud and opulent city, was anything but encouraging. Of his feelings at this time he says: "I was with you in weakness, and in fear, and in much trembling." (2: 3.) He was keenly sensitive of the weakness of his situation; he feared a failure similar to that of Athens; and he trembled at the thought that the salvation of so many souls was dependent on so weak and feeble an instrumentality.

Whether Aquila and Priscilla were Christians when Paul met them is not stated, but it is not probable that Luke would have called Aquila "a certain Jew," had he been a disciple of Christ; yet nothing is said of their becoming Christians. It is certain, however, if they were not Christians, they soon became such, and Paul found in them truehearted worshipers of God, and formed a personal attachment to them, which lasted to the close of his life, and henceforward they are his earnest fellow workers in the gospel.

The preaching in the synagogue which continued through several Sabbaths seems to have been slower in its effect than usual. Silas and Timothy arrived from Macedonia while he was engaged in this work. Shortly after their arrival, on account of the opposition of the Jews, he found it expedient for him to leave the synagogue. Fortunately, a proselyte was favorably impressed by Paul; and as he had a house which "joined hard to the synagogue," tendered it to Paul for his subsequent meetings. Although Paul left the synagogue in apparent disappointment, he was not without fruits of his labor, for Luke says: "Crispus, the ruler of the synagogue, believed in the Lord with all his house; and many of the Corinthians hearing believed, and were baptized." (Acts 18: 8.) It was much to the credit of Crispus that he became obedient unto the Lord, and at this time when the opposition and blasphemy of the other Jews were so pronounced. He was the kind of material to form the nucleus for a congregation.

Notwithstanding the fact that Paul's success when leaving the synagogue must have been a source of great comfort and encouragement to him, he was far from being relieved, for he says, "I was with you in weakness, and in fear, and in much trembling." (2: 3.) Most likely a part of this distress was due to his failure to save these Jews who were now reviling him, and who, he was sure, would do everything in their power to defeat his efforts to bring them to the obedience of faith. It was at this crisis that the Lord Jesus said to him by a night vision: "Be not afraid, but speak and hold not thy peace: for I am with thee, and no man shall set on thee to harm thee: for I have much people in this city." (Acts 18: 9, 10.) The comfort which this gave was not the assurance of personal safety alone, but the assurance that his labors and sufferings in Corinth would be rewarded by the salvation of many people. Supported by this assurance, Paul continued his labors with renewed zeal and earnestness; great success attended his labors which increased the determination of the Jews to defeat his purpose.

The attempt of the Jews to suppress the preaching, which Paul had been expecting ever since he left the synagogue, came at last, but it came in an unusual form, and with unusual results. The occasion was the coming of Gallio, the new proconsul, who was perhaps unfamiliar with the duties of his office and whose desire for popularity at the beginning of his government might have made him courteous to prosperous Jews, who thought they could with impunity excite a tumult. They rose in a body, seized Paul and dragged him before the proconsul. It was evident that they had presumed on his probable inexperience, and his reputation for mildness; and with all the turbulent clamor of their race, they charged Paul with persuading "men to worship God contrary to the law." (Acts 18: 13.) Though Claudius had expelled the Jews from Rome, their religion was licensed by the State; but the religion of "this man," they urged, though it might pass itself off under the name of Judaism, was not Judaism at all—it was a spurious counterfeit of Judaism. They seemed to have thought, if this violation of the Jewish law could be proved, Paul would become amenable to the criminal law of the Empire; or, perhaps, they hoped, that he would be given up into their hands for punishment.

Their chief speaker was Sosthenes, the successor of Crispus, the ruler of the synagogue. The Greeks were standing around to hear the result, and hating the Jews, were ready to be partisans. At the moment "when Paul was about to open his mouth" to make his defense, Gallio, taking no notice of him, by contemptuous dismissal of the Jews and their charge, stopped the proceedings with the remark: "If indeed it were a matter of wrong or of wicked villany, O ye Jews, reason would that I should bear with you: but if they are questions about words and names and your own law, look to it yourselves; I am not minded to be a judge of these matters." Having thus quashed the case, Gallio ordered his officers to clear the court.

The effect of this proceeding must have produced humiliation and disappointment among the Jews. With the Greeks and other bystanders the result was very different. They were very gratified. They held the forbearance of Gallio as proof that their own religious liberties would be protected under the new administration; and, with the disorderly impulse of a mob which had been kept up to this time in suspense, rushed upon the "ruler of the synagogue, and beat him before the judgment-seat." Meanwhile, Gallio took no notice of the injurious punishment they thus inflicted on the Jews, and with characteristic indifference left Sosthenes to his fate. Thus the accusers were themselves involved in disgrace. Gallio obtained a high popularity among the Greeks, and Paul was enabled to pursue his labors in safety.

Had he been driven away from Corinth, the whole Christian community might have been put in jeopardy. But the result of this onslaught was to give protection to the infant church, with opportunity of safe and continued growth. As for Paul, his credit rose with the disgrace of his persecutors, the most imminent peril was turned into safety and honor; and the assurance communicated in the vision was abundantly fulfilled.

Though bitter enemies had "set on" Paul, no one had harmed him. The Lord was with him, and "much people" turned to the Lord, "and he dwelt there a year and six months, teaching the word of God among them." (Acts 18: 11.) This shows that during that period he was executing chiefly the second part of the commission, "teaching them to observe all things whatsoever I commanded you." (Matt. 28: 20.) From this we can see that, notwithstanding the many disorders which were afterwards found in the Corinthian church, it was probably the best taught church of all the churches thus far planted by Paul. If they had been less fully instructed, what might have been their later condition?

III. OCCASION OF WRITING THE EPISTLE

After Paul's departure from Corinth, events moved rapidly, and far from satisfactorily. The distance from Ephesus by sea was about an eight days' journey, and in the constant travel between the two cities news of what was transpiring must frequently have come to his ears. Members of the household of Chloe are distinctly mentioned as having brought tidings of the contentions that prevailed (1: 11), and there was most likely other information. Paul was so concerned by the information received that he sent Timothy on a mission to them with many commendations (4: 17; 16: 10), although the present epistle reached them first. He had also felt impelled, in a letter (5: 9), which is now lost, to send earnest warnings against companying with fornicators. Moreover, Apollos, after excellent work in Corinth, had returned to Ephesus, and was received as a brother. (3: 5, 6; 16: 12.) Equally welcome were the messengers consisting of Stephanas, Fortunatus, and Achaicus (16: 17), from whom the fullest information could be gained, and who were probably bearers of a letter from the church at Corinth itself (7: 1), requesting advice and direction on a number of points. This letter has not been preserved, but it was evidently the immediate occasion of this epistle, and its tenor is clearly indicated by the nature of Paul's reply. So this epistle treats of a condition fully understood, and, on the whole, of a most distressing situation. The church was divided into factions, and was disturbed by party cries. Some of its members were living openly immoral lives, and discipline was practically in abeyance. Others had quarrels over which they dragged one another into the heathen courts. Great differences existed with regard to marriage and the social relations generally, to food offered to idols, to the behavior of the women in the assemblies, to the Lord's Supper, to the use and value of spiritual gifts, and with regard to the hope of the resurrection. Resisting the impulse to visit them at once "with a rod," he wrote this epistle with the purpose of arousing them to the seriousness of their condition, and delayed his own visit to Corinth till after his visit to Macedonia, so as to leave time for his injunctions and warnings to have their proper effect, and prepare the way for his own coming, after his visit to Macedonia.

IV. PLACE OF WRITING

The place where the epistle was written can be no other than Ephesus, for in closing he says: "But I will tarry at Ephesus until Pentecost; for a great door and effectual is opened unto me." (16: 8, 9.) And again, he sends salutations from the churches of Asia, and likewise from Aquila and Priscilla, who had sailed with Paul from Corinth to settle at Ephesus.

V. TIME OF WRITING

The entire sojourn of Paul at Ephesus continued about three years. (Acs 20: 32.) The thing to settle is, What time of this sojourn did he write the epistle? On this point there are several facts which will enable us to definitely set the date.

(1) Paul says: "I will tarry at Ephesus until Pentecost." (16: 8.)

(2) At the time of writing, Apollos, who had returned from Corinth, was with Paul. (16: 12.) Now Apollos, unto whom Priscilla and Aquila had expounded "the way of God more accurately," shortly after their arrival in that city, and before that of Paul, had gone thence to Achaia, with a letter of commendation to continue the work there begun by Paul, and had exerted a great influence, after which he returned to Ephesus. (Acts 18: 24-28.) This all supposes a considerable time to have elapsed since Paul's arrival at Ephesus, and brings us to an advanced period of his sojourn in that city.

(3) Luke tells us (Acts 19: 8, 10, 21) that after having labored two years and three months at Ephesus he purposed in the spirit to go to Rome. But before proceeding there he felt bound to visit Jerusalem once more, and to offer to the church a solemn testimony of love and fellowship from all the churches founded by him among the Gentiles. He therefore determined to send Timothy and Erastus from Ephesus to make preparations, in Macedonia and Achaia, for the execution of the plan. (Acts 19: 21, 22.) Now this sending of Timothy to Corinth coincides perfectly with that which is twice mentioned in this epistle. (4: 17; 16: 10.) It took place at the time when Paul was composing it, and shortly before leaving Ephesus, for in it he announces the sending of Timothy as an accomplished fact.

(4) The collection for which Timothy was to prepare, and which is expressly mentioned (16: 1, 2; 2 Cor. 8: 1 to 9: 15), can only be that with which Paul closes his ministry in the East, and of which he speaks in Rom. 15: 24, 33; Acts 24: 17. Here is a new indication which again brings us to the same date.

As it is impossible for all these reasons to suppose a date previous to the circumstances mentioned, it is no less so to suppose a later one. In fact, when the epistle was written, Paul was yet freely going whithersoever he chose, but it is a well-known fact that shortly after, when he had delivered the gift of the Gentile churches into the hands of the elders at Jerusalem, he was arrested and thrown into prison, and from that time remained a prisoner for more than four years.

If the sojourn of Paul in Asia, by the time this epistle was written, had continued two years and three months (Acts 19: 8-10), dating from the year 54 when Paul arrived at Ephesus, it was written just before Pentecost, possibly at the time of the Passover of the year 57.

COMMENTARY ON THE FIRST EPISTLE TO THE CORINTHIANS

SECTION ONE

INTRODUCTION
1: 1-9

1. THE APOSTOLIC GREETING
1: 1-3

1 Paul, called *to be* an apostle of Jesus Christ through the will of God,

---

1 **Paul, called to be an apostle of Jesus Christ through the will of God,**—Paul had first preached the gospel at Corinth (Acts 18: 1); had planted the church there, yet his authority as an apostle had been denied, and in this letter he vindicates his claim to be an apostle. He therefore begins the letter with the assertion that he was an apostle and called of Jesus Christ to the apostleship. "Paul, an apostle of Jesus Christ through the will of God," is a simple and literal translation, giving the idea clearly. Jesus called Paul to be an apostle to the Gentiles when he appeared to him on the way to Damascus. Hence, it is said: "Paul, an apostle (not from men, neither through man, but through Jesus Christ, and God the Father, who raised him from the dead)." (Gal. 1: 1.)

and Sosthenes our brother,—Sosthenes is doubtless the same person mentioned in Acts 18: 17, who as ruler of the synagogue was set upon by the Jews. He became a follower of Christ, was persecuted at Corinth, and likely went with Paul when he left the city under persecution, and when Paul wrote this letter to the church at Corinth, Sosthenes joined him in it, probably acting as amanuensis. To this position it is objected that it was he, who, as ruler of the synagogue, had dragged Paul himself before Gallio, the Roman proconsul, and who, when Gallio refused to meddle with the case, as out of his jurisdiction, was set upon and roughly handled by the Jews, even before the judgment seat. (Acts 18: 12-17.) But since the name of Sosthenes occurs nowhere else but in this

and Sosthenes [1]our brother, 2 unto the church of God which is at Corinth,
   [1]Gr. *the brother.*

epistle addressed to the Corinthians as one with whom they were familiar, and since it is often that the most violent opposers of the truth, when once won by it, become, like Paul himself, its most enthusiastic promoters, I can but conclude that the position here taken is correct.

2 **unto the church of God**—The church is a divine name for the disciples of Christ in a city or community. The term church is used in a general and universal sense, also in a specific and local sense. In its universal sense it embraces all the spirits in the universe that obey God as the ruler and the lawgiver. (Heb. 12: 22-29.) In its local sense it embraces all persons in a community who have been called out, separated from the world by the gospel, and who are bound together by a common faith in Jesus Christ. While in the world we can know and approach this church only in its local manifestations. So far as this church is composed of spirits that are invisible, the church is invisible; so far as it is composed of visible men and women, it is a visible body. No visible being can be a part or a member of an invisible church, any more than visible arms and legs can compose an invisible body. If a visible material person is a member of the church, he is a member of the visible local church where he lives. All Christians in the days of the apostles were members of the local churches. They became so by obedience to God. These local churches were bodies distinct and separate, without any organic connection with one another. Each was a distinct body within itself. The members of these local assemblies, under the direction of the Holy Spirit, chose their own overseers and workers. The local congregation was the highest and only manifestation of the church. Each congregation stood on a perfect equality with all others. The elders of the local congregation were the highest "dignitaries" of the church, and they were chief servants and ruled by example rather than by authority.

which is at Corinth,—The members of the church at Corinth had fallen into many sinful habits, yet Paul recognized them as a church of God.

even them that are sanctified in Christ Jesus, called *to be* saints, with all that call upon the name of our Lord Jesus Christ in every place, their *Lord* and

even them that are sanctified in Christ Jesus,—The sanctified are set apart or separated to a sacred service of purpose. It does not mean that they were sinless, or free from temptation from sin; but consecrated to the service of God. All who have entered into Christ, and have obligated themselves to serve him, are said to be sanctified in Christ Jesus regardless of their degree of consecration or perfection of character. There are degrees of sanctification just as there are degrees of Christian knowledge and fidelity to Christ. The growth in sanctification and holiness is to be attained by a constant and persistent study of God's will, and a daily effort to bring oneself into obedience to the same.

The claim that religion in any of its parts is to be obtained otherwise than through learning the word of God and striving faithfully to do the things commanded is a sad mistake that results in the perversion of religion from a faithful, self-denying service to a spasmodic feeling or impulse of excitement. True religion is to be felt and appreciated, not as fleshly excitement or emotion, but as the result of right thinking and doing. It is the abiding consciousness of duty performed to the best of one's ability. This feeling of joy and happiness that thus comes is permanent and enduring. All excitement of the fleshly emotions are short lived and deceptive.

called to be saints,—All who accept the invitation offered in the gospel are the called of Jesus Christ. Saints are sanctified ones, set apart to the service of God.

with all that call upon the name of our Lord Jesus Christ— [To call upon is to invoke his aid. To call upon the name of Jesus Christ our Lord is to invoke his aid as the Christ, the Messiah predicted by the prophets, and as our almighty and sovereign possessor and ruler. It is in that sense that Jesus is Lord. All authority in heaven and on earth was committed unto him (Matt. 28: 18) after he died and rose again that he might be the Lord of the dead and of the living; that is, that he might acquire that peculiar right of possession in his people which arises from his having purchased them with his own blood. (Acts 20: 28.) To call upon the name of Jesus as

ours: 3 Grace to you and peace from God our Father and the Lord Jesus Christ.

Lord is therefore to worship him. It looks to him for that help which God only can give. All Christians, therefore, are the worshipers of Christ. And every sincere worshiper is a true Christian. The phrase expresses not so much an individual act of invocation, as an habitual state of mind and its appropriate expression.]

in every place,—This shows that while the epistle was written directly to, and for the instruction of the church at Corinth, it was also intended for the instruction and use of all who call upon the name of Jesus Christ at all times and in all places. In other words, it was an epistle for universal use.

their Lord and ours:—This means that Jesus is at once the Lord and Savior of all God's children wherever they be.

3 Grace to you and peace from God our Father and the Lord Jesus Christ.—This is a prayer that favor be unto them and peace that God and Christ have and alone can give should be given unto them. This peace nothing can destroy.

2. THANKSGIVINGS ON ACCOUNT OF THEIR SPIRITUAL ADVANTAGES
1: 4-9

4 I thank [2]my God always concerning you, for the grace of God which

[2]Some ancient authorities omit my.

---

4 I thank my God always concerning you, for the grace of God which was given you in Christ Jesus;—He thanked God for the great favor that had been shown them as servants of Christ Jesus. [He congratulates them on the abundant gifts and graces bestowed on them from God, and to express his hope as to their spiritual progress; in order, by a praise calculated to conciliate their good will, to introduce, with less offense, the reproofs which their state rendered is necessary for him to administer, and which he skillfully introduces. There was much to be thankful for, and hopeful about, in the Corinthian church. And on this he first dwells, in order to appeal to their better feelings, and thus place the contrast in stronger relief, and so fix a deep conviction of sin.]

was given you in Christ Jesus; 5 that in everything ye were enriched in him, in all ³utterance and all knowledge; 6 even as the testimony of Christ was confirmed in you: 7 so that ye come behind in no gift; waiting for the reve-

³Gr. *word.*

5 that in everything ye were enriched in him,—In the fourteenth chapter Paul mentions the many gifts bestowed on the church at Corinth, showing that in everything they, as a church of Jesus Christ, had received blessings and favors that spiritually enriched them, or placed the rich gifts of the favors unto which these gifts brought.

in all utterance—The ability to speak the gospel in different tongues.

and all knowledge;—The spiritual gifts that would bestow all knowledge needful for salvation and the power of imparting it to others by the gift of tongues had been freely bestowed on the members of the church at Corinth. These gifts had been so distributed to the members of the church that they would supply the knowledge of God's will to them.

6 even as the testimony of Christ was confirmed in you:— The testimony concerning Jesus was confirmed by the miracles wrought and the gifts bestowed, making sure that the things spoken were from God.

7 so that ye come behind in no gift;—The gifts were so freely bestowed that they fell behind other churches in no gift. "For what is there wherein ye were made inferior to the rest of the churches, except it be that I myself was not a burden to you?" (2 Cor. 12: 13.)

waiting for the revelation of our Lord Jesus Christ;—These gifts were to impart all instruction and knowledge while they waited the coming, or restitution, of the Lord Jesus Christ. It is difficult to determine whether this coming refers to the destruction of Jerusalem, which would be a full confirmation of all that had been said of Christ and the apostles; or whether to "when he shall come to be glorified in his saints, and to be marvelled at in all them that believed . . . in that day." (2 Thess. 1: 10.) [That it has reference to the latter there can be but little doubt, since the Lord promised his anxious disciples when he was about to leave them that he would return, and this promise was renewed by the angel on the

lation of our Lord Jesus Christ; 8 who shall also confirm you unto the end,
that ye be unreprovable in the day of our Lord Jesus Christ. 9 God is faithful, through whom ye were called into the fellowship of his Son Jesus Christ
our Lord.

very day that he ascended into heaven. (Acts 1: 11.) It became the settled hope of Christians that he would return.
(Tit. 2: 12, 13; 2 Pet. 3: 12; Heb. 8: 28.) And the apostle
John, who was present when Jesus ascended, closed the volume of inspiration with the earnest prayer that he would
come quickly. (Rev. 22: 20.) The expectancy of the coming
of the Lord steadied and strengthened the Christian life, and
probably here it is introduced as the motive by which they
were kept from anything that would impoverish their spirituality. This earnest desire and expectation is the greatest
proof of maturity and richness of the Christian life.]

8 **who shall also confirm you unto the end, that ye be unreprovable in the day of our Lord Jesus Christ.**—God would so
confirm them in the truth of what had been taught them that
they would remain steadfast and be blameless when Christ
should come to judge the world. [This would cause them to
hold themselves in readiness for that great day, not knowing
when it might come.]

9 **God is faithful,**—He assures them that God is faithful to do
what he has promised. If they continued steadfast in their
obedience to him, he would preserve them without blame,
through the power he exerts in Christ Jesus.

through whom ye were called into the fellowship—Fellowship with Christ means a partnership with him, a merging our
individuality in the body of Christ. Earthly partnerships are
limited. Business partnerships are limited to the business
proposed in the combination. The relation of husband and
wife is the most extended partnership of this life, yet it is limited. The partnership in Christ is unlimited as to time or objects of accomplishments. The completeness of the partnership is indicated by the comparison to the union of the fleshly
in one body. They are indissolubly joined together; the interest of the one is the interest of all. One cannot possibly prosper at the cost or detriment of another. If "one member suffereth, all the members [the whole body] suffer with it."

(12: 26.) If one member prospers, all rejoice with it, the union is complete.

of his Son Jesus Christ our Lord.—Of that partnership Christ is Head. He is Head in the sense that from him all the strength and power come, all the wisdom descends. He is the center to which all the members are bound, from him all the impulses and guidance flow. [Paul's whole desire was to rivet the mind of the Corinthian church to the name of Jesus Christ. He makes no mention of any apostle or teacher, but evermore of Jesus. Nowhere in any other epistle is the name of Jesus Christ so often repeated. In these introductory verses, he repeats the name nine times, making it the connecting link of the whole introductory part of the epistle. The frequent mention of his name doubtless grew out of the desire of the apostle to draw them away from their party admiration of particular teachers to Christ alone.]

SECTION TWO

PARTISAN STRIFE AND ITS CONSEQUENCES
1: 10 to 4: 21

1. EXHORTATION TO UNITY AND REPROOF OF PARTY SPIRIT
1: 10-17

10 Now I beseech you, brethren, through the name of our Lord Jesus Christ, that ye all speak the same thing, and *that* there be no ¹divisions among you; but *that* ye be perfected together in the same mind and in the same judgment. 11 For it hath been signified unto me concerning you, my brethren, by them *that are of the household* of Chloe, that there are conten-

---
¹Gr. *schisms.*

---

10 Now I beseech you, brethren, through the name of our Lord Jesus Christ,—Paul, as a brother in Christ, tenderly entreats them from God, speaking for Jesus Christ and by his authority (2 Cor. 5: 20), [not to let any other name eclipse the name of Jesus Christ, by making it a rallying point around which to gather.]

that ye all speak the same thing,—To speak the same thing is to speak only as they were taught by the Holy Spirit, with which he had told them they had been richly endowed.

and that there be no divisions among you;—They were divided over their favorite teachers or ministers. [The divisions which existed in Corinth were not of the nature of hostile sects refusing communion with each other, but such as may exist in the bosom of the same congregation, consisting in alienation of feeling and party strife.]

but that ye be perfected together in the same mind and in the same judgment.—To be of the same mind and the same judgment must be practical among Christians, else Paul would not have urged it. But it is practical only when all follow the things taught by the Lord. By deferring our judgment to his teaching and following the same we can be one. When we change things which God directs or add things not taught by God, we will differ and divide. In any matter not taught by God involving no fidelity to his laws or to institutions, each must defer to the other.

11 For it hath been signified unto me concerning you, my brethren, by them that are of the household of Chloe, that

tions among you. 12 Now this I mean, that each one of you saith, I am of
Paul; and I of Apollos; and I of Cephas; and I of Christ.   13 ²Is Christ
divided? was Paul crucified for you? or were ye baptized into the name of

²Or, *Christ is divided! Was Paul crucified for you?*

---

there are contentions among you.—Chloe and her house are
mentioned only here. They had probably come from Corinth
to Ephesus where Paul was when he wrote this letter and had
told him that contentions had arisen among them at Corinth,
that divided them into factions and parties.

**12 Now this I mean, that each one of you saith, I am of
Paul;**—Some Judaizers had come among them and denied
that Paul was an apostle. Others became so zealous in his defense that they claimed to be his followers. He had planted
the church, was plain, direct, and uncompromising in his
teaching, withal was not commanding in appearance or elegant in speech. His enemies said: "His bodily presence is
weak, and his speech of no account." (2 Cor. 10: 10.)

and I of Apollos;—Apollos, an eloquent speaker and learned
in the Scriptures, had gone among them, become popular and
a party had sprung up claiming him as their teacher. At this
writing he was with or near Paul (16: 12)., in communication
with him and likely cognizant of the condition at Corinth, and
of the writing of this letter.

and I of Cephas;—Others had come from Jerusalem and
were now at Corinth. They claimed Peter as their leader and
teacher, as he had been the leader at Jerusalem and in Judea.

and I of Christ.—Others still claimed to ignore all teachers
and to be of Christ. This could be done in a partisan spirit.
To ignore the teachers sent of Christ, and while doing this to
claim to be of Christ, was to be a party. Jesus said: "He that
heareth you heareth me; and he that rejecteth you rejecteth
me; and he that rejecteth me rejecteth him that sent me."
(Luke 10: 16.)

13 Is Christ divided?—This was said in condemnation of
their divided state. To divide and rend the church of Christ
into parties is to divide Christ. The church is his spiritual
body, to establish which he sacrificed his fleshly body. Then
it is a greater sin to divide the church of Christ than it was to
pierce and mutilate his fleshly body. He who introduces

Paul? 14 ³I thank God that I baptized none of you, save Crispus and
Gaius; 15 lest any man should say that ye were baptized into my name. 16
And I baptized also the household of Stephanas: besides, I know not whether

³Some ancient authorities read *I give thanks that.*

things not required by God, that cause division and strife, is
guilty of the strife. All the divisions in the churches arise
over the introduction of teachings, orders, and institutions
not ordained of God. Hence the followers of Christ cannot divide—cannot introduce things not required by God.

**was Paul crucified for you? or were ye baptized into the
name of Paul?**—That is, they should be followers of none,
save him who died to redeem them, and into whose name they
had been baptized. He does not mention Apollos, but shows
the folly of human leaders by showing the sin of following
himself instead of Christ. [To be "baptized into the name of"
signifies to be baptized while engaging henceforth to belong
to him in whose name the rite is performed. In the name is
summed up all that is revealed regarding him who bears it,
consequently all the titles of his legitimate authority.
Baptism is therefore a taking possession of the baptized on
the part of the one whose name is invoked on him. Never did
Paul think for a moment of arrogating to himself such a position in relation to those who were baptized by him.]

14 I thank God that I baptized none of you,—He said this
on account of their divisions and strife,

save Crispus and Gaius;—Crispus was one of the first converts (Acts 18: 8), and was baptized before Timothy and Silas
reached Corinth. Of Gaius we know but little. In the epistle
to the Romans (16: 23), he calls him "my host, and of the
whole church." He was doubtless one of the first converts.

**15 lest any man should say that ye were baptized into my
name.**—Had he baptized in his own name he would have
taken unto himself the honor that belonged to Christ alone.

16 And I baptized also the household of Stephanas:—The
household of Stephanas were the first fruits of Achaia. (16:
15.) Because it is said that Paul baptized the households of
Stephanas, Lydia, and the jailer (Acts 16: 15, 34), some endeavor to prove that infant baptism was practiced in the apostolic age, on the ground that these families contained infants

I baptized any other.   17 For Christ sent me not to baptize, but to ⁴preach

⁴Gr. *bring good tidings.* Comp. Mt. 11. 5.

and that when Paul baptized the household he must have baptized the infants. But that these three persons, one a woman
in business of whose husband nothing is said, had infant children is far from certain. Nor does the phrase "baptized the
household" make it certain that the infants, if there were any,
were baptized. [For we are told that the nobleman "believed,
and his whole house" (John 4: 53) ; that Crispus "believed in
the Lord with all his house" (Acts 18: 8) ; that the jailer "rejoiced greatly, with all his house, having believed in God"
(Acts 16: 34) ; that Cornelius "feared God with all his house"
(Acts 10: 2) ; and that "the house of Stephanas . . . is the firstfruits of Achaia, and that they have set themselves to minister unto the saints" (1 Cor. 16: 15). But this by no means implies that in these five houses there were no infants, or that
infants believed the gospel, feared god, or rejoiced but that
those capable of understanding the gospel believed it and rejoiced. Just so in reference to baptism. Consequently these
passages render no aid whatever to those contending for infant
baptism.]

besides, I know not whether I baptized any other.—[Paul
guards against the statement being taken absolutely, so that
any slight error in it could be used against him. The Spirit
was given to the apostles to lead them into all the truth (John
16: 13) ; but it was truth relative to man's salvation which
was thus made known to them, and not truth like the fact
here mentioned, the certain knowledge of which was of no use
to the world.]

17 For Christ sent me not to baptize,—By this he did not
mean to deprecate baptism, or to say it was not important.
An inspired man could not preach Christ without preaching
baptism. Usually Paul was accompanied by his companions
in labor who baptized those who believed under his preaching ; but he went into Corinth unaccompanied by any of them
(Acts 17: 14; 15; comp. 18: 5), and "reasoned in the synagogue every sabbath, and persuaded Jews and Greeks" (Acts
18: 4), and those persons most likely believed before the arrival of Silas and Timothy. So he baptized with his own hands

the gospel: not in wisdom of words, lest the cross of Christ should be made void.

---

those who believed, and after their arrival he baptized no more of them. They ministered to him by doing such service. Paul, no matter who were his companions, was the chief leader and teacher. His pre-eminence was marked and always recognized.

but to preach the gospel:—To preach the gospel is to preach Christ as God's representative, and no one can preach Christ as he is represented in the Scriptures without teaching all he taught. Paul could only claim to be free from the blood of all men by declaring the whole counsel of God. (Acts 20: 26, 27.)

not in wisdom of words,—Christ sent him to preach the gospel, not with the wisdom of learning, nor by the philosophy of human wisdom, nor with eloquent and persuasive speech, but with the simple facts of the gospel.

lest the cross of Christ should be made void.—The simple facts of the gospel, with the requirements growing out of them, told in an earnest and loving spirit, and not eloquence and learning, should be relied on to win men from their sins to serve the living God. [To a people thoroughly vitiated in their taste, the preacher of the gospel is open to the temptation of shading off those features of the gospel which are repulsive to the pride of the heart, and of urging the reception of it rather on the ground of its own "sweet reasonableness" than on its being an authoritative message from heaven.]

2. THE DOCTRINE OF THE CROSS AND ITS MODE OF PRESENTATION AS OPPOSED TO PARTISAN TENDENCIES
1: 18-31

18 For the word of the cross is to them that ⁵perish foolishness; but unto

⁵Or, *are perishing*

---

18 **For the word of the cross is to them that perish foolishness;**—To those who reject the story of the cross, the death of Jesus for the deliverance of man from sin is all foolishness. They regard it so, treat it so, and it, standing to them as foolishness, has no influence or power to save.

us who are ⁶are saved it is the power of God. 19 For it is written,
   ⁷I will destroy the wisdom of the wise.
   And the discernment of the discerning will I bring to nought.
20 Where is the wise? where is the scribe? where is the disputer of this

   ⁶Or, *are being saved*
   ⁷Is. xxix. 14.

---

but unto us who are saved it is the power of God.—The cross, which stands for the facts and truths of the gospel, is the power to save from sin. The idea that to humble himself as a servant, to suffer and die as a criminal, is the way to exert influence and power to overcome man and to lead him away from selfishness and sin is contrary to all feelings and propensities of human nature. While Christ reveals in his humanity a new power to men, and through thus humbling himself he can lead others away from sin, he also reveals to men a new and living way to happiness. The only sure way to happiness is to help others in the name of him who became a sin offering for the whole human family.

19 For it is written, I will destroy the wisdom of the wise, —The wisdom of the world is folly in the sight of God. The great living principle of salvation is that man must hear God and be guided by his wisdom. God is the Creator and Ruler of the universe and all things must be brought into harmony with his will and be subject to his laws. All God's dealings with man are intended to bring about this end. The trouble with man is that he prefers to walk by his own wisdom rather than surrender to the wisdom of God. All God's dealings with man from the beginning have been to show that man's own wisdom has brought him to ruin. Therefore he must eschew it and seek the wisdom of God. (Isa. 29: 14; Jer. 8: 9; Rom. 1: 16.)

And the discernment of the discerning will I bring to nought.—So God has foretold that he would bring all the devices and inventions of human wisdom to nought by the things that seemed to men weak and foolish.

20 Where is the wise?—The wise doubtless were the Greek philosophers who sought after wisdom and claimed to be its chief upholders.

where is the scribe?—The scribes were a learned body of

⁸world? hath not God made foolish the wisdom of the world? 21 For
seeing that in the wisdom of God the world through its wisdom knew not
God, it was God's good pleasure through the foolishness of the ⁹preaching to

⁸Or, *age*
⁹Gr. *thing preached.*

men, otherwise denominated lawyers, whose influence over
the Jewish people was very great.

where is the disputer of this world?—The disputers were
the Epicureans, Stoics, and other schools of philosophy devoted especially to disputation.   None of these classes, the
learned and wise of their nations, accepted the truth.   Jesus
said: "I thank thee, O Father, Lord of heaven and earth, that
thou didst hide these things from the wise and understanding,
and didst reveal them unto babes: yea, Father; for so it was
well-pleasing in thy sight." (Luke 10: 21.)

hath not God made foolish the wisdom of the world?—
When properly used, learning, instead of being a hindrance, is
a great help in coming to a knowledge of the truth; but if a
man is puffed up by it, so as to think he is wise and not dependent upon God, it hinders.   God has shown by his teachings and dealings with the world that all such wisdom is foolishness.

**21 For seeing that in the wisdom of God the world through
its wisdom knew not God,**—To know God is to know his character, will, judgments, and his manner of dealings with man,
when he will bless and when he will curse.   It was a part of
the wisdom of God, in ordering all things, that man by his
own wisdom should not thus know God.

**it was God's good pleasure through the foolishness of the
preaching to save them that believe.**—Nothing in man can
teach him these things.   He is dependent upon God made
known through the preaching of the gospel which seems foolishness to man. The gospel is a revelation of God and of his
will made known through Christ.   Those who believe in
Christ and accept him and his teachings as the true wisdom of
God will be saved by it.   The things suggested by human wisdom cannot save.

22 Seeing that Jews ask for signs,—The Jews had been
trained to accept the revelation of God attested by signs and

save them that believe. 22 Seeing that Jews ask for signs, and Greeks seek
after wisdom: 23 but we preach [10]Christ crucified, unto Jews a stumbling-

[10]Or, a Messiah

miracles. It was the test of one claiming to be a teacher of
the truth. The Jews repeatedly asked signs of Jesus. (Matt.
12: 38; 16: 1; Mark 8: 11, 12; 4:.48.)

and Greeks seek after wisdom:—The Greeks asked philosophy—wisdom of the world. The religion of the Jews was
based on signs and miracles; [but the more they got of them;
the less they were satisfied; contrariwise, the Greeks looked
with philosophic indifference on the whole field of the supernatural, regarding even the resurrection of Christ as adding
but one more of the already plentiful childish fables, fit only
for the simple-minded. "Give us wisdom" was their cry—anything that will carry its own evidence on its face. Nor was
this state of things a peculiarity of that time. Every age has
its blind devotees of supernatural interposition and its self-
sufficient worshipers of human reason.]

23 But we preach Christ crucified,—This they did as the
only means offered to man to escape sin and its penalties.

unto Jews a stumblingblock,—Jesus was a living miracle
and sign in his life, his teaching, and his works. The life
and teaching of Jesus are as much a miracle, above human
power, as were the works he performed. They are not so
striking to the unthinking mind, but the life and teaching of
Jesus are just as far above the capacities of man as it is beyond the power of man to raise the dead. The Jews could not
account for his wonderful life. [It is well known that to the
Jews no doctrine was more offensive than that the Messiah
was to be put to death, and that there was to be salvation in
no other way. It was so in the time of Paul, and it has been
so ever since.]

and unto Gentiles foolishness:—His whole teaching and
manner of helping man was without reason or sense to th
philosophic Greeks. They could see neither reason nor sens
in it. [Nothing in the apprehension of the modernist can b
more absurd than that the blood of the cross can remove si

block, and unto Gentiles foolishness; 24 but unto [11]them that are called, both
Jews and Greeks, Christ the power of God, and the wisdom of God. 25 Because the foolishness of God is wiser than men; and the weakness of God is
stronger than men.
26 For [12]behold your calling, brethren, that not many wise after the flesh,

[11]Gr. *the called themselves*
[12]Or, *ye behold*

promote virtue, and secure salvation; or that the preaching of
that doctrine is to convert the world.]

24 **but unto them that are called, both Jews and Greeks,**—
The called were those who believed in Jesus and accepted the
invitation to come unto him. And those who accepted him
were not those filled with the conceit of their own wisdom and
self-sufficiency; but those conscious of their own weakness,
willing to hear, and be guided by his wisdom.

Christ the power of God, and the wisdom of God.—The
provisions made in Christ for the salvation of men embodied
what God in his wisdom saw was best to save man, and in
these provisions the full power of God to save is found.

25 **Because the foolishness of God is wiser than men;**—The
things provided by God that seem foolish to man have much
more true wisdom than the things that seem to man the greatest wisdom.

and the weakness of God is stronger than men.—The things
of God that seem to man weak have more strength in them
than the mightiest of man's devices. The seemingly weakest
of God's appointments, used in God's name for God's honor
and glory as he directs, have all the power and strength of
God in them.

26 **For behold your calling, brethren, that not many wise
after the flesh, not many mighty, not many noble, are called:**
—This will bear two constructions. One is, not many worldly
or great ones accept the divine call and become servants of
God. The other is, that not many wise, noble, or great ones
of earth are chosen of God to preach the gospel. Both propositions are true. The latter one seems more in harmony with
the context.

27 **but God chose the foolish things of the world, that he
might put to shame them that are wise;**—God to show his

not many mighty, not many noble, *are called*: 27 but God chose the foolish things of the world, that he might put to shame them that are wise; and God chose the weak things of the world, that he might put to shame the things that are strong; 28 and the base things of the world, and the things that are despised, did God choose, *yea* [13]and the things that are not, that he might

[13]Many ancient authorities omit *and*.

power and presence, and to manifest the folly of man's wisdom, and the weakness of his greatest inventions, chose the things that to human wisdom appear foolish to confound or confuse the wisdom of the great ones.

and God chose the weak things of the world, that he might put to shame the things that are strong;—Jesus himself came as a helpless babe among the poorer classes of the people and without human power or greatness, and undertook the rescue of the world from the dominion of the evil one. All the appointments of God correspond to the character of Jesus and his condition, lack worldly wisdom. When man uses means fitted to the end sought, he is prone to attribute the result to the means used, to his wisdom in choosing the means. But when the conditions are inadequate to produce the end, then he who ordains the means is looked upon as the source of the power. Of such character was the separating the waters of the Red Sea, the throwing down the walls of Jericho, and the healing of Naaman of leprosy, and this is characteristic of God's work generally. The things that seem foolish and weak to the wisdom of man are chosen by God to overturn the works of man, and to effect what his wisdom chooses to accomplish.

28 and the base things of the world, and the things that are despised, did God choose, yea and the things that are not,— God chose the things that seem base, that man despised as unworthy, and even things that are not—are dead—as Rachel weeping for her children; and she would not be comforted, because they are not—dead.

that he might bring to nought the things that are:—God depended upon a dead Christ to call them to repentance, to establish the reign and authority of God, overturn the mighty works of man that had been built up in the world in rebellion against God.

bring to nought the things that are: 29 that no flesh should glory before
God. 30 But of him are ye in Christ Jesus, who was made unto us wisdom
from God, ¹⁴and righteousness and sanctification, and redemption: 31 that,

¹⁴Or, *both righteousness and sanctification and redemption*

---

29 that no flesh should glory before God.—God requires
man to work through means unfitted to the end to be accomplished, to show him that the power is of God, that God does
the work, that man might not glory as though he did it himself; but his glorying was in God the giver of all good. The
great end of God's dealings with man is to cause him to trust
God, and lead him to walk in accordance with his will. God
imposes on man conditions which in themselves are inadequate to the accomplishment of the end sought, that man may
show his faith in God and his willingness to obey him, and in
this obedience show his fitness to receive the blessings of God,
and that no man should glory in himself in the presence of
God. Man had so sinned, so fallen from God's favor, that
God would receive him only as he distrusted self and trusted
God who redeemed him.

30 But of him are ye in Christ Jesus,—By the provisions of
God we are brought into Christ Jesus through faith. Faith affects the heart, the emotions, and directs the confidence and
trust toward Christ. Faith carries into Christ only as it leads
us to perform the acts that place us in Christ. Faith perfected
by obedience is the bringing the whole man—"spirit and soul
and body"—into harmony with the faith of the heart. Faith
perfected by obedience embodied and expressed by repentance
and baptism (Acts 2: 38), puts us in Christ. "For ye are all
sons of God, through faith, in Christ Jesus. For as many of
you as were baptized into Christ did put on Christ." (Gal.
3: 26, 27.)

who was made unto us wisdom from God,—Jesus Christ
with his works, teachings, and requirements is the perfection
of divine wisdom to save man. When man acts according to
his teaching and follows his ways, he appropriates and uses
God's wisdom to guide his steps. This lifts the humble man of
earth above the weakness of his own wisdom and ignorance,
and enables him to walk by the wisdom of God. When Solo-

according as it is written, [15] He that glorieth, let him glory in the Lord.

[15]Jer. ix. 23 f.

mon gave divine sanction to the wise proverbs of nations and peoples, he enabled every one who has faith in God to appropriate this wisdom as his own and to walk by it. So Jesus Christ is to us the wisdom of God. "Behold, a greater than Solomon is here." (Matt. 12: 42.)

and righteousness—Jesus suffered and died as though he was a sinful man that sinful men might stand clothed with the righteousness of God, and live as though he had never sinned. God is righteous, and for man to become righteous, he must live according to the will of God, that in character he may be like him. Man by faith enters into Christ, drinks into his spirit, walks as he walked, and so clothes himself with the righteousness of Christ, thus has God made him righteousness to us.

and sanctification,—Jesus sanctified himself that in him man might be sanctified or set apart to the service of God. Only in Christ, and walking in his wisdom, can man be set apart or sanctified to the services of God. Out of Christ man cannot serve God.

and redemption:—Jesus Christ came to rescue man from the thralldom of sin, and gave his life to rescue him from death. In Jesus Christ as his servant God will accept him. Thus is Christ made unto us redemption.

31 that, according as it is written, He that glorieth, let him glory in the Lord.—All these blessings came to man, not in his own name, or by walking in his ways, but as a servant of Jesus Christ, redeemed, sanctified, saved by him in fulfillment of the Scripture: "Thus saith Jehovah, Let not the wise man glory in his wisdom, neither let the mighty man glory in his might, let not the rich man glory in his riches; but let him that glorieth glory in this, that he hath understanding, and knoweth me, that I am Jehovah who exerciseth lovingkindness, justice, and righteousness, in the earth: for in these things I delight, saith Jehovah." (Jer. 9: 23, 24.) There is no room for man glorying in himself. His own wisdom, his own ways, his own strength brought death, and still bring only ruin. So he cannot glory in himself. He that glorieth in honors won, or in blessings enjoyed, must do it in the Lord, as he alone can guide with wisdom, clothe with righteousness, sanctify man to his service, and redeem him from his iniquities and from death.

3. EXEMPLIFICATION OF THESE PRINCIPLES IN PAUL'S PREACHING AT CORINTH
2: 1-5

1 And I, brethren, when I came unto you, came not with excellency of [16]speech or of wisdom, proclaiming to you the [17]testimony of God. 2 For I determined not to know anything among you, save Jesus Christ, and him

[16]Or, *word*
[17]Many ancient authorities read *mystery.*

1 **And I, brethren, when I came unto you, came not with excellency of speech or of wisdom, proclaiming to you the testimony of God.**—Paul was not a man of commanding appearance or an eloquent speaker, further than the importance of his message and his anxiety to save gave him eloquence. He refers to these when he says that his opponents will say, "His letters, they say, are weighty and strong; but his bodily presence is weak, and his speech of no account." (2 Cor. 10: 10.) God chose a man of this character to bear his testimony to the Gentiles that the salvation might be of God and not of human wisdom, learning, or eloquence.

2 **For I determined not to know anything among you, save Jesus Christ, and him crucified.**—This embraced his mission to the world, his teaching, his sufferings, death, burial, and resurrection, with all the teaching he gave to the world and sealed with his blood. No appeals of eloquence, no working upon the sympathies by death scenes other than that of Jesus. No human philosophy, but simply love of God to lost men, and the provisions made through Christ Jesus for salvation from sin, would Paul make. Of certain characters the Lord has said, "Their fear of me is a commandment of men which hath been taught them." (Isa. 29: 13.) These he would not accept. The fear of Jehovah must rest upon the fear and love of God. The gospel is God's wisdom for the salvation of the world. That is, the gospel according to God's wisdom was the

crucified. 3 And I was with you in weakness, and in fear, and in much
trembling. 4 And my ¹⁶speech and my ⁹preaching were not in persuasive
words of wisdom, but in demonstration of the Spirit and of power: 5 that
your faith should not ¹⁸stand in the wisdom of men, but in the power of God.

¹⁸Gr. *be.*

---

best thing to save man from his sins, and it was God's power
vested to save.

3 **And I was with you in weakness, and in fear,**—[The
weakness of which he here speaks was not bodily weakness;
for although elsewhere he speaks of himself as weak in body
(2 Cor. 10: 10), and as suffering under bodily infirmity (Gal.
4: 14), yet here the whole context shows that he refers to his
state of mind.]   His deportment was that of a man humble
and distrustful of his powers, and with a fear lest his work
should be vain.

and in much trembling.—[It was not the gospel he had to
preach that made him tremble; he was not ashamed of that
(Rom. 1: 16), neither was it fear of personal danger; but he
was keenly sensitive of the weakness of his situation; he
feared a failure similar to that in Athens; and trembling at the
thought of the infinite importance of his work—that the salvation of so many men and women was dependent on so feeble
an instrumentality.]

. ̣... ̣.y speech **and my preaching were not in persuasive
words of wisdom,**—His speech and preaching were without
the persuasiveness of eloquence and worldy wisdom, but
rested upon God, declared by the presence of his Spirit working miracles.

but in demonstration of the Spirit and of power:—The truth
was revealed by the Spirit, and confirmed by the miracles performed and gifts imparted to them.   Paul relied upon these to
carry convictions to their hearts that what he taught was
from God.   The matter contained in the Gospels, the revelations made, are above human wisdom, and their adaptedness
to the needs of the soul shows an origin from God.

5 **that your faith should not stand in the wisdom of men,
but in the power of God.**—These testimonies that God gave to
the word spoken by Paul were relied on that their faith might

not rest on the reasonings of man, but on the power of God, manifested by his Spirit.

4. CONCERNING GOD'S WISDOM AND THE METHOD OF ITS IMPARTATION
2: 6-16

6 We speak wisdom, however, among them that are fullgrown: yet a wisdom not of this [19]world, nor of the rulers of this [19]world, who are coming to nought: 7 but we speak God's wisdom in a mystery, *even* the *wisdom* that hath been hidden, which God foreordained before the [19]worlds unto our glory;

---

[19]Or, *age:* and so in ver. 7, 8; but not in ver. 12.

---

6 **We speak wisdom, however, among them that are fullgrown:**—Paul had been disavowing that he had spoken after the wisdom of the world; and now avows that what he had spoken was according to the wisdom of the full grown—those filled with the wisdom of God. [The full grown are those who have advanced beyond the position of beginners in the Christian life into the higher sphere of thorough and comprehensive insight into its duties, privileges, and blessings. While admitting their knowledge (1: 5), he appeals to their contentions (3: 1), in proof that they were still babes in Christ, and therefore not prepared for solid food which is "for fullgrown men, even those who by reason of use have their senses exercised to discern good and evil" (Heb. 5: 14). Jesus himself teaches the principle of adaptation to the various stages in the Christian life, when he said to his sorrowing disciples: "I have yet many things to say unto you, but ye cannot bear them now." (John 16: 12.)]

yet a wisdom not of this world, nor of the rulers of this world,—In this he keeps before them that what the world calls wisdom is foolishness with God and his servants.

who are coming to nought;—They must fall and their wisdom perish.

7 **but we speak God's wisdom in a mystery, even the wisdom that hath been hidden, which God foreordained before the worlds unto our glory:**—The gospel is God's wisdom for the salvation of man. It was provided before the world was —before man was created, it is generally interpreted—to bring man to glory. A mystery was not something that could

8 which none of the rulers of this ¹world hath known: for had they known it, they would not have crucified the Lord of glory: 9 but as it is written,
²Things which eye saw not, and ear heard not,
And *which* entered not into the heart of man,
Whatsoever things God prepared for them that love him.
10 ³But unto us God revealed ⁴*them* through the Spirit: for the Spirit searcheth all things, yea, the deep things of God. 11 For who among men knoweth the things of a man, save the spirit of the man, which is in him? even

¹Or, *age:* and so in ver. 7, 8; but not in ver. 12.
²Is. lxiv. 4; lxv. 17.
³Some ancient authorities read *For*
⁴Or, *it*

not be explained or understood, but something unrevealed and unknown. The gospel before it was revealed in Christ was the mystery.

8 which none of the rulers of this world hath known:—The reference is to the Jewish and Roman rulers who engaged in the crucifixion of Jesus Christ. It was the world in its princes who rejected the Savior.

for had they known it, they would not have crucified the Lord of glory:—Had they known and understood this mystery, they would not have committed the awful deed.

9 but as it is written,—This was done in fulfillment of the prophecy.

Things which eye saw not, and ear heard not, and which entered not into the heart of man, whatsoever things God prepared for them that love him.—The things spoken of in this passage that eye had not seen nor ear heard were the great blessings of salvation through Jesus Christ our Lord. Before he came no human being by human wisdom ever had any conception of what these blessings would be; but they are now revealed to us by the Holy Spirit through the New Testament. Hence they are no longer mysteries, but matters of plain revelation.

10 But unto us God revealed them through the Spirit:—The Spirit who dwelt with and knew the mind of God came to the apostles, dwelt in them, and revealed God's will to them.

for the Spirit searcheth all things, yea, the deep things of God.—The Spirit of God knew the deep, unrevealed things of God, and made them known to the apostles; and they, through their writings, have made them known to us.

11 For who among men knoweth the things of a man, save

so the things of God none knoweth, save the Spirit of God. 12 But we received, not the spirit of the ⁵world, but the spirit which is from God; that we
might know the things that were freely given to us of God. 13 Which
things also we speak, not in words which man's wisdom teacheth, but which
the Spirit teacheth; ⁶combining spiritual things with spiritual *words.* 14

⁵See ver. 6.
⁶Or, *interpreting spiritual things to spiritual* men

the spirit of the man, which is in him?—No man knows the
things that are in man save the spirit dwelling in him which
pervades his whole being and knows all the secrets and purposes of his heart, soul, and body.

**even so the things of God none knoweth, save the Spirit of
God.**—The Spirit of God alone knows the mind and purposes
of God and searches its deep things, just as none but the spirit
of man which is in him knows the things of man.

**12 But we received, not the spirit of the world, but the
spirit which is from God;**—The apostles had received the
spirit not of the world, but the Spirit that dwelt with and
knew the mind of God.

**that we might know the things that were freely given to us
of God.**—The Spirit of God was given to the apostles, that
they might know the mind or will of God, and the things that
are freely given to them in Christ Jesus. That is, the Spirit
which had dwelt with and in God, and so knew his whole
mind, was transferred to the apostles and revealed to them
the things of God. The Spirit revealed to them the mind,
will, and purposes of God with all the blessings freely given
to men in Christ Jesus.

13 Which things also we speak,—The things they received
of the Spirit they spoke to the world. This is the way others
learned of these truths.

not in words which man's wisdom teacheth,—They spoke
them not in the words suggested by the wisdom of the world.

but which the Spirit teacheth;—The salvation of man was
wholly of and from God. Man's wisdom was not permitted to
furnish words through which the mind of God was spoken.
[The Spirit taught these things in words, and thus revealed
them to the apostles who spoke them in the same words. So
the Spirit guided them into the truth revealed (John 16: 13).]

combining spiritual things with spiritual words.—They

Now the [7]natural man receiveth not the things of the Spirit of God: for they are foolishness unto him; and he cannot know them, because they are spiritually [8]judged. 15 But he that is spiritual [9]judgeth all things, and he himself

[7]Or, *unspiritual* Gr. *psychical*
[8]Or, *examined*
[9]Or, *examineth*

spake spiritual ideas in the terms or words of the Spirit. The Spirit chose words suitable to the spiritual truths made known.

14 **Now the natural man receiveth not the things of the Spirit of God:**—Man by his natural faculties, without revelation, could not learn the will of God; but in order that he might know it, the Spirit of God, who knows the things of God, was transferred to the apostles and made known to them God's will, and they revealed it to the people. The natural man, then, is the man who has never heard the will of God, for he has no means of knowing till those who received the revelation make it known to him. Having once been revealed by the Spirit of God, it was committed to writing under the guidance of the Spirit, so that man may come to it and learn it. It means about the same as "seeing that in the wisdom of God the world through its wisdom knew not God, it was God's good pleasure through the foolishness of the preaching to save them that believe." (1: 21.)

for they are foolishness unto him;—The manifestations are without meaning to him.

and he cannot know them,—This does not mean that men to whom the revelation is declared by those possessing the Spirit cannot understand and obey it. It was revealed to the inspired men that they might teach it to others that they might understand and know the way of salvation.

because they are spiritually judged.—This endowment of the Spirit enabled the endowed to judge or discriminate whether things revealed were of God or not. Without this they could not.

15 **But he that is spiritual judgeth all things,**—He that is endowed with the Spirit discerns and discriminates what is of God, and teaches all things God reveals.

and he himself is judged of no man.—Those not endowed with the presence of the divine Spirit are not capable of dis-

is ⁸judged of no man. 16 For who hath known the mind of the Lord, that
he should instruct him? But we have the mind of Christ.

---

criminating and determining whether the things taught by the
inspired men are of God or not. An inspired man alone could
judge of the fidelity of inspired men in teaching the will of
God. This refers to the original revelations. Men now test
all teaching by the truths delivered by the inspired men.
They instruct us to "believe not every spirit, but prove the
spirits, whether they are of God; because many false prophets
are gone out into the world." (1 John 4: 1.)

16 **For who hath known the mind of the Lord,**—Who, save
those endowed with the Spirit of God, know the mind of the
Lord? Those having the Spirit of God know his mind. The
Spirit revealed it to them.

**that he should instruct him? But we have the mind of
Christ.**—This does not seem to make sense nor to harmonize
with the context. How could knowing the mind of God enable one to instruct God or Jesus? Adam Clarke translates it:
"For who hath known the mind of the Lord, that he should
teach it?" The *nous,* the Greek for mind, is masculine gender,
and *auton,* translated *him,* is masculine, but might agree with it.
This would give a clearer idea, but I believe the trouble is in
the word translated *to instruct.* It is translated *to instruct* or
teach only in this one place.

The word occurs in the following passages: "But Saul increased the more in strength, and confounded the Jews that
dwelt at Damascus, *proving* that this is the Christ" (Acts 9: 22);
"Concluding that God had called us to preach the gospel unto
them" (Acts 16: 10); "From whom all the body fitly framed and
knit together through that which every joint supplieth" (Eph. 4:
16); "That their hearts may be comforted, they being *knit* together
in love" (Col. 2: 2); "From whom all the body, being supplied
and *knit* together through the joints and bands, increaseth with
the increase of God" (Col. 2: 19). In these passages it means to
understand or know so as to be *joined together with him.*

In the passage before us, it means, "Who of you uninspired
hath known the mind of God, so as to be joined together with
him? But we inspired men so understand him that we are

united in him in teaching his will, we are laborers together with God." (2: 9.) The whole trend and meaning of the chapter is that none could know or teach the will of God by human wisdom. They were dependent upon the revelation made by God's spirit through the apostles for a knowledge of his will, and only through receiving this could any become co-workers with him in saving men. This does not refer to the work of preaching what has been revealed.

Adam Clarke gives these judicious thoughts: "This chapter might be considered a good model for a Christian to regulate his conduct by, or his public ministry; because it points out the mode of preaching used by Paul and the apostles in general. This great apostle came not to the people with ex-cellency of speech, and of wisdom, when he declared unto them the counsel of God. They know little, either of the spirit of Paul, or the design of the gospel, who make the chief ex-cellence of their preaching to consist in the eloquence of lan-guage, or depth of human reasoning. That may be their testi-mony, but it is not God's. The enticing words of man's wis-dom are seldom accompanied by the demonstration and power of the Holy Spirit. One justly remarks that 'the foolishness of preaching has its wisdom, loftiness, and eloquence; but it consists in the sublimity of its truths, the depths of its mys-teries, and the ardor of the Spirit of God.' In this respect Paul may be said to have preached wisdom among those who are perfect," or inspired.

5. REPROOF FOR LACK OF SPIRITUAL WISDOM AS EVINCED BY THEIR CARNAL DIVISIONS
3: 1-4

1 And I, brethren, could not speak unto you as unto spiritual, but as unto

---

1 **And I, brethren, could not speak unto you as unto spiri-tual, but as unto carnal,**—Paul had told them that they were dependent on the inspired apostles for the knowledge of the truth by which they might become spiritual beings. He could not speak unto them as though they were taught by the Spirit, but as though they were fleshly, or led by the impulse of the flesh.

carnal, as unto babes in Christ. 2 I fed you with milk, not with meat; for
ye were not yet able *to bear it*; nay, not even now are ye able; 3 for ye are

as unto babes in Christ.—Not grown, were undeveloped
under the instruction of the Spirit. As the spiritual element
in them is developed under the instruction of the Spirit the
flesh loses its rule, but they had learned slowly, had not
grown in spirituality as they should have done, so he chides
them that they are yet carnal when they ought to be spiritual.
He uses the term here in a modified sense. [The term is
sometimes used in a good sense. (1 Pet. 2: 2.) Here, however, it is taken in a bad sense, as referring to the understanding. For we must be children in malice, but not in understanding. (14: 20; Eph. 4: 14.)]

2 I fed you with milk,—Babes are fed with milk, food suited
to the digestive powers of their weak and helpless condition.

not with meat;—After they grow stronger they are fed with
stronger, more strengthening food, suited to their infantile
state, and not with stronger spiritual food suited to a greater
spiritual growth.

for ye were not yet able to bear it:—Sufficient time had
elapsed for them to have reached a more vigorous and health-
ful growth, but they had not improved and grown in the spiritual life as they should, so were babes unfit to receive the
stronger spiritual food. He had treated them with tenderness,
had not been chargeable to them as he might have been when
laboring among them, and had not fully impressed on them
the obligation to deny themselves all fleshly lusts and appetites, and sacrifice all things for the sake of Christ.

nay, not even now are ye able:—Men fail to improve themselves so that when they ought to be skilled in the word, eat
meat and grow strong, able to bear heavy burdens and help
others, they are yet weak babes, needing themselves to be
nursed on milk and carried by others. This was the condition
of these Corinthians; and many yet always remain babes to be
nursed, fed, and carried by others.

[Christ is at the same time milk to babes and strong meat
to those who are of full age (Heb. 5: 13, 14), the same truth of
the gospel is administered to both, but so as to suit their ca-

yet carnal: for whereas there is among you jealousy and strife, are ye
not carnal, and do ye not walk after the manner of men?   4 For when one
saith, I am of Paul; and another, I am of Apollos; are ye not men?   5

pacity. Hence it is the part of the wise teacher to accommodate himself to the capacity of those whom he has undertaken
to instruct, so that in dealing with the weak and ignorant, he
begins with such principles as they are able to understand,
and does not go higher than they are able to follow. (Mark
4: 33; John 16: 12.) At the same time these principles will
contain everything necessary to be known, no less than the
further advanced lessons that are communicated to those that
are stronger. Some, however, present Christ at such a distance, and cover over with so many disguises, that they constantly keep their hearers in destructive ignorance.]

3 **for ye are yet carnal:**—They had not grown from under
the rule of fleshly passions. [This word has a wide scope. It
is not confined to sexual, or even sensual sins, but covers
those tempers and dispositions that express themselves in
strife and dissensions.]

**for whereas there is among you jealousy and strife, are ye
not carnal, and do ye not walk after the manner of men?**—
This refers to the parties noticed in 1: 11, 12. These all grow
out of the predominance of the works of the flesh. Paul gives
the natural fruits of the flesh: "Now the works of the flesh are
manifest, which are these: fornication, uncleanness, lascivi-
ousness, idolatry, sorcery, enmities, strife, jealousies, wraths,
factions, divisions, parties, envyings, drunkenness, revellings,
and such like." (Gal. 5: 19-21.) Where these exist, the flesh
rules. Had they been spiritual, they would have looked to
Christ and not been partisans of men.

4 **For when one saith, I am of Paul; and another, I am of
Apollos;**—Their divisions and strifes had arisen concerning
the teachers that had labored among them, especially over
Paul and Apollos. Neither of these countenanced this parti-
sanship in his favor. An idea has gone abroad that there was
great rivalry between Paul and Apollos that gave rise to the
parties in the church at Corinth; but there is no ground whatever for this conclusion, for Paul always speaks of Apollos
with the highest esteem and affection. At the time of the

writing of this epistle, he was with Paul, or in easy reach of
him, and knew of his writing, for Paul says: "But as touching
Apollos the brother, I besought him much to come unto you
with the brethren: and it was not at all his will to come now;
but he will come when he shall have opportunity." (16: 12.)
Paul was writing to condemn the divisions that had grown up
concerning him and Apollos and desired Apollos to go help
correct the evils.

are ye not men?—He places before them the truth that divisions and parties, even for inspired men, are sinful, and grow
out of the lusts and passions of the flesh.

6. PROPER ESTIMATE OF MINISTERS AS DETERMINED BY THEIR WORK
3: 5-15

What then is Apollos? and what is Paul? Ministers through whom ye believed; and each as the Lord gave to him. 6 I planted, Apollos watered; but

---

5 **What then is Apollos? and what is Paul?**—What position does Apollos and Paul occupy that they should divide
over them? [From the answer given it is implied that the par-
tisanship of their followers does not accord with the spirit of
the leaders they have chosen, and is condemned as carnality.]

Ministers through whom ye believed;—Here is an emphatic
statement that Apollos and Paul were nothing else than mere
ministers, servants of God. [They are thereby designated as
instruments in God's hands for the production of faith, and
such they were in their function as preachers and teachers of
the truth.]

and each as the Lord gave to him.—Each ministered as the
Lord gave him ability and knowledge, so God, not his servant,
is the leader to follow.

6 **I planted,**—Paul first preached the word of God, which is
the seed of the kingdom (Luke 8: 11), among them, and
planted the church there.

Apollos watered;—Apollos taught afterward, encouraging
the disciples, so watered. Others came in likely under his
teaching. A seed is sometimes planted, but germinates or
grows and bears fruit only as it is watered and cultivated.

God gave the increase. 7 So then neither is he that planteth anything, neither he that watereth; but God that giveth the increase. 8 Now he that planteth and he that watereth are one: but each shall receive his own reward according to his own labor. 9 For we are God's fellow-workers: ye are God's [10]husbandry, God's building.

[10]Gr, *tilled land.*

---

but God gave the increase.—While each had done the part for which he was fitted by God, and to which God had called him, God gave the increase. [Paul's generous reference to Apollos here, as following up the work which he himself had begun, is a rebuke of the Corinthian party spirit, which set them up as rivals.]

7 So then neither is he that planteth anything, neither he that watereth;—The work that each did as servants of God was necessary to the growth of the plant, but all the power that produced the fruit come from God.

but God that giveth the increase.—God does what is accomplished through the provisions he makes and the agents he uses, both in the natural and spiritual world. He gave the increase through the works of these, his servants, as he gives increase of fruit in the material world.

8 Now he that planteth and he that watereth are one:— They are one in position and relation. They are servants through whom God works. They are equal—not one to be exalted above another. Neither is entitled to any credit.

but each shall receive his own reward according to his own labor.—They only do what God directs them to do, and each shall be rewarded according to his faithfulness in doing the will of God.

9 For we are God's fellow-workers:—The apostles and faithful teachers are God's fellow workers, working together with him, doing and teaching what he directs.

ye are God's husbandry,—The church is God's husbandry, is the field planted with the seed God gave, and is cultivated and nourished by God's servants. [This metaphor is frequently used in the Scripture which shows that it plainly rests upon a far-reaching harmony of things natural and spiritual. (See Isa. 5: 1-7; Matt. 13: 3-30; Luke 13: 6-9; John 15: 1-6.) All agriculture is man working together with God. For every

10 According to the grace of God which was given unto me, as a wise masterbuilder I laid a foundation; and another buildeth thereon. But let each man take heed how he buildeth thereon. 11 For other foundation can

pious farmer feels that his harvest is a result and reward proportionate to his own toil and skill, and yet altogether God's gift to him. Just so, the servant of the Lord places the word of God in its appropriate soil, the human heart, and from the word, in virtue of its life-giving power, there springs up a fruitful plant of an obedient believer and a devoted Christian life.]

God's building.—The church is the temple of God, builded of living stones. (1 Pet. 2: 5.) Jesus Christ is the chief cornerstone. God is fitting the stones and placing them into the building through his workmen. God builds the house, and through the Spirit dwells in it. As we give honor, not to the workmen who execute, but to him who planned and provided for the building, so the honor for this spiritual house belongs to God.

10 **According to the grace of God which was given unto me, as a wise masterbuilder I laid a foundation;**—According to the gifts and spiritual blessings bestowed on Paul as a wise master builder under God, he laid the foundation of the church at Corinth by preaching that Jesus is the Christ, the Son of God. He first preached that truth in Corinth.

and another buildeth thereon. But let each man take heed how he buildeth thereon.—He warns every one to take heed, be careful how he builds. There is danger by false teaching, or false methods, of building unworthy material upon the foundation which Paul had laid.

11 **For other foundation can no man lay than that which is laid, which is Jesus Christ.**—There is but one foundation on which a church of Christ can be laid. Paul had laid that foundation when he preached in Corinth that Jesus is the Christ. When Peter confessed his faith in Jesus, saying: "Thou art the Christ, the Son of the living God," Jesus said unto him: "Upon this rock I will build my church; and the gates of Hades shall not prevail against it." (Matt. 16: 16-18.) There is controversy as to what constitutes the rock on which Christ

no man lay than that which is laid, which is Jesus Christ. 12 But if any man buildeth on the foundation gold, silver, costly stones, wood, hay, stubble; 13 each man's work shall be made manifest: for the day shall declare it, because it is revealed in fire; [11]and the fire itself shall prove each man's work of what sort it is. 14 If any man's work shall abide which he built thereon, he

[11]Or, and each man's work, of what sort it is, the fire shall prove it.

would build his church; but Paul says that Christ is the only foundation that can be laid.

12 But if any man buildeth on the foundation—The church is compared to a building into which may be builded both good and bad material.

gold, silver, costly stones, wood, hay, stubble;—The members built into the church are compared to these two classes of material.

13 each man's work shall be made manifest:—Every man's work will be tried with fire, and so its character will be revealed or made known. If tried by fire, the wood, hay, and stubble will be burned up.

for the day shall declare it, because it is revealed in fire;—There is some doubt as to what day is meant. It is a day of testing to the unfaithful that is coming whether in this world or in the world to come. Some think it is the day of persecution that will come upon the church as a fiery trial that will destroy and purge out the unworthy. Others interpret it as referring to the day of judgment.

and the fire itself shall prove each man's work of what sort it is.—The point of comparison is: fire will purge and purify the gold, silver, and precious stones. It will burn up and consume wood, hay, and stubble. So the day of trial will purge and purify the good, and they will shine the brighter; but it will bring to ruin the unworthy. This is true of the classes, whether it refers to a time of persecution and trial here or to the future judgment.

14 If any man's work shall abide which he built thereon, he shall receive a reward.—If the work done in building up the church of Christ abides, he who does it will receive a reward. [Paul is here speaking of the material built into the church upon the one foundation, which may be good or bad. When a laborer builds wood, hay, and stubble upon the foundation, all

shall receive a reward. 15 If any man's work shall be burned, he shall suffer loss: but he himself shall be saved; yet so as through fire.

such will turn back to the world, yield to its temptations, and thus be overcome by fiery trials; and in such cases the laborer loses his reward. On the other hand, those of his converts who prove themselves to be as gold, silver, and costly stones in the service of God will be admitted "into the eternal kingdom of our Lord and Saviour Jesus Christ" (2 Pet. 1: 11), and this will be a reward to him.]

15 **If any man's work shall be burned, he shall suffer loss: but he himself shall be saved; yet so as through fire.**—When this test by fire is made has been a question of some doubt. It seems to be that if one brings in ill-prepared material, it will be destroyed. Paul says of his converts: "Ye are our epistle, written in our hearts, known and read of all men"; (2 Cor. 3: 2), and "For what is our hope, or joy, or crown of glorying? Are not even ye, before our Lord Jesus at his coming? For ye are our glory and our joy." (1 Thess. 2: 19, 20.) If these converts were to be the ground of his reward, the loss of them would cause him to suffer a corresponding loss, yet he would be saved, but the fire that destroyed his bad work would test him. This teaching of Paul was clearly intended to warn the church he had planted and taught and among whom he had determined to know nothing but "Jesus Christ, and him crucified," against teachers who would come into their midst and teach the commandments of men, that would corrupt and defile the temple of God.

7. INDICATIONS OF THE SOURCE OF THE PERNICIOUS TENDENCIES AT CORINTH AND ADMONITIONS RESPECTING THE SAME
3: 16-23

16 Know ye not that ye are a [12]temple of God, and *that* the Spirit of God

[12]Or, *sanctuary*

16 **Know ye not that ye are a temple of God,**—Solomon erected a temple in Jerusalem, that was recognized as "the house of Jehovah," "the house of God," and "Jehovah's house." In it was Jehovah's name recorded; in it was the mercy seat; in it must the offering of prayer or praise be pre-

dwelleth in you? 17 If any man destroyeth the [12]temple of God, him shall God destroy; for the [12]temple of God is holy, [13]and such are ye.

[13]Or, *which* temple *ye are*

sented. The temple itself, with its corner and foundation stones and comely stones of its walls, was typical of the spiritual temple, the church, "built upon the foundation of the apostles and prophets, Christ Jesus himself being the chief corner stone" (Eph. 2: 20), of which every Christian is a living stone "builded together for a habitation of God in the Spirit." [The lessons of care and sanctity and reverence taught concerning the temple of God in Jerusalem are examples to teach how reverential and careful we must be in reference to the spiritual temple and how we should make it after the pattern given. It must not be neglected; it must not be defiled; it must not be made secondary to anything in the world.]

and that the Spirit of God dwelleth in you?—God's Spirit in the beginning had dwelt upon the earth with man. Man sinned, the earth was defiled, and his Spirit ceased to dwell with man. Altars were built and consecrated where he met the worshipers. Then the tabernacle, then the temple in Jerusalem, now the spiritual temple or the church of God. In this spiritual temple he makes his permanent dwelling place among men. (See 6: 19; 2 Cor. 6: 16; Heb. 3: 6; 1 Pet. 2: 5.)

17 If any man destroyeth the temple of God,—The church is destroyed as God's temple by so defiling it that God will not dwell in it. The earth was defiled by man introducing practices into it not ordained of God, following the evil one instead of God, by substituting the will of man for the will of God. The same course will destroy the church as a temple of God. In the tabernacle, and the temple in Jerusalem, every person who served, and every vessel and instrument of service were sanctified by the typical blood of bulls and goats. To bring persons or things not sealed by this blood into the temple so defiled it that God would not dwell in it. Every person built into the spiritual temple of God must be sanctified by the blood of Christ. Every ordinance and appointment of service is consecrated by that blood. To bring a person or service into the church not sealed by the blood defiles it. The persons who enter according to the terms laid down in the New

18 Let no man deceive himself. If any man thinketh that he is wise among you in this ¹⁴world, let him become a fool, that he may become wise.

¹⁴Or, *age*

Testament, and the ordinances and the provisions there made for serving God, are sealed by the blood of Christ. None others are. To bring into the church those not admitted by the law of Christ is to defile the temple of God, so that God refuses to dwell in it. The temple of God is holy, consecrated to God's service. All its appointments and ordinances have been sealed by the blood of Christ.

him shall God destroy; for the temple of God is holy, and such are ye.—As Nadab and Abihu brought strange fire into the earthly tabernacle and were destroyed by that fire, so also shall whosoever brings into the church of God, or performs any service not ordained, and so consecrated by God, be destroyed by that unconsecrated, unordained service.

18 **Let no man deceive himself.**—He warns against the danger of the wisdom of this world. It is intimately connected with this defilement of the temple. To introduce things resting on human wisdom defiles the temple of God. To use those ordained by the wisdom of God, sealed by the blood of Christ, is to keep the temple holy and sacred.

If any man thinketh that he is wise among you in this world, let him become a fool,—If a man seems or affects to be wise after this world and so thinks he may bring things resting on this wisdom into the church of God, let him become a fool to this world.

These admonitions are most needful to men, for they often deceive themselves. God is never deceived as to man's character or as to his ability or to the motives that actuate him in anything he does. Self-deception is the most common phase of deception among men. Our neighbors as a rule understand us better than we understand ourselves. They see us more clearly than we see ourselves. Paul cautions: "Be not deceived; God is not mocked: for whatsoever a man soweth, that shall he also reap. For he that soweth unto his own flesh shall of the flesh reap corruption; but he that soweth unto the Spirit shall of the Spirit reap eternal life." (Gal. 6: 7, 8.)

19 For the wisdom of this world is foolishness with God. For it is written,

---

This warning grows out of man's tendency to deceive himself. Many of us while gratifying the flesh imagine we are following the Spirit. Many preachers preach for money and ease and imagine they are preaching to save souls. Often we build fine houses to gratify our pride and persuade ourselves that we are doing it to serve God. Most of life's failures come from self-deception. We deceive ourselves as to our abilities, and undertake to do things we have no capacity to do. After years of close observation I feel sure that nine-tenths of the failures in life come from overweening confidence in self. One so self-confident never stops to investigate or properly consider the difficulties in the way of his carrying out a work. Solomon in his counsels of wisdom cautions: "Trust in Jehovah with all thy heart, and lean not upon thine own understanding. . . . Be not wise in thine own eyes" (Prov. 3: 5-7) ; and Paul says: "Be not wise in your own conceits" (Rom. 12: 16). Self-conceit causes men to depend upon their own wisdom and strength instead of that of God, and leads them to ruin financially and spiritually.

that he may become wise.—To learn that the wisdom of this world is foolishness is to prepare oneself to accept the wisdom of God.

19 **For the wisdom of this world is foolishness with God.**— He here applies the truths presented in the conclusion of the first chapter. To be wise after the world is to be a fool before God. To be wise with God is to be a fool with the world. God has ordained that every institution and organization by man shall be engulfed in the destroying vortex of ruin. The disposition to introduce things into the service of God based on human opinions or judgments has been the besetting sin of man from the beginning. It has been the fatal rock on which he has made shipwreck of his faith and on which he has forfeited the favor of God, and the same thing is true even to this day.

Men become infidels by introducing their own opinions into the service and worship of God. It is done first with a view to adding interest and efficiency to the service. This trains men to rely more and more upon their opinions and judgment, less and less upon the institutions of God until they erect their own judgment and opinions into the standard of right, and whatever in the word of God does not agree with this standard of their own, they reject. Whenever men reject the word of God, or any part of it, because it does not agree with their own conceptions of what is right, they are in essential elements infidels. When a man tests the Bible and its truth, or any part of it, by his own judgment and opinions of what is right or wrong, he has rejected the word of God as the rule of faith for man. God has ordained that those who thus walk shall come to ruin. He shall fall into the pit he has digged.

For it is written, He that taketh the wise in their craftiness: —God so overrules as to destroy men with that by which they had devised to save themselves.

20 and again, The Lord knoweth the reasonings of the wise, that they are vain.—God knows all the plans of the wise that they are vain, and will lead to ruin. All the provisions of human wisdom for the advancement of the church of God result in evil to the church and to the world. There never has been an age in the past when there were so many and such costly attractions to draw people to church—fine and luxuriously equipped houses, fine mechanical musical instruments furnishing the best music, well-paid and eloquent ministers, preaching on topics of current interest, with all the societies and helps to attract and entertain the young and the old—yet the people cease to attend. Never before have there been so many human devices and so much money expended at home and abroad to hold and convert the people, and yet the denominational churches are growing relatively weaker and are losing ground.

The Lord has taken the wise men of the churches in their own craftiness. They have thought that they could improve, by their wisdom, on the ways of God, and God has shown them that they bring weakness to the churches and drive men

eth the reasonings of the wise, that they are vain. 21 Wherefore let no one glory in men. For all things are yours; 22 whether Paul, or Apollos, or Cephas, or the world, or life, or death, or things present, or things to come;

from God and the church. The church of God is defiled, and it is growing weaker day by day under the addition of these human organizations and helps. They are parasites that sap the life from the church, while for a time seeming to add to its vigor and life. Yet with all these warnings of God in the Scriptures confirmed by the examples of the destructive effects of the human inventions, churches and men claiming to be wise, and to believe in the Bible, follow the same path of ruin. There have drifted into the churches many who do not believe the Scriptures. The disposition to bring human organizations into the work and worship of the church comes from a feeling of wordly wisdom which is foolishness with God. It is a manifestation of unbelief and it must be thrust out of the churches before they can be blessed of God.

21 **Wherefore let no one glory in men.**—Do not glory in men or follow the works and inventions of men. [To glory in men is to boast of one's relation to them, to trust in them as the ground of confidence, or as the source of honor. Thus men are said to glory in the cross because Christ, as crucified, is regarded as the ground of confidence and the source of blessedness. The Corinthians gloried in men when they said, "I am of Paul; and I of Apollos; and I of Cephas."]

For all things are yours;—All that the men sent from God teach is the common heritage of all who believe in God. They all minister good to all who seek to know and do the will of God. No revelation to man was for personal use, but for the good of all the children of God.

22 **whether Paul, or Apollos, or Cephas,**—He makes special application of this truth to himself and others. Paul, Apollos, and Cephas are all sent for the good of all the children of God, and every child of God should receive all the teachings of all the faithful teachers if they would grow into a well-rounded likeness of Jesus Christ in character.

This truth is applicable now. Uninspired teachers are more liable to be one-sided and imperfect than the inspired ones were. And often what of God's teachings is presented by one

all are yours; 23 and ye are Christ's; and Christ is God's.

teacher is not preached by another, and often men would be
benefited by learning from different teachers, and men of di-
verse temperaments, and characteristics. All should be watchful to learn and do the will of God.

or the world,—[This denotes the material universe and all
its providential arrangements. All things that are in it that
are not sinful may be made serviceable to the happiness and
progress of the Christian, and to the glory of God. However
evil men may usurp possession meanwhile, it is the saints that
inherit the earth. (Matt. 5: 4.) It is maintained for their use,
ordered with a view to their spiritual welfare.]

or life,—[The term of our sojourn on earth, with all that it
brings, is ours. Life is a mighty gift—a great field in which to
sow eternal seed. It is ours for two purposes—being and
doing, the culture of the new life within us and the promotion
of our neighbor's well-being—in these two directions life is
our opportunity. "For to me to live is Christ." (Phil. 1: 21.)
There are ways of promoting God's glory which are peculiar
to this life, and which can never come to us again.]

or death,—[That grim, horrid thing, whose face strikes terror to the stoutest heart, and whose icy grasp freezes the fountains of life—that, too, becomes our servant, ministers to our
advancement. "To die is gain." (Phil. 1: 21.) It releases
from pains, and toils, and conflicts, and limitations of this mortal state, and ushers us into the enjoyment of the eternal inheritance.]

or things present, or things to come; all are yours;—[The
present and the future in the most comprehensive sense. Our
actual lot is ours, whether it be easy or hard, pleasant or distressing. It is ours to serve us, if we will only let it do its
work and turn it to the best account. The future is still hid
from us, but it can bring us nothing which shall not be for our
good. Whatever form the things to come may take, we are
assured that they are ours. (Rom. 8: 28.)]

23 and ye are Christ's; and Christ is God's.—So that in becoming Christ's, they become God's. "And we know that to
them that love God all things work together for good, even to

them that are called according to his purpose." (Rom. 8: 28.)
[What a climax! How the last words light up the whole situation and show how unworthy, how indescribably foolish and wrong was the party strife of the Corinthians. As there is one God over all, and one Lord Jesus Christ, so there is one church, in whose unbroken life the peace of God should find itself reflected.]

8. COROLLARY OF THE FOREGOING DISCUSSION SETTING FORTH THE TRUE VIEW OF MINISTERIAL WORTH AND RESPONSIBILITY
4: 1-5

1 Let a man so account of us, as of ministers of Christ, and stewards of the mysteries of God. 2 Here, moreover, it is required in stewards, that a

1 **Let a man so account of us, as of ministers of Christ,**—Paul returns to the question, in what esteem the inspired teachers of the gospel should be held. Let all esteem them as servants, underworkers of Christ to whom has been committed the things heretofore unrevealed, to be made known by them to men.

and stewards of the mysteries of God.—The office of a steward is to receive from the master and distribute as he directs. Of themselves, and apart from Christ, they had nothing, and could give nothing.

2 **Here, moreover, it is required in stewards, that a man be found faithful.**—God entrusted to the inspired men the truths he revealed to them through the Spirit. These truths were given to them to be taught to others for their salvation and edification. They were entrusted with the great spiritual truths brought to light in Christ Jesus for the salvation of the world. So Peter tells the Corinthians: "According as each hath received a gift, ministering it among yourselves, as good stewards of the manifold grace of God." (1 Pet. 4: 10.) Paul says: "For the bishop must be blameless, as God's steward." And Luke (16: 1-12) gives an account of the unjust steward who was not honest in the use of the master's goods. So it is important that those entrusted as stewards with the truth of God should be honest and faithful in teaching to the world all

man be found faithful. 3 But with me it is a very small thing that I should be ³judged of you, or of man's ⁴judgment: yea, I ⁵judge not mine own self. 4 For I know nothing against myself; yet am I not hereby justified: but he

³Or, *examined*
⁴Gr. *day.* See ch. 3. 13.
⁵Or, *examine*

---

that God has revealed for the salvation of the world. Not to teach all God's commands is to leave the world in condemnation with its blood on the stewards who failed to teach the truths God committed to them. So Paul, to the elders at Ephesus, in leaving them, said: "Wherefore I testify unto you this day, that I am pure from the blood of all men. For I shrank not from declaring unto you the whole counsel of God." (Acts 20: 26, 27.) Paul was an honest steward, distributing to others what God had entrusted to him for their good.

Teachers today are in a limited sense stewards of God to deliver his teaching to the world. He who refuses to teach the whole will of God is dishonest toward God and unfaithful to man. [Nothing short of an unswerving adherence to the simple gospel of Christ is divinely regarded as filling the required measure of this faithfulness as may be seen by the following exhortation: "And the things which thou hast heard from me among many witnesses, the same commit thou to faithful men, who shall be able to teach others also." (2 Tim. 2: 2.) "Take heed to thyself, and to thy teaching. Continue in these things; for in doing this thou shalt save both thyself and them that hear thee." (1 Tim. 4: 16.)]

3 **But with me it is a very small thing that I should be judged of you,**—[It was a matter of little concern to Paul that he should be judged by any of the Corinthians as to his faithfulness or unfaithfulness. His responsibility was not to them. They had not sent him; he was not their steward.]

or of man's judgment: yea, I judge not mine own self.—He leaves all to the judgment of God. He had no standard by which to judge himself save by the will of God.

4 **For I know nothing against myself;**—He was conscious of no failure to do his duty as a minister of God.

yet am I not hereby justified:—His failure to know any-

that ⁶judgeth me is the Lord. 5 Wherefore judge nothing before the time, until the Lord come, who will both bring to light the hidden things of darkness, and make manifest the counsels of the hearts; and then shall each man have his praise from God.

⁶Or, *examineth*

thing against himself did not make it sure that he was guiltless.

but he that judgeth me is the Lord.—God might know something against him even if his own heart did not condemn him. John said: "Hereby shall we know that we are of the truth, and shall assure our heart before him: because if our heart condemn us, God is greater than our heart, [and will make our condemnation the greater], and knoweth all things. Beloved, if our heart condemn us not, we have boldness toward God [that he will not condemn us]." (1 John 3: 19-21.) So Paul here, while knowing nothing against himself gives him hope, it does not make it certain that God will not see something wrong in him and condemn him.

5 Wherefore judge nothing before the time, until the Lord come, who will both bring to light the hidden things of darkness,—Wait for the Lord's judgment when he will bring to light all things now hidden in darkness.

and make manifest the counsels of the hearts; and then shall each man have his praise from God.—He will then open to view the secret motives of the heart and then every man, faithful as a steward, shall have the praise of God. Paul had confidence that God would justify him and Apollos in all the things over which the Corinthians had divided and for which they had been condemned. This does not mean that men should not test themselves by the word of God by which God will judge them.

9. REASON FOR LOWLINESS ENFORCED BY A CONTRAST BETWEEN THE ASSUMED SELF-SUFFICIENCY OF THE CORINTHIANS AND THE REAL CONDITION OF THE APOSTLES
4: 6-13

6 Now these things, brethren, I have in a figure transferred to myself and Apollos for your sakes; that in us ye might learn not *to go* beyond the things which are written; that no one of you be puffed up for the one against the other. 7 For who maketh thee to differ? and what hast thou that thou didst not receive? but if thou didst receive it, why dost thou glory

---

6 **Now these things, brethren, I have in a figure transferred to myself and Apollos for your sakes; that in us ye might learn not to go beyond the things which are written;**—This was said to impress upon them that in their esteem for teachers they should not follow them further than they do the will of God as it is written. Bishop Pierce paraphrases the verse thus: "I have made use of my own and Apollos' name in my arguments against your divisions, because I would spare to name those teachers among you who are guilty of making and leading parties, that in us you might learn not to follow any one with a party." Paul and Apollos did not make the parties. Other ambitious men fomented the parties and used the names of Apollos and Paul to do it.

that no one of you be puffed up for the one against the other.—This may mean that the division was not concerning Paul, Apollos, or Peter; but that he had used their names to show the evil of following men. If it was not right to follow them, much less the uninspired men.

7 **For who maketh thee to differ?**—Who made them leaders of parties arrayed one against another? [This glorification and depreciation of rival teachers sprang from unwarrantable arrogance. It involved a claim to superiority, and a right to sit in judgment, which they did not possess.]

and what hast thou that thou didst not receive?—What did they have in the way of gifts and knowledge that they did not receive from those to whom God gave his Spirit?

but if thou didst receive it, why dost thou glory as if thou hadst not received it?—If they received it from the apostles, why did they boast and set themselves against them, and set

as if thou hadst not received it? 8 Already are ye filled, already ye are become rich, ye have come to reign without us: yea and I would that ye did reign, that we also might reign with you. 9 For, I think, God hath set forth us the apostles last of all, as men doomed to death: for we are made a spec-

themselves as leaders as though they had not received it from those whom they now oppose?

8 **Already are ye filled, already ye are become rich, ye have come to reign without us:**—In this he reproaches them for their assumption of worldly wisdom. They acted as though they were already filled of all the good things of earth, had become rich in spiritual things, and were reigning as kings without those from whom they had received all they had from Christ. [The strong irony in these expressions, taken in connection with what he had already said, must have stung them to the heart. For there is a striking contrast between the comfortable, full-fed, self-satisfied Corinthians and the depression and the scorn in the midst of which the apostles lived. It is not an unusual thing for many people to forget, if not despise, the men through whom they were brought to the knowledge of the truth; and take up others to whom, in things of God, they owe nothing.]

yea and I would that ye did reign, that we also might reign with you.—He would have rejoiced at their reigning as real kings and priests of the Lord that those who had converted them and had bestowed on them all the real good they possessed might reign with them instead of suffering want and persecution as they were then suffering.

9 **For, I think,**—[The Corinthians thought themselves wise, and Paul, in contrast, thought God had set forth the apostles the lowest in this world. They fared worse than even the prophets, who, though grievously afflicted and tormented, were sometimes honored.]

God hath set forth us the apostles last of all, as men doomed to death:—He speaks this in view of the great persecutions the apostles were called upon to suffer before the world. [The word translated "doomed" occurs nowhere else in the New Testament, and denotes the certainty of death. It implies that such were their continued conflicts, trials, and persecutions, that it was certain that they would terminate in

tacle unto the world, ⁷both to angels and men. 10 We are fools for Christ's
sake, but ye are wise in Christ; we are weak, but ye are strong; ye have

⁷Or, *and to angels, and to men.*

their death. This is a very strong expression, and denotes the
continuance and intensity of their sufferings in the cause of
Christ.]

**for we are made a spectacle unto the world, both to angels
and men.**—They were appointed to suffer unto death for
Christ's sake, a spectacle before heaven and earth. [It is
quite likely that the reference here is to the ancient amphitheatre, whose arena was surrounded by circular seats, capable of accommodating thousands of spectators. In this arena
trained athletes struggled for prizes in the games, at the close
of which, when the spectators had been sated with bloodless
performances, criminals condemned to death were brought in
to fight with wild beasts or with one another. They came
into the arena knowing that they could never leave it alive.
While others sat comfortably looking on, with curtains to
shade them from the heat and refreshments to save them from
exhaustion or from faintness at the sight of blood, they were
in the arena, exposed to wounds, ill-usage and death. On
such an arena Paul speaks of himself and fellow laborers as
struggling, the objects not only of human, but angelic, spectators. Such were the sufferings of the apostles that men and
angels gazed on them with wonder.]

10 **We are fools for Christ's sake,**—According to the world's
wisdom, the apostles were fools for Christ's sake.

but ye are wise in Christ;—By the same rule, while claiming to be the servants and teachers of Christ, they enjoyed
honor, plenty, and every worldly good.

**we are weak, but ye are strong; ye have glory, but we have
dishonor.**—The apostles were among them "in weakness, and
in fear, and in much trembling" (2: 3), and thought not of
themselves, but of their Master's message, and this humbled
them; whereas their opponents assumed stately airs and
claimed to be strong in Christ, and were honored by the heathen around them. The apostles, who gloried in no such pretensions, were dishonored by those teachers and the world.

[The contrast between the two situations enunciated in verses 8 and 9 is expressed in this verse in three antitheses which are withering blows to the proud Corinthians. These words are addressed especially to these proud party leaders, but at the same time to all the members who sympathized with them :

(1) As to teaching, the apostles had to face the reputation of foolishness which the gospel brought upon them, while at Corinth there was found a way of preaching Christ so as to procure a name for wisdom, the reputation of profound philosophers and men of most reliable judgment. Paul might have become as celebrated as Gamaliel; but for Christ's sake he consented to pass as a fool. The Corinthians knew better how to manage—they made the teaching even of the gospel a means of gaining celebrity for their lofty wisdom.

(2) As to conduct. They came before the public with the feeling of their strength. There is in them neither hesitation nor timidity. They succeeded in becoming wise, strong, and honorable in consequence actually of their being Christians. They had turned their relationship to Christ in an effective means to restore them to worldly greatness, in another form, which they once surrendered in order to become Christians. The apostles did not condescend to these grand lordly airs. They thought not of themselves, but of their Master and his message, and this, instead of exalting, humbled them. For Paul says of himself, and he expressed the sentiment of all : "Most gladly therefore will I rather glory in my weaknesses, that the power of Christ may rest upon me. Wherefore I take pleasure in weaknesses, in injuries, in necessities, in persecutions, in distresses, for Christ's sake : for when I am weak, then am I strong." (2 Cor. 12 : 9, 10.)

(3) The welcome received from the world by the one and the other. The proud party leaders were honored, feted, and regarded as the ornament of cultivated circles ; there was rivalry to do them honor, while the apostles were reviled and calumniated.]

In verses 11-13 he tells them how the true teachers who converted them and taught them all they knew of Christ— who while among them lived in want working with their own hands that they might not burden them—are still persecuted,

glory, but we have dishonor.   11 Even unto this present hour we both hunger, and thirst, and are naked, and are buffeted, and have no certain dwelling-place; 12 and we toil, working with our own hands: being reviled, we
bless; being persecuted, we endure; 13 being defamed, we entreat: we are

---

reviled, despised, suffering for want of all things, and in it all
they returned good for evil, blessings for curses, while these
unworthy teachers enjoyed good. This was a reminder that
they were not following the teachings of Jesus.

11 **Even unto this present hour**—[The emphasis is on the
ceaselessness of the hardships, privations, sufferings, and hu-
miliations to which the apostles were subjected. The fact
that Paul gladly submitted to all these afflictions presented
his case in glaring contrast with that of his opposers at Corinth, who exposed themselves to no such sufferings out of zeal
for Christ.]

we both hunger, and thirst,—Like their Master, the apostles
were poor, and in traveling from place to place, it often happened that they scarcely found entertainment of the poorest
kind. Of this his own language is the best comment: "In
hunger and thirst, in fastings often." (2 Cor. 11: 27.)

and are naked,—[They were insufficiently clad. In their labors their clothing became old and badly worn, and they had
no friends to replace them, neither had they money with
which to buy new ones.]

and are buffeted,—[Slapped in the face. Such insults, together with scourgings, frequently fell to the lot of Paul (Acts
16: 23; 23: 2), and the other apostles. It shows the utter contempt with which they were treated.]

and have no certain dwelling-place;—[This homelessness
was among the severest of all trials. They wandered in dis-
tant lands; when driven from one place they went to another;
and thus they led a wandering, uncomfortable life amidst
strangers and foes. All this was for the sake of the gospel
that men might have eternal life.]

12 **and we toil, working with our own hands:**—[Paul supported himself and his companions in labor by the dreary toil
and scant earnings of a tentmaker, in the express determination to be no burden to those who accepted the gospel under
his preaching in Corinth. (2 Cor. 11: 7-9.) Such conduct was

made as the [8]filth of the world, the offscouring of all things, even until now,

[8]Or, *refuse*

---

more noble because all mechanical trades were looked down upon by the Greeks. It is quite likely that this is mentioned to put the false teachers at Corinth to shame, who not only demanded maintenance from them, but were living in ease and luxury through their liberality to them.]

being reviled, we bless; being persecuted, we endure;— [The picture of the ignominious condition of Paul and his fellow laborers is continued, and its effects heightened by the contrast of their demeanor. They are so utterly empty and devoid of all honor with others that, as respects those who reviled, persecuted, and slandered them, they did not in any wise defend themselves or seek vengeance against them.]

13 **being defamed, we entreat:**—They wished good to their revilers, remained quiet and patient towards their persecutors, and gave beseeching words to their slanderers. In all this they followed the example of their Master: "Who, when he was reviled, reviled not again; when he suffered, threatened not; but committed himself to him that judgeth righteously."

we are made as the filth of the world, the offscouring of all things, even until now.—[This has reference to that which is collected by sweeping a house, or that which is collected and cast away by purifying or cleansing anything; hence any vile, worthless, and contemptible object. It was applied to men of the most vile, abject, and worthless character. This shows in a very strong light the indignities and sufferings which Paul and his fellow laborers endured in the service of Christ. Notice how severely this description rebukes the self-conceited disturbers among the Corinthians. In the presence of such tremendous earnestness and such forgetfulness of self, they could not but feel how utterly contemptible was all thought of their own learning or skill. What are we doing for him for whom Paul did and suffered so much!]

10. EXPLANATION OF THE CHARACTER AND SPIRIT OF HIS REPROOFS AND ADMONITIONS
4: 14-21

14 I write not these things to shame you, but to admonish you as my beloved children. 15 For though ye have ten thousand tutors in Christ, yet *have ye* not many fathers; for in Christ Jesus I begat you through the

---

14 **I write not these things to shame you,**—He does not write these things to shame them for their neglect of him and his fellow laborers.

but to admonish you as my beloved children. He warns them that they are not following Christ and are in danger of making shipwreck of their profession. A holy, devoted life would bring upon them the sufferings and persecutions the apostles were enduring; hence the Corinthians were deceived in supposing that they were serving God while enjoying the worldly good. [Paul's object in drawing such a contrast between their case and his was not to mortify them; but out of his love to them as children to bring the truth to their minds, and let them see what they really were, as contrasted with what they imagined themselves to be.]

15 **For though ye have ten thousand tutors in Christ, yet have ye not many fathers;**—They had many teachers in Christ, yet they had but one father in the gospel. The father cared more for them than any teacher, especially those making gain of them.

for in Christ Jesus I begat you through the gospel.—By the Holy Spirit sent down from heaven, Paul preached the gospel, the word of God, which is the seed of the kingdom, to the Corinthians; they received it into the heart as the incorruptible seed, and by it they were begotten or made alive. James says: "Of his own will he brought us forth by the word of truth, that we should be a kind of firstfruits of his creatures." (James 1: 18.) Peter says: "Having been begotten again, not of corruptible seed, but of incorruptible, through the word of God, which liveth and abideth. . . . And this is the word of good tidings which was preached unto you." (1 Pet. 1: 23-25.) Connect with this what Jesus said to Nicodemus (John 3: 3-5), and it is clear that the Holy Spirit begets by imparting

⁹gospel. 16 I beseech you therefore, be ye imitators of me. 17 For this
cause have I sent unto you Timothy, who is my beloved and faithful child in
the Lord, who shall put you in remembrance of my ways which are in
Christ, even as I teach everywhere in every church. 18 Now some are

⁹Gr. *good tidings.* See marginal note on Mt. 4. 23.

---

the word of God, the incorruptible seed, to the heart of man
through the gospel.

16 I beseech you therefore, be ye imitators of me.—Here he
asserts his fidelity to Christ, his nearness to them as their
father, and so pleads with them for their own good as beloved
children to imitate him in Christ, [in humility, self-denial, and
faithfulness. To what extent he wished them to imitate him,
he shows in these words: "Be ye imitators of me, even as I
also am of Christ." (11: 1.)]

**17 For this cause have I sent unto you Timothy, who is my
beloved and faithful child in the Lord,**—To the end that they
imitate him, he sent Timothy, who also was his son in the
gospel, and faithful in the Lord, who as his son imitated him
as he besought them to do.

**who shall put you in remembrance of my ways which are in
Christ, even as I teach everywhere in every church.**—[Timo-
thy's description of Paul's conduct would correspond with
Paul's actual behavior as a Christian and a teacher, which he
declares emphatically to be the same everywhere. This was
said to assure them that, in laying upon them the necessity of
unanimity and humbleness of mind, he did not inculcate what
he did not universally teach and practice himself. His public
teaching and private life were the same everywhere. What he
taught in Corinth was the same that he taught and practiced
in Philippi and everywhere else.]

**18 Now some are puffed up, as though I were not coming to
you.**—These false teachers were puffed up, haughty, thinking
he would not come unto them. [His sending Timothy was no
indication whatever that he did not intend to visit Corinth, as
some in their pride and self-importance affirmed. Paul's writings clearly indicate that the false teachers in different ways
endeavored to destroy his influence among them by calling in
question his apostleship (9: 1-3; 2 Cor. 12: 12); accusing him
of fickleness (2 Cor. 1: 17); and asserting that his "bodily

puffed up, as though I were not coming to you. 19 But I will come to you shortly, if the Lord will; and I will know, not the word of them that are puffed up, but the power. 20 For the kingdom of God is not in word, but in power. 21 What will ye? shall I come unto you with a rod, or in love and a spirit of gentleness?

presence is weak, and his speech of no account" (2 Cor. 10: 10). These detractors and their followers were the ones who were puffed up. They were so conceited as to their own importance, and as to the success of their injurious representation respecting him, as to make it appear that he was afraid to come to Corinth, and therefore sent Timothy in his stead.]

19 **But I will come to you shortly,**—[It was from no fear of them that he was kept away; and to convince them of this] he firmly asserts that he would come to them soon.

if the Lord will;—[With Paul this expression was far more than a mere form. It was a recognition both of the providential and spiritual government of the Lord. He recognized that the accomplishment of any purpose depended on his will and felt that his life was in his hands.]

and I will know, not the word of them that are puffed up, but the power.—He would know not the eloquence and pretensions of the false teachers, but would test their power. They claimed to be greater than Paul, and denied that he was an apostle sent of God. The test that one's apostleship was from God, and that God approved him, was manifested in God's presence in enabling him to work miracles. Paul proposed to test their power as to whether the presence of God was with them.

20 **For the kingdom of God is not in word,**—God's kingdom does not rest on eloquent and persuasive words. (2: 4.) [The kingdom of God implies here, as usual in the language of Paul, the living fellowship established by the Savior, which lives in the soul, and manifests itself in the essential character of the loving obedience of those belonging to it.]

but in power.—The presence of God's Spirit with the teachers, which is the power to work miracles.

21 **What will ye?** shall I come unto you with a rod,—This divine power was sometimes used to punish pretenders, as in the case of Ananias and Sapphira (Acts 5: 1-11); and Elymas,

the sorcerer (Acts 13: 8-12). Some think Paul meant something of this kind. It certainly meant that Paul would show the presence and power of the Spirit with him in contrast with the lack of it in the false teachers. It was with them to say by the course they pursued whether he would come to them with a rod of authority and power to assert his claims as an apostle, or should he come to them as a father to his children.

or in love and a spirit of gentleness?—God is gentle, kind, forgiving to the penitent; but will by no means clear the guilty. Is stern and unyielding in his punishment of the wicked. His servants should cherish his spirit.

SECTION THREE
CONCERNING LICENTIOUSNESS
5: 1 to 6: 20

1. CENSURE OF THE DELIBERATE TOLERATION OF A GROSS CASE OF INCEST
5: 1-8

1 It is actually reported that there is fornication among you, and such fornication as is not even among the Gentiles, that one *of you* hath his father's wife. 2 And [10]ye are puffed up, and [11]did not rather mourn, that he

[10]Or, *are ye puffed up?*
[11]Or, *did ye not rather mourn, . . . you?*

---

1 It is actually reported—[It was a matter of common notoriety, talked among the people generally and caused great scandal.]

that there is fornication among you,—With the confluence of strangers and of commerce, were associated the luxury and licentiousness which gave the name of Corinth an infamous notoriety, and which connected in the case of the Temple of Aphrodite with religious rites, requiring licentious acts in its devotees, it is not surprising that such sins would be committed by some of those who professed to be followers of Christ. For sins that are common and popular in a community will trouble a church in that community.

and such fornication as is not even among the Gentiles,—Here is a type of licentiousness in the church that was not tolerated among the heathen. [It was held in detestation by them as a shameful and abominable monstrosity.]

that one of you hath his father's wife.—It is probable that the father had been guilty of the folly of marrying a woman better suited in age for his son. But it was a gross outrage upon chastity and virtue, and yet the church was tolerating it and glorying over it. [The marriage of a son to his stepmother was forbidden among the Jews under the penalty of death (Lev. 18: 8, 20: 11; Deut. 22: 30; 27: 20); and it was a violation of the Roman law and held in abhorrence by them. From the complete silence as to the crime of the woman, it is inferred that she was a heathen.]

2 And ye are puffed up,—Looseness in faith, heresy, division and strife breed indifference to morality and virtue, and

that had done this deed might be taken away from among you. 3 For I
verily, being absent in body but present in spirit, have already as though I

---

open the way for all shames and sins to follow. So these people in their departures from the faith had admitted all types of
immorality. This case was probably among the wealthy and
influential, or belonged to an influential party, and instead of
condemning him for the sin, they were arrogant, defied criti-
cism, and did not feel that his course was a source of sorrow
and shame for the persons sinning and for the church so dis-
graced and humiliated by the crime. [It does not mean that
they were puffed up because of this outrage, but in spite of it.
It ought to have humbled them to the dust, and yet they retained their self-satisfied complacency. Their morbid self-importance, which made them so intolerant of petty wrongs (6:
7), made them tolerant of deep disgrace.]

and did not rather mourn,—[The church should have risen
as one man, and gone into a common act of humiliation and
mourning, like a family for the death of one of its members.
It should have been a day of repentance, on which the whole
church before the Lord deplored the scandal committed, and
cried to him to lead them to expel the guilty person from the
fellowship in irrepressible horror at his conduct.]

**that he that had done this deed might be taken away from
among you.**—That he should be refused fellowship or recognition in the church. Loss of fellowship involved loss of recognition and association among Christians. It should be considered a great disgrace and shame yet to be excluded from the
membership of the church of Christ. It is noteworthy that
God always holds the man the more guilty party in such sins.
It is to the shame of society that this order has been reversed
in modern times.

3 **For I verily, being absent in body but present in spirit,**—
[Paul was fully informed by the Spirit of God in all the circumstances, and instructed by him in the way he should act.]

**have already as though I were present judged him that hath
so wrought this thing,**—His spirit was present with them and
he had already decided as to the guilt and condemnation of
him who had done the deed. [This is a remarkable assertion

we. ¯esent judged him that hath so wrought this thing, 4 in the name of our L.rd Jesus, ye being gathered together, and my spirit, with the power of our Lord Jesus, 5 to deliver such a one unto Satan for the destruction of the flesh, that the spirit may be saved in the day of the Lord ¹Jesus. 6 Your

¹Some ancient authorities omit *Jesus.*

of apostolic power. After reading this letter, they would know that he who had wrought miracles with such power among them was spiritually and effectually present, and weak though he was in personal appearance and speech, was able to exercise sharp discipline on the whole body, unless they submitted to the voice of God through his mouth.]

4 in the name of our Lord Jesus,—Acting for and in the stead of the Lord Jesus. [The phrase includes, on the one hand, the denial that the thing was done by virtue of his own authority; and on the other, the claim of the right to act as the representative of Christ.]

ye being gathered together, and my spirit, with the power of our Lord Jesus,—When they were gathered together, Paul himself present in spirit gave his decision in this letter, with the power of the Lord Jesus Christ. When the church acts according to his directions, its action is clothed with the power of Christ. The act of the body in such case is the act of Christ. [A question of much importance is, Does the apostle by the words, "ye being gathered together," mean that he waits for their assent to his ruling in this matter? Most assuredly not. The whole tone, not only the passage which is now before us, but of the whole epistle up to this point, is that he would have them look upon him as the apostle—the special messenger of Christ—standing towards them in the place of Christ. There is not the faintest hint of making the pronouncing of the sentence dependent on the vote of the assembly which is to be held, as if the apostle's decision could be annulled by the contrary opinion of a majority. For his part everything is decided, and with his apostolic competency he has judged to deliver over the offender. There will be joined to Paul, in the assembly which he convokes, "the whole church" (Acts 15: 22), to take part in this act.]

5 to deliver such a one unto Satan for the destruction of the flesh, that the spirit may be saved in the day of the Lord Je-

sus.—What the deliverance of the body to Satan may mean, how the flesh is destroyed, and what the day of the Lord Jesus is, are questions of doubt and have produced much discussion. It probably means that he was separated from the fellowship of the church, from all association with the brethren in Christ, regarded and treated as a heathen; that by these influences he might be brought to realize the enormity of his sin, and turn from fleshly lusts, and be restored to a life of holiness, and to the fellowship of the church that he might at last be saved. The church by the direction of Paul put him away from among them (2 Cor. 2: 10), and at a later period he directs them to forgive and comfort the one who had been separated from the fellowship, supposed to be the same person, "lest by any means such a one should be swallowed up with his overmuch sorrow." (2 Cor. 2: 7.) The exclusion from the fellowship of the saints and the privileges of the house of God is a serious and awful matter. When one has been excluded from the fellowship of the church, Christians should make him feel that he forfeits the esteem and association of all the members of the church, yet he should be warned and admonished as a brother. (2 Thess. 3: 15.)

[Disorderly conduct must be dealt with by the church in the way the Lord appoints. Immorality is not to be tolerated among the followers of Christ. The whole action of the church is moral and spiritual, and the extremest infliction it can impose in any case is exclusion from the fellowship. The necessity for exercising such discipline is for the following reasons:

(1) The honor of Christ, which is sadly impeached when open sin is allowed among those who profess to be his followers. To make Christ a minister of sin is a grievous offense.

(2) The welfare of the offender himself is never to be lost sight of. The wise, kindly, deliberate action of the church may save the erring one. And hence, however humiliating and terrible the exclusion may have been, the door is always left open for return. Its object, so far as the offender is concerned, is his recovery, and if he repents and comes to a right state of mind, nothing stands in the way of his restoration to the fellowship.

glorying is not good. Know ye not that a little leaven leaveneth the whole lump? 7 Purge out the old leaven, that ye may be a new lump, even as ye are unleavened. For our passover also hath been sacrificed, *even* Christ: 8

(3) The welfare of the church requires that the transgressors shall be dealt with. For sin is a spreading leprosy. It may begin in a small obscure place, but unless speedily arrested will increase and diffuse itself till the whole body is infected. A moral gangrene must be cut out.]

6 **Your glorying is not good.**—The glorying and self-justification were not good. If not put away from among them, it would soon work the corruption of the whole body.

Know ye not that a little leaven leaveneth the whole lump? —As a small quantity of leaven pervades the entire mass of dough and communicates its nature to the whole of that with which it comes in contact, so the least sin tolerated affects the whole church, and communicates its nature to the whole of that with which it comes in contact. It is therefore applied to all sin voluntarily tolerated by the individual or the church. To be indifferent to grave misbehavior is to become partly responsible for it, and to lower the standard of Christian living. [Here the stress of the argument lies less in the evil example of the offender than in the fact that toleration of this conduct implies concurrence (Rom. 1: 32), and debases the standard of moral judgment and instinct. To be indifferent to grave misbehavior is to become partly responsible for it. A subtle atmosphere, in which evil readily springs up and is diffused, is the result. The leaven that was infecting the Corinthian church was a vitiated public opinion.]

7 **Purge out the old leaven,**—Here is an allusion to the order given by Moses (Ex. 12: 15, 20; 13: 7) to remove all leaven from the Jewish house before the Passover, and carried out with such scrupulous care that on the fourteenth day of the month they searched with lighted candles even the darkest places in their houses to see whether any remained.

that ye may be a new lump,—The position of Christians is analogous to that of Israel, and they should put away the evil and purge out the leaven of sin that is among them that they may be a pure unleavened lump of holiness.

wherefore let us ²keep the feast, not with old leaven, neither with the leaven of malice and wickedness, but with the unleavened bread of sincerity and truth.

²Gr. *keep festival.*

---

even as ye are unleavened.—They were purged of the leaven of evil in coming into Christ.

For our passover also hath been sacrificed, even Christ:— As when the passover lamb was sacrificed they must put away the leaven, so Christ is our passover, a perpetual sacrifice for us, so we must put from us the leaven of evil as the children of God.

8 wherefore let us keep the feast, not with old leaven,— Since Christ is our passover, sanctified for us, let us keep the feast perpetually. That is, live holily. The whole life of the Christian should be a joyous and pure feast of services to God in sincerity and truth, none of the old leaven of heathenism being retained in the body, the church. [To the Christian, Christ is a perpetual sacrifice, an ever-present paschal Lamb, demanding and enforcing constant vigilance and unceasing cleanliness. The individual must put away every sinful habit of the old life. The church must purge itself of all whose lives are sources of corruption.]

neither with the leaven of malice and wickedness,—[Malice is ill will in the mind; wickedness is ill will expressed in action.]

but with the unleavened bread of sincerity—[The word "sincere" sets forth before the mind the material image from which the spiritual quality takes its name. The honey free from the smallest particle of wax, pure and transparent. The word used here conveys a similar idea. It is derived from the custom of judging the purity of liquids or the texture of cloths by holding them between the eye and the sun. What is here set forth as necessary to the Christian character is a quality which can stand this extreme test, and does not need to be seen only in an artificial light. It brings before us a pure transparent sincerity which is genuine; and acceptance of Christ which is real, and which is rich in real results.]

and truth.—[This means far more than veracity. In its subjective sense, it means the inward state which answers to truth; fullness, straightforwardness, integrity of purpose; that moral and spiritual condition which conforms to the law and character of God. All corresponds to an unsullied, uncontaminated, and genuine Christian character.]

2. CORRECTION OF THEIR MISUNDERSTANDING OF A COMMANDMENT PREVIOUSLY GIVEN AS TO ASSOCIATION WITH FORNICATORS
5: 9-13

9 I wrote unto you in my epistle to have no company with fornicators; 10 [3]not at all *meaning* with the fornicators of this world, or with the covetous and extortioners, or with idolaters; for then must ye needs go out of the

[3]Or, *not altogether with the fornicators &c.*

---

9 **I wrote unto you in my epistle**—Some think he means that he had so written them in this letter. This the expression would not allow, for he intends to modify now directions hitherto given. So Paul had doubtless written a letter to them before this, in which he had given the directions here noted.

to have no company with fornicators;—A fornicator is one who has sexual intercourse with an unmarried person, but the word is frequently used to denote all unlawful intercourse. (Matt. 5: 32; 19: 9.) To have company with is to associate with and treat one as worthy of companionship and association. The Christian is not to treat the guilty person as such. The object, no doubt, is to make the fornicator feel the disgrace and shame of his course and bring him to repentance.

10 **not at all meaning with the fornicators of this world,**— He now modifies the command so as to apply to fornicators in the church and not to those in the world.

or with the covetous—The covetous are those who seek to obtain what is another's in an unlawful way. The man who sacrifices honesty to the acquisition of wealth is heinous in the sight of God. He cannot be a Christian and should not be recognized as such.

and extortioners,—An extortioner is one who by power or threats takes what is not his own or more than is right. The

world: 11 but *as it is, I wrote unto you not to keep company, if any man that is named a brother be a fornicator, or covetous, or an idolater, or a reviler, or a drunkard, or an extortioner; with such a one no, not to eat. 12 For what have I to do with judging them that are without? Do not ye

*Or, *now I write*

man who takes advantage of another's poverty, or his necessities, to obtain exorbitant gain, is an extortioner.

or with idolaters;—Prior to the preaching of the gospel in Corinth, by Paul, all the inhabitants therein, with the exception of a few Jews, were idolaters.

for then must ye needs go out of the world:—He did not mean to so treat those guilty of the sins just mentioned. They were so common among the people that if they refused to associate with them it would be like going out of the world, withdrawing as a recluse, having no association or dealing with mankind.

11 but as it is, I wrote unto you not to keep company, if any man that is named a brother be a fornicator, or covetous, or an idolater, or a reviler, or a drunkard, or an extortioner; with such a one no, not to eat.—Personal association with those claiming to be Christians guilty of these sins is prohibited. [Christians must tolerate no such sins among themselves; they must exclude from the social circle any one who, bearing the name of Christ, indulges in these vices of the heathen world. The church is to be the light of the world and not the recipient of the world's darkness.]

The question is sometimes raised as to whether the eating means the Lord's Supper or a common meal. The context plainly shows that it means the latter. The association here forbidden with the sinner calling himself a Christian is permitted to men of the world guilty of the same sins. But we are not permitted to eat the Lord's Supper with the sinners without. Therefore, this cannot refer to the Lord's Supper, but must refer to an ordinary meal. Then, too, to eat a common meal with a man was to acknowledge him as a worthy equal. The Jews would not eat with the publicans and sinners, and strongly condemned Jesus for doing so.

12 For what have I to do with judging them that are without?—[They should have easily understood his meaning, for it

judge them that are within? 13 But them that are without God judgeth.
Put away the wicked man from among yourselves.

---

was well known to them that] he had nothing to do with
judging those not members of the church. [The phrase "them
that are without" is frequently used by Paul (1 Thess. 4: 12;
Col. 4: 5), and their awful condition he graphically describes
as follows: "Ye were at that time separate from Christ, alien-
ated from the commonwealth of Israel, and strangers from the
covenants of the promise, having no hope and without God in
the world." (Eph. 2: 12.)]

Do not ye judge them that are within?—As churches they
were to look after and deal with those within that they might
be kept from evil influences. [Their own practice should have
saved them from misunderstanding him. It is possible that
his meaning had been purposely wrested by interested persons
to bring discredit upon his teaching concerning fornicators.]

13 But them that are without God judgeth.—They were to
leave those without to the judgment of God.

Put away the wicked man from among yourselves.—In pursuance of the truth set forth here, he commands them to put
from them this wicked person, who had taken his own father's
wife. There was no choice left the church. It must do just
what Paul under the guidance of the Spirit directed them to
do. There was no voting, but obedience to plain directions in
carrying out the case.

3. LITIGATION BEFORE CIVIL COURTS FORBIDDEN
6: 1-11

1 Dare any of you, having a matter against [5]his neighbor, go to law be-
[5]Gr. *the other.* See Rom. 13. 8.

---

1 Dare any of you,—[The word "dare" implies that the re-
sort to civil courts to settle differences between Christians is
wholly inconsistent with the will of Christ, and that even one
case would be outrageous.]

having a matter against his neighbor, go to law before the
unrighteous,—To neglect or reject the authority of God at one
point prepares the way and leads to the setting aside his au-

fore the unrighteous, and not before the saints? 2 Or know ye not that the

thority at all points. The Corinthians turned from adherence to the law of God, and became followers of men. They gave up the high regard for morality and palliated the grossest forms of licentiousness. They set aside the leaders of the congregation as the divinely appointed tribunal for deciding differences that might arise among them, and resorted to the tribunals of the heathen, or the government of the unbelievers; and Paul now comes to remonstrate with them for setting aside the divine authority.

and not before the saints?—It was anticipated that Christians would have troubles or differences in their affairs, and Jesus gave (Matt. 18: 15-20) rules by which to settle them. The judgment of the saints was obtained when the directions given were followed. Paul regarded it as a daring sin in Christians to neglect the law of Christ and seek the tribunals of the State. This did not conflict with Paul's own course of appealing to Caesar's court for protection, when the servants of Caesar were used to persecute him. He appealed to the protection Caesar's laws guaranteed when those were perverted and abused to punish him by the laws of Caesar. Caesar's courts are recognized as the courts of unbelievers; the decisions of the church as courts of the believers. Since the days of the union of "Church and State," and while believers participate in State affairs, this distinction is lost sight of, and the admonition is disregarded. The decisions of the church are brought into disrepute, because they are so often mere efforts at compromise instead of decisions of justice. Compromise of right, truth, and justice can never command the respect of God or man.

2 Or know ye not—[A form of expression often used by Paul when he wished to bring to mind important truth, which his readers knew, but disregarded. The knowledge of the great future which was in store for the children of God was the strongest argument against the humiliating degradation to which their appeal to the civil courts to settle their differences had subjected them.]

that the saints—All Christians are called saints whether they

saints shall judge the world? and if the world is judged by you, are ye un-

live lives of consecration to God or not. They have separated themselves to the service of God and that sanctifies them.

shall judge the world?—What this verse and the next means is a matter of doubt. When, how, and where the saints are to judge the world and angels, is difficult to determine. Macknight holds that the saints are now judging the world through presenting the gospel to it, because by it the world is justified or condemned, as it receives or rejects its teachings. But the judgment here seems to be a deciding, according to that word, who is guilty and who is innocent. Matthew says: "And Jesus said unto them, Verily I say unto you, that ye who have followed me, in the regeneration when the Son of man shall sit on the throne of his glory, ye also shall sit upon twelve thrones, judging the twelve tribes of Israel." (Matt. 19: 28.)

Another position occupied by many commentators is that the saints will be associated with Christ when they reign with him and when he judges the wicked. The doctrine, they claim, glimmered faintly to Daniel and came as a message of consolation and hope in the time of national suffering and shame, "and judgment was given to the saints of the Most High, and the time came that the saints possessed the kingdom." (Dan. 7: 18-22.) Christ's people will share his royalty (Rom. 8: 18; 2 Tim. 2: 12); and therefore they will share the government (Matt. 19: 28; Luke 22: 30), which the Father has committed to the Son (John 5: 22). In the great day the saints will intelligently and cordially approve and endorse the sentence pronounced by Christ on the millions on earth. Possibly this approval may be divinely appointed an essential condition, without which sentence would not be pronounced by man upon men, but by men themselves redeemed from their own sins, upon those who have chosen death rather than life. They further claim that it may be that final sentence cannot, according to the principles of the divine government of the universe, be pronounced upon the lost without the concurrence of the saved, that is, without a revelation of the sentence so clear as to secure the full approbation of the saved. If so, the concurrence of the saved is an essential element in

worthy ⁰to judge the smallest matters? 3 Know ye not that we shall judge

⁰Gr. *of the smallest tribunals.*

the final judgment; and they may truly be said to judge both men and angels. That the sentence which the saints will pronounce is put into their lips by Christ does not make their part in the judgment any less real; for even the Son says, "I can of myself do nothing: as I hear, I judge." (John 5: 30.) As summoned by Christ to sit with him, the saints will approve and endorse the measures of reward to be given to themselves. To appeal to human courts of law was to appeal to men upon whom, as upon all men, they themselves, amid the splendor of the great assize, will pronounce an eternal sentence.

How and when the saints will judge the world seems difficult to determine, but as a truth it is accepted, and the apostle argues that they are competent to judge the differences arising among themselves.

and if the world is judged by you, are ye unworthy to judge the smallest matters?—[This appeal is quite intelligible. It may be asked: "What has all this to do with the matter in hand? The rule of the saints is not yet." The answer is that this judgment of the world is no private privilege arbitrarily bestowed. The saints are to share our Lord's activity, because they share his mind (2: 15, 16), and this mind is in part already formed in them. Thus of necessity their disputes ought to be referred to them, rather than to courts, since they are competent to judge and adjust their differences.]

3 Know ye not that we shall judge angels? how much more, things that pertain to this life?—Some think "we" in this verse refers to the apostles, and not to the saints generally; but the latter clause seems to show that it was written to vindicate the right of the saints to judge the temporal questions that come up between Christians. If so, it must refer to them. Angels are generally understood to mean the fallen angels, demons, as the angels ministering for God hardly need to be judged. Some think the saints are to judge these by preaching the gospel, as the power of Christ through it "should spoil demons of their oracles and idols; should de-

angels? how much more, things that pertain to this life? 4 If then ye have
[7]to judge things pertaining to this life, [8]do ye set them to judge who are of
no account in the church? 5 I say *this* to move you to shame. [9]What,
cannot there be *found* among you one wise man who shall be able to decide
between his brethren, 6 but brother goeth to law with brother, and that be-

[7]Gr. *tribunals pertaining to.*
[8]Or, *set them . . . church*
[9]Or, *Is it so, that there cannot &c.*

prive these of their seats and strip them of their domain."
The power of the demon is supposed to have been curtailed,
and the demons ceased to dominate persons on earth. These
views seem strained and farfetched, hence are unsatisfactory,
yet I have nothing better to offer.

4 **If then ye have to judge things pertaining to this life, do
ye set them to judge who are of no account in the church?**—
The meaning of this verse has also been involved in doubt.
Does it mean that the least experienced and efficient members
of the church shall be set to judge these temporal affairs?
This cannot be true as the following verse shows. Some
think the question was asked to reproach them for setting
heathen tribunals over them.

5 **I say this to move you to shame.**—He shames them for
leaving the Christian tribunals and going before those notorious for their mercenary character as were the civil.

**What, cannot there be found among you one wise man who
shall be able to decide between his brethren,**—By their course
they said this, and it was a slander and a reproach in the
church. They boasted of their knowledge and spiritual gifts
and acted as if there was not a prudent and intelligent person
among them competent to settle their differences.

6 **but brother goeth to law with brother, and that before unbelievers?**—[This question was most humiliating. It is the
climax. That there should be disputes about property is bad;
that they should go to law is worse; that they should do this
before unbelievers is extremely humiliating and sinful.] This
is the sinful end they had reached.

7 **Nay, already it is altogether a defect in you, that ye have
lawsuits one with another.**—He insisted that going to law was
wholly wrong—a reproach and a shame to the church.

fore unbelievers? 7 Nay, already it is altogether [10]a defect in you, that ye have lawsuits one with another. Why not rather take wrong? why not rather be defrauded? 8 Nay, but ye yourselves do wrong, and defraud, and that *your* brethren. 9 Or know ye not that the unrighteous shall not inherit the kingdom of God? Be not deceived: neither fornicators, nor idolaters, nor adulterers, nor effeminate, nor abusers of themselves with men, 10 nor

[10]Or, *a loss to you*

Why not rather take wrong? why not rather be defrauded?
—A part of the religion of the church of Christ is to suffer and endure wrong for his sake. [The law of Christ contains principles according to which all such may be set at rest. And the difference between the laws governing worldly courts of justice and that of Christ is the difference of diametrical opposition. Law says, "You shall have your rights"; the law of Christ says, "Defraud not your neighbor of his rights." The law says, "You must not be wronged"; Christ says, "It is better to suffer wrong than to do wrong."]

8 **Nay, but ye yourselves do wrong, and defraud, and that your brethren.**—Unless there were efforts to wrong and defraud one another there would be but slight cause for differences among brethren. If each would look to his brother's interest instead of his own, the occasions of difference would be greatly lessened. The same sin exists today for the same causes. Men are covetous and selfish. They are anxious for more than belongs to them. They look every man to his own things, not to the things of others. (Phil. 2: 4.) This leads them to differ and to appeal to the tribunals of Caesar in order to obtain them. Some think there is less wrong in going to law now than in the apostolic days, because the tribunals are somewhat more liable to do justice than then, and because Christians sometimes take part in political affairs. But the latter is only a step further in the wrong prohibited. If Christians cannot appeal to the tribunals of the State to settle differences that arise between them, much less can they manage, control, and participate in the operation of these tribunals.

9 **Or know ye not**—[Some of them acted as if the gospel gave license to live in sin, instead of being intended to deliver from its power. All such persons are warned of their fatal mistake. He assures them that one who allows himself the indulgence of any sin cannot be saved.]

that the unrighteous shall not inherit the kingdom of God?
—Paul here, as did Jesus when he was appealed to to settle differences between two brothers (Luke 12: 14), lays down principles that will remove the causes that produce the contentions about property. Those who act unrighteously in doing
his brother wrong, or in going before the tribunals of unbelievers, cannot inherit the kingdom of God, that is, the heavenly kingdom. It is the heritage of these who are faithful as
the sons of God in the world.

Be not deceived:—[There was great danger of their being
led to think lightly of sins which were daily committed by
those amongst whom they were living, hence these words of
warning] lest they should think one could inherit the kingdom
while practicing the sins mentioned.

neither fornicators, nor idolaters, nor adulterers.—Much of
the idol worship consisted in most degrading forms of de-
bauchery and licentiousness. These sins were encouraged both
as acts of worship and by the examples of their idols.   [No-
tice how he distinguishes between fornication and adultery.
Though both will exclude from the inheritance, the latter is in
many respects the worst crime, because through it the family
is broken up, and a third person is irretrievably injured.]

nor effeminate,—[This word occurs in Matt. 11: 8; Luke 7:
25, where it is applied to clothing, and rendered "soft rai-
ment"—luxurious livers, who pamper their body. Applied to
morals, it denotes those who give themselves up to a soft, and
indolent way of living; who make self-indulgence the grand
object of life. In the classics the word is applied to those who
are given up to wantonness and sensual pleasures, or who are
kept to be prostituted to others.]

nor abusers of themselves with men,—Those who lie with a
male as with a female.

**10 nor thieves, nor covetous, nor drunkards, nor revilers,
nor extortioners, shall inherit the kingdom of God.**—Christians should heed this warning and be sure that they are
guilty of none of these crimes, "for because of these things
cometh the wrath of God upon the sons of disobedience."
(Eph. 5: 6.) It is difficult for people to realize to what extent

thieves, nor covetous, nor drunkards, nor revilers, nor extortioners, shall inherit the kingdom of God. 11 And such were some of you: but ye [11]were washed, but ye were sanctified, but ye were justified in the name of the Lord Jesus Christ, and in the Spirit of our God.

[11]Gr. *washed yourselves.*

these most degrading practices of licentiousness prevailed among the more enlightened classes of the heathens.

11 And such were some of you:—The Corinthians were noted for their indulgence in all these crimes. Their idols were of the licentious order, and Corinth was noted for its profligacy and crimes. Many of these Christians had been guilty of them before they obeyed the gospel. [The threefold "but" in the clause which follows emphasizes strongly the contrast between their present state and their past, and the consequent demand which their changed condition makes upon them.]

but ye were washed,—They had through faith in Jesus Christ died to sin, had been buried with him in baptism, wherein they were also raised with him to walk in newness of life. [They had washed away their sin exactly as Paul was commanded to do. (Acts 22: 16.) Their seeking baptism was their own act, and they entered the water as voluntary agents just as Paul did (cf. 2 Tim. 2: 21), seeking the forgiveness promised in the gospel, fulfilling the divinely ordained condition, and they actually received the remission of their sins (Mark 16: 15, 16; Acts 2: 38).]

but ye were sanctified,—They were set apart to a life of holiness. [The crisis, of which their baptism was the concrete embodiment, had marked their transition from the rule of self to the service of God.]

but ye were justified in the name of the Lord Jesus Christ,—As servants of Jesus Christ they were justified [having passed from the condition of guilty sinners to that of pardoned children of God.]

and in the Spirit of our God.—They were led by the Spirit of God which they had received.

4. REMONSTRANCE AGAINST CONFOUNDING GENTILE LIBERTINISM WITH CHRISTIAN LIBERTY
6: 12-20

12 All things are lawful for me; but not all things are expedient. All things are lawful for me; but I will not be brought under the power of any.

---

12 **All things are lawful for me;**—All things have a lawful use. [It is probable that Paul used these words of himself. Starting from the doctrine taught by Jesus Christ (John 8: 32, 36), and proclaimed by the mouth of the apostles (Acts 15: 10; James 2: 12; 1 Pet. 2: 16), he declared that the Christian was bound to a service of perfect freedom (Rom. 8: 2). But this principle needed very careful statement, if the Greeks were not to abuse it. No actions in themselves were unlawful provided (1) that they were in accordance with God's design in creation; (2) that they were calculated to promote the general welfare of all; and (3) that we were the masters of our own actions, not they of us.]

but not all things are expedient.—It is not always expedient to use them. [The word "expedient" signifies originally the condition of "one who has his feet free"; and hence that which frees from entanglements, helps on, and expedites. Its opposite, that which entangles, is similarly called an impediment. The sense, "serving to promote a desired end of interest, for the sake of personal advantage, as opposed to what is based on principle," in the modern sense of the word. Hence the meaning here is profitable for others as well as for ourselves. The derivative of the word here used is translated "profit" in the following passages: 1 Cor. 7: 35; Heb. 12: 10; and "profitable" in Matt. 5: 29; 18: 6; Acts 20: 20.]

All things are lawful for me; but I will not be brought under the power of any.—There is a lawful use of all appetites, desires, and lusts; but none of them must obtain the mastery over us. All appetites, passions and lusts are for our good, if properly used and restrained. If they enslave us, they degrade and destroy us. An improper use or direction of the appetites and desires brings evil, not good. [If we sacrifice the power of choice which is implied in the thought of liberty,

13 Meats for the belly, and the belly for meats: but God shall bring to

---

we cease to be free; we are brought under the power of that
which should be in our power.]

13 **Meats for the belly, and the belly for meats:**—Food is for
the stomach. [Paul now proceeds to explicitly apply these
principles to the matter in hand. The language indicates that
some argued that if meats were morally indifferent, a man
being morally neither the better nor the worse for eating the
food which had been offered in an idol's temple, so also a man
was neither better nor worse for fornication. To expose the
monstrous error of this reasoning, he draws a distinction between the digestive, nutritive organs of the body and the body
as a whole. The body is an essential part of human nature,
and in the future the natural body will give place to the spiritual body. The spiritual body is connected with, and has its
birthplace in, the natural body, so that the body that we now
wear is to be represented by that finer and more spiritual organism in which the righteous are hereafter to be clothed. (15:
44.) The connection of the future body with the physical
world and its dependence on material things we do not understand; but in some way it is to carry on the identity of our
present body, and thereby it reflects a sacredness and significance of this body. The body of the aged is very different
from that of the newborn babe, but there is a continuity that
links them together and gives them identity. So the future
body may be very different from and yet the same as the present. At the same time, the organs which serve for the maintenance of the natural body will be unnecessary and out of
place in the future body, which is spiritual in its origin and in
its maintenance. There is therefore a difference between the
organs of nutrition and that body which is part of our permanent individuality, and which by the power of God is to be
made into an everlasting body. The digestive organs have
their use and their destiny, and the body as a whole has its use
and destiny. The two differ from one another; and if we
argue from one to the other we must keep in view this distinction. By eating we are not perverting the digestive organs of

the body to a use not intended for them; but we are putting them to the use God meant them to serve.]

but God shall bring to nought both it and them.—Both the food and the stomach—the appetite for food—are to perish. They end with our earthly being. [They serve a temporary purpose, like the house in which we live, or the clothes we wear.]

But the body is not for fornication,—This is not its lawful use. [There is a vital difference between the satisfaction of hunger and the gratification of the sexual appetite. The latter is only possible in the bonds of matrimony. Fornication is an abuse of the body, a defilement of Christ's member, an insult to the Lord himself, whose property is not only taken by theft from him, but handed over to a harlot. This is very plain speaking on the part of the apostle. But it is just; and if it was necessary in those days, it is equally necessary now.]

but for the Lord;—[Here lies the true purpose of the body.] It is for the service of the Lord, who has an appropriate use and sphere for it. [It is destined to be the vehicle of spiritual faculties and the efficient agent of the Lord's purposes. It was through the body of the Lord that the great facts of our redemption were accomplished. It was the instrument of the incarnation, and of the manifestation of God among men, of the death and resurrection by which we are saved. And as in his body Christ was incarnate among men, so now it is by means of the bodily existence and energies of his people on earth that he extends his kingdom among men.] And to this great end it should be used instead of abused, and destroyed by fornication.

and the Lord for the body:—[The Lord dwells in and acts and provides for the body. He thus sustains and keeps it from vanity and sin and corruption. It would be a wicked thing to tear away our body from that sacred connection and give it over to licentiousness.]

14 **and God both raised the Lord, and will raise up us through his power.**—The body, unlike the belly, has an eter-

Lord; and the Lord for the body: 14 and God both raised the Lord, and will raise up us through his power. 15 Know ye not that your bodies are members of Christ? shall I then take away the members of Christ, and make them

---

nity before it, and as evidence of this Paul says: "And if Christ is in you, the body is dead because of sin; but the spirit is life because of righteousness. But if the Spirit of him that raised up Jesus from the dead dwelleth in you, he that raised up Christ Jesus from the dead shall give life also to your mortal bodies through his Spirit that dwelleth in you." (Rom. 8: 10, 11.) If the appetites, passions, and lusts are held in proper restraint and used as is good, then the Spirit of God will dwell in and be with us, and God, who raised Jesus, will by his Spirit raise us up to reign with him. ["Will raise up us" here stands in contrast with "shall bring to nought" in verse 13.]

15 **Know ye not that your bodies are members of Christ?**— Their bodies, with the Spirit of God dwelling in them, are the members of the body of Christ. (12: 27.) [This solemn truth, that there is a real community of spiritual life between Christ and the true believer, is employed here to remind them of the restrictions placed upon their liberty. The body of the Christian is Christ's, nay in a sense, it is a part of himself (Eph. 5: 30), so that the same Spirit which possessed Christ is the same which possesses the Christian. It is in Christ that he seeks to live, and it is the consuming desire of his heart that Christ would use his body to the accomplishment of his purposes even as he used his own body while on earth.]

shall I then take away the members of Christ, and make them members of a harlot?—Sexual intercourse is the act that the Bible recognizes as making man and woman one. When a man who is a member of the body of Christ is guilty of fornication he [forms this union in an unlawful way and] makes the member of Christ one with a harlot.

God forbid.—[If the Christian is as truly a member of Christ's body as were the hands and feet and eyes he wore on earth, the mind shrinks, as from blasphemy, from the very thought of being joined to a harlot as is done by one guilty of fornication.]

members of a harlot? God forbid. 16 Or know ye not that he that is joined
to a harlot is one body? for, [12]The twain, saith he, shall become one flesh.
17 But he that is joined unto the Lord is one spirit. 18 Flee fornication.
Every sin that a man doeth is without the body; but he that committeth

[12]Gen. ii. 24.

**16 Or know ye not that he that is joined to a harlot is one
body?**—When a man takes a woman unto himself they become one flesh.

for, The twain, saith he, shall become one flesh.—"Therefore
shall a man leave his father and his mother, and shall cleave
unto his wife: and they shall be one flesh." (Gen. 2: 24.)
[That these words refer originally to marriage does not lessen
their appropriateness here. For they teach that the union of
the sexes in the marriage relation was divinely ordained at the
creation of the race, in order to unite husband and wife so
closely that in them even personal distinction should in some
respects cease. Intercourse with harlots desecrates this divine relation to a means of sin. Therefore in a Christian, it
robs Christ of a member of his own body in order to place it
in union with one utterly opposed to him, a union so close
that they are one flesh.]

17 But he that is joined unto the Lord is one spirit.—[To be
united in one spirit to Christ and at the same time to be
united to impurity is impossible.] To be one with Christ in
spirit and at the same time in body with a harlot would make
the Lord one with the harlot. This is the outrage of such a
course of sin. A man marries a good woman; they are one
flesh; he afterwards commits adultery and thus becomes one
with a harlot; does not that make the wife one with the harlot? Has a Christian woman the right to become one with a
harlot by living with a husband that is guilty of adultery?
Fornication or adultery justifies a husband or wife in putting
away the guilty party. Does it not go further and demand it?
Has a Christian husband or wife the right to live with one
guilty of adultery?

18 Flee fornication.—In view of the great sin, flee from it,
keep out of the way of temptation to commit it.

Every sin that a man doeth is without the body;—Other

fornication sinneth against his own body. 19 Or know ye not that your body
is a [13]temple of the Holy Spirit which is in you, which ye have from God?

[13]Or, *sanctuary*

---

sins are without or apart from the body. [That is, all other
sinful acts which affect the body approach it from without and
affect particular members. They require some motive or
weapon other than the body. The body is the subject.]

**but he that committeth fornication sinneth against his own
body.**—[Fornication takes the body as a whole and makes it
the instrument of sin. It joins the body of sinful union to a
body of death, so that it becomes one flesh with the condemned harlot, thereby severing itself from the life in Christ,
and thus it strikes directly at the body's future state. When a
man and woman are united in marriage according to God's
law, there is no such alienation from the Lord's body, and
consequently no sin. This view is confirmed by the fact that
the word here translated "sinneth" means to "go astray," to
"miss the mark"; so the words "sinneth against his own
body" imply the running counter to the object for which the
body was created.] The oneness of the body of two persons
that cohabit is more than a formal union. How much of the
real nature and being of a man does a woman partake of in intercourse with him and especially in carrying children begotten by him in her womb with a circulation of blood through
her whole body, and how much he is affected by her will likely
never be definitely determined, yet there is more in becoming
one than we usually think. So a man guilty of fornication
sins against his own body.

**19 Or know ye not that your body is a temple of the Holy
Spirit which is in you, which ye have from God?**—The body
of a Christian is a temple or a dwelling place of the Holy
Spirit, it is therefore a terrible thing to make a temple of God
one with a harlot. [What has before been asserted of the
church as a whole (3: 16) is now asserted of every member of
it, and the Christian's body is the most sacred thing on earth,
and every dishonor to it is an insult to him who has chosen it
for his dwelling place.] Three epochs are marked by the
word temple. In the Old Testament it means the material
temple, the sign of localized worship and a separate people

and ye are not your own; 20 for ye were bought with a price: glorify God
therefore in your body.

(Ex. 20: 24; Deut. 12: 5, 11, 13, 14); in the Gospels Jesus uses
it of his own body (John 2: 19-21); here it is used of every
baptized believer, sanctified by the indwelling of the Holy
Spirit.

and ye are not your own:—[Christians do not belong to
themselves, even if they could commit fornication without
personal contamination or self-violation. Christianity makes
unchastity dishonor both sexes. There is no double standard
of morality. The plea here is to Christians to be clean as
members of Christ's body.]

20 **for ye were bought with a price:**—Man had sinned and
was under the sentence of death. Jesus interposed and gave
his life to secure a respite from the sentence and to open the
way by which he might return to the favor of God and enjoy
eternal life. The only way man can come to appropriate the
cleansing efficacy of the blood of the Son of God is to come by
faith and take the laws given by Jesus Christ into the heart
and let them control and govern his life. Those who accept
this offer of mercy are bought, redeemed, purchased.

glorify God therefore in your body.—Inasmuch as they had
been redeemed by Jesus Christ, he exhorts them that they
should with their bodies glorify him. Live so as to honor
him, and not through fornication defile the temple of God by
making it one with a harlot. [We should so use the body as
to please and do the service of God. To glorify God is to exalt
and honor him as worthy of the highest praise and most faithful service. Our only and supreme desire should be to know
the will of God that we may do it. For we show forth his
praise by obedience to his law. "The heavens declare the
glory of God" in obedience to the law of creation, and much
more do men glorify him by willing obedience to "the law of
the Spirit of life in Christ Jesus." This being so, what a pro-
fanation it is when we take this body, which is built to be his
temple, and put it to uses which it were blasphemous to associate with God! Let us rather find our joy in realizing the
ideal set before us, in keeping ourselves pure as a temple of
God and in glorifying him in our body.]

SECTION FOUR

CONCERNING MARRIAGE
7: 1-40

1. RIGHTS AND OBLIGATIONS OF MARRIED LIFE
7: 1-7

1 Now concerning the things whereof ye wrote: It is good for a man not to touch a woman. 2 But, because of fornications, let each man have his

---

1 **Now concerning the things whereof ye wrote:**—The Corinthians had written to the apostle inquiring in reference to certain matters of duty. Among others, the relation of husband and wife, when they could separate, when they were guilty of fornication, and other questions connected with the marriage relation.

It is good for a man not to touch a woman.—Not to be connected with woman in marriage. This he teaches not as a general truth, for he does not contradict God, who said: "It is not good that the man should be alone; I will make him a help meet for him." (Gen. 2: 18.) In verse 26, he explains, "that this is good by reason of the distress that is upon us, namely, that it is good for a man to be as he is." The "distress" means the persecution then raging against the Christians. On account of these it was best if a man could restrain his lusts not to be married. There are some special cases, as of Paul himself, in which a man can devote himself without the care and distractions of a family to the service of God. But more evil than good comes of attempting it by those who cannot be continent. It is true now, as in the beginning, that "it is not good that the man should be alone." And the universality of marriage is a mark of the morality and virtue of a community.

2 **But, because of fornications, let each man have his own wife, and let each woman have her own husband.**—Recognizing that but few men can be continent and that the lusts with men and women are strong and liable to lead to sin, he tells them the best way to avoid sin is for every man to have his own wife and every woman to have her own husband. He recognizes that both men and women are liable to be led into

own wife, and let each woman have her own husband. 3 Let the husband
render unto the wife her due: and likewise also the wife unto the husband.
4 The wife hath not power over her own body, but the husband: and likewise, also the husband hath not power over his own body, but the wife. 5
Defraud ye not one the other, except it be by consent for a season, that ye
may give yourselves unto prayer, and may be together again, that Satan
tempt you not because of your incontinency. 6 But this I say by way of

---

sin by the strength of lusts. They are both restricted to one
companion.

3 **Let the husband render unto the wife her due:**—After
their marriage, the husband must satisfy the wife in her desires, lest she be tempted to do wrong with other men.

and likewise also the wife unto the husband.—The wife
must please the husband in his desires lest he be tempted to
seek unlawful gratification of his passions with other women.

4 **The wife hath not power over her own body, but the husband:**—The wife has not power over her own body to refuse
the marriage privileges to the husband.

**and likewise also the husband hath not power over his own
body, but the wife.**—The husband has not the power over his
body to refuse the marriage privileges to the wife, neither has
he the right to bestow them upon others. In the marriage obligations they surrender the power over their bodies to the
other. [Marriage is not a capricious union, but a holy bond,
in which separate ownership of person ceases, and neither
without the other realizes the perfect ideal of man. This
equality of the sexes is clearly presented as the way to keep
marriage undefiled.]

5 **Defraud ye not one the other, except it be by consent for a
season,**—They are not to deprive each other of these marriage
rights to which each is entitled except by mutual consent.

that ye may give yourselves unto prayer,—It is proper by
agreement to refrain from indulgence in this fleshly enjoyment or gratification while engaged in special seasons of
prayer.

**and may be together again, that Satan tempt you not be-
cause of your incontinency.**—After the period of self-denial
has passed they must come together, lest through inability to

concession, not of commandment. 7 ¹Yet I would that all men were even as I myself. Howbeit each man hath his own gift from God, one after this manner, and another after that.

¹Many ancient authorities read *For.*

restrain their lusts, Satan should tempt one or both to sin with others.

6 But this I say by way of concession, not of commandment.—[He leaves the details of their lives, whether married or unmarried, to their individual circumstances, for what is suitable in one case may be the reverse in another.]

7 Yet I would that all men were even as I myself.—He again expresses the wish that all were as he was, able to live without marriage.

Howbeit each man hath his own gift from God, one after this manner, and another after that.—One has ability or strength to control one appetite or lust, another is gifted with abilities to do some kind of work, another after a different kind. So each must act as he is able. He who can live and control himself without marriage should do so. One who is not able to control himself had better marry.

2. COUNSEL FOR THE UNMARRIED AND IMPERATIVE INJUNCTIONS FOR THE MARRIED
7: 8-16

8 But I say to the unmarried and to widows, It is good for them if they

8 But I say to the unmarried and to widows, It is good for them if they abide even as I.—It is good for them to remain single even as he did. [Paul had vividly before his mind the trials and persecutions to which the Christians were subjected. What was expedient "by reason of the distress" might not be desirable under other conditions. And similarly "good" might cease to be so under changed conditions. Elsewhere Paul says, "Let marriage be had in honor among all." (Heb. 13: 4.) And he speaks of marriage with the greatest respect when he elevates it to the loftiest position by employing it as a type of the union between Christ and the church. (Eph. 5: 23-32.) He also pronounces the prohibition of marriage to be one of the signs of the great apostasy. (1

abide even as I. 9 But if they have not continency, let them marry: for it is better to marry than to burn. 10 But unto the married I give charge, *yea* not I, but the Lord, That the wife depart not from her husband 11 (but should she depart, let her remain unmarried, or else be reconciled to her husband) ; and that the husband leave not his wife. 12 But to the rest say I,

---

Tim. 4: 3.) We are, therefore, driven to the conclusion that the statement here in no way conflicts with "it is not good that the man should be alone." (Gen. 2: 18.) A single life is good in the sense of being in itself honorable, and under certain circumstances expedient.]

9 **But if they have not continency, let them marry :**—If they have not power over themselves to restrain their sexual passions, let them marry.

for it is better to marry than to burn.—It was better to marry even under the distress in which they were living than to burn with lusts [raging, consuming, and exciting] which they were not able to subdue. [The one, though disadvantageous, is innocent, the other is sinful.]

10 **But unto the married I give charge, yea not I, but the Lord,**—He now gives command from the Lord to those already married. Under the law of Moses they had been permitted to be separated when displeased. But Jesus told the Pharisees that Moses permitted this because of the hardness of their hearts, but it was not God's law of marriage as ordained in the beginning. The man must leave all others and cleave unto his wife, "and the two shall become one flesh." (Matt. 19: 3-9.)

That the wife depart not from her husband—Paul, following the teaching of Jesus, commands the wife not to depart from her husband.

11 **(but should she depart, let her remain unmarried,**—If she and her husband cannot live harmoniously together let her remain unmarried. She is not permitted to marry again. That would be adulterous.

or else be reconciled to her husband) ;—If the wife who has separated from her husband finds that, after all, she cannot live a single life in purity the only course open to her is to be reconciled to the husband whom she has injured. The same

not the Lord: If any brother hath an unbelieving wife, and she is content to

thing applies to the husband under similar circumstances.

and that the husband leave not his wife.—This passage undoubtedly teaches that the believer is to take no steps to hinder the restoration of the marriage relations, but to be ready to seek to restore them. Divorce is intended to make the separation permanent and to make unlawful marriage possible. No Christian can do this. Nothing severs the marriage relationship between Christians save the sin of adultery.

No man or woman with a living wife or husband not guilty of adultery can marry another without adultery, and no lapse of time will purge the cohabitation of its sinfulness. The one who separates from the other tempts the other to commit adultery. One in a state of sin cannot become a Christian or live a Christian life without making an earnest endeavor to correct that wrong. Repentance involves the confession of all our sins as occasion may demand, and of our undoing our wrongs, as far as in our power. A failure to do so shows a lack of faith from the heart and of genuine repentance towards God. Neither the woman nor the man with whom she cohabits can live the Christian life without ceasing their adulterous relationship. No service is acceptable to God unless done because God requires it, and done to obey him. The great trouble on this question is not a failure to understand the teaching of the Bible, but a lack of faith and courage to do what it requires.

12 But to the rest say I, not the Lord:—[The contrast here and in verse 10 is not between commands given by Paul as an inspired apostle and as a private individual. He expressly claims that all "the things which I write unto you, that they are the commandment of the Lord" (14: 37), and he speaks of that knowledge into which he was guided as given by the Holy Spirit, as "by the word of the Lord" (1 Thess. 4: 15). He must therefore not be regarded as here claiming apostolic authority for some things he writes and not for others. The real point of the contrast is between a subject on which the Lord while on earth gave direct instruction, and another sub-

dwell with him, let him not leave her. 13 And the woman that hath an unbelieving husband, and he is content to dwell with her, let her not leave her husband. 14 For the unbelieving husband is sanctified in the wife, and the unbelieving wife is sanctified in the brother: else were your children unclean; but now are they holy. 15 Yet if the unbelieving departeth, let him

ject on which he now gives his commands through an inspired apostle, as was promised by Jesus on the night of his betrayal: "Howbeit when he, the Spirit of truth, is come, he shall guide you into all the truth." (John 16: 13.) The Lord had given instructions regarding divorce (Matt. 5: 31, 32; 19: 3-9; Mark 10: 2-12; Luke 16: 18), and Paul here has only reiterated what he had already commanded.]

If any brother hath an unbelieving wife, and she is content to dwell with him, let him not leave her.—Hitherto his direction has been to them when both husband and wife were Christians. He now introduces another class. Sometimes in the preaching of the gospel, a husband would believe and the wife would not. The fact that the provision is here made by Paul for them to separate when the unbeliever is unwilling to live with the believer, with the direction that a widow may marry "only in the Lord" (verse 39), and that Christians are forbidden to be "unequally yoked with unbelievers" (2 Cor. 6: 14)—to be so tied to them as to be controlled by them— clearly suggests that it is not well for believers to marry unbelievers, nor to enter into any relation by which they would be controlled by unbelievers. But he gives directions to those who found themselves so married to them. If the unbelieving wife is content to dwell with the believing husband, let him not depart.

13 And the woman that hath an unbelieving husband, and he is content to dwell with her, let her not leave her husband. —The same law applies to husband and wife alike; but it seems to me if it had been anticipated that believers would marry unbelievers such provisions would not have been made for separation when one becomes a believer after marriage.

14 For the unbelieving husband is sanctified in the wife, and the unbelieving wife is sanctified in the brother: else were your children unclean; but now are they holy.—What is meant by the unbelieving being sanctified by the believing

depart: the brother or the sister is not under bondage in such *cases*: but God hath called ²us in peace. 16 For how knowest thou, O wife, whether thou

²Many ancient authorities read *you*.

companion has been much discussed. Macknight says: "When infidels are married to Christians, if they have a strong affection for their Christian spouses, they are thereby sanctified to them, they are fitted to continue married to them; because their affection to the Christian party will insure to that party the faithful performance of every duty; and that if the marriages of infidels and Christians were to be dissolved, they would cast away their children as unclean; that is, losing their affection for them, they would expose them after the barbarous custom of the Greeks, or at least neglect their education. But that by continuing their marriages, their children are holy; they are preserved as sacred pledges of their mutual love, and educated with care." That is, if an unbelieving husband or wife is regarded so unclean that you cannot live with him or her, you must for the same reason regard your unbelieving children as unclean, but now under the rule he lays down, they are holy. The unbeliever is held as so sanctified by being one flesh with the believer, the relation is to be borne by the believer. Both husband and wife in the marriage relationship are sanctified or made sacred to each other. So when the unbeliever is willing, the marriage is to be held sacred. [It means that the marriage relation is sanctified so that there is no need of divorce. If either husband or wife is a believer and the other agrees to remain, the marriage is holy and need not be set asunder. If it is otherwise, their children are illegitimate. If the relations of the parents be holy, the child's birth must be holy also (not illegitimate.)]

15 **Yet if the unbelieving departeth, let him depart:**—[If the desire for separation is pressed by the unbeliever, making it intolerable for the Christian, he or she must be passive; and, if the unbeliever withdraws from such a union, let him not be hindered in so doing. The unbeliever is not constrained to keep up the union.]

the brother or the sister is not under bondage in such cases: —There has been doubt as to the meaning of this expression.

Does it mean that bond is not binding in such cases? The Roman Catholic Church and most of the Protestant churches allow remarriage in the case of willful desertion. The meaning most likely is that the believer can regard the unbeliever's act as final, and need not seek to live with him, while yet in such cases remarriage is not approved. The Christian should be prepared to restore the marriage relation when possible, and this certainly is safe ground. If, however, the unbeliever should marry another person, he would by the act commit adultery and in that case the wife or husband would be at liberty to marry.

Just here I wish to emphasize the thought that there is so much looseness in the churches on the marriage relation, so little regard for Scripture teaching, it is well to guard the point that the violation of the marriage vow not only must exist, but it must be the cause and ground of separation—or the adultery of the unbeliever as in the case before us—to justify remarriage of the separated party. Frequently the guilt of a husband is known, the crime is condoned by the wife, she lives with him knowing his guilt. Finally other causes lead to a separation; and then, when she wishes to marry again, the infidelity of the husband, which did not cause the separation, is made the excuse to justify the new marriage. Unless the separation took place on account of the lewdness of the companion, it cannot be ground for remarriage. Frequently a woman lives with a lewd husband who is one with a harlot. She becomes one with him who is one with a harlot—lives this life of doubtful virtue, and some other trouble grows up. She separates from him for this, and makes his lewdness merely the excuse for marrying again. This is not allowable. She is in adultery all the time. Not only must she have separated from the former husband because of his adultery, to justify her, but the present husband must have been satisfied that was the cause of it when he married her, else his marriage was in intent and at heart adultery. The intention has everything to do with obedience to the command of God. It must not be an incidental happening to obey God when we go and do as we please, but a clear and distinct purpose to be gov-

shalt save thy husband? or how knowest thou, O husband, whether thou

erned by the law, to justify it. For a man and woman to reck-
lessly rush ahead in marriage, determined to do it, law or no
law, and after it is done to look around and see if they can
find any ground to justify, does not relieve them from inten-
tional guilt of marrying whether there be law or no law.

but God hath called us in peace.—The believer must make
all the efforts in his power to live in peace with the unbeliever, sacrifice everything save obedience to God. Jesus
said: "If any man cometh unto me, and hateth not his own
father, and mother, and wife, and children, and brethren, and
sisters, yea, and his own life also, he cannot be my disciple."
(Luke 14: 26.)

16 **For how knowest thou, O wife, whether thou shalt save
thy husband?**—If the unbelieving husband so will, the Christian wife must live with him because it is possible that she
may be able to save him. "In like manner, ye wives, be in
subjection to your own husbands; that, even if any obey not
the word, they may without the word be gained by the behavior of their wives; beholding your chaste behavior coupled
with fear." (1 Pet. 3: 1, 2.)

**or how knowest thou, O husband, whether thou shalt save
thy wife?**—The unbelieving wife may often be won by the
godly behavior of the husband. When a believer finds him or
herself with an unbeliever, instead of seeking a separation, the
believer should live in peace and seek by a godly behavior to
win the unbelieving companion to Christ.

3. THE GENERAL PRINCIPLES JUST SET FORTH APPLIED
TO OTHER CIVIL RELATIONS
7: 17-24

shalt save thy wife?   17 Only, as the Lord hath distributed to each man, as

17 **Only, as the Lord hath distributed to each man, as God
hath called each, so let him walk.**—Whatever relation or sur-
rounding one is in when he is called to the belief of the gospel,
in that let him abide and seek to do the will of God, striving

God hath called each, so let him walk. And so ordain I in all the churches.
18 Was any man called being circumcised? let him not become uncircumcised. Hath any been called in uncircumcision? let him not be circumcised.
19 Circumcision is nothing, and uncircumcision is nothing; but the keeping of

by his godly walk to win those to salvation with whom he comes in contact.

[The mighty effect of the gospel when first proclaimed is only slightly appreciated. The equality of men which it announced; the precious and exceeding great promises which it contained; the short-lived character it ascribed to all earthly things; and the certainty of the coming of the Lord to judge the world in righteousness, which is predicted, produced a commotion in the minds of the people which was never experienced either before or since. It is no surprise, therefore, that many were disposed to break away from their old relationships. This was an evil that called for repression. Paul endeavored to convince his readers that their relation to Christ was comparable with any social relation or position not sinful in itself. Their conversion to Christ involved, therefore, no necessity of breaking asunder their social ties. The gospel is not a revolutionary, disorganized element; but one which is designed to eliminate all evil, and exalt and purify that which is good.]

And so ordain I in all the churches.—[This principle was of universal application, and so he lays it down authoritatively for all the churches. He now proceeds to give specific instances to which this rule applies.]

18 **Was any man called being circumcised? let him not become uncircumcised.**—[Reference is here made to certain efforts which were attempted by those who were ashamed of having been circumcised.] If any man has been circumcised, let him not seek to become uncircumcised or to be regarded as a Gentile.

Hath any been called in uncircumcision? let him not be circumcised.—If a Gentile is called, let him remain one, let him serve God in the relation in which he finds himself, and seek to reach and save whom he can in the relation.

19 **Circumcision is nothing, and uncircumcision is nothing;**

the commandments of God. 20 Let each man abide in that calling wherein

—[They have no influence either favorable or unfavorable on
our relation to God. No man is either the better or worse for
being either circumcised or uncircumcised. This, of course,
was said with reference to the standing before God in Christ
Jesus. Before his coming it could not have been said without
contravening the express command of God. (Gen. 17: 9-14;
Lev. 12: 3.)] Being a Jew does· not commend a man to God
neither does it condemn him. The same is true of the Gentile.
Circumcision as a family mark is not condemned; but as an
act of service to God, it has no weight. The dispensation of
which circumcision was the seal was contrary to the people of
Israel, "and he [Christ] hath taken it out of the way, nailing
it to the cross." (Col. 2: 13-15.)

but the keeping of the commandments of God.—[The great
question concerning which the Christian should be solicitous
above everything else is as to whether he brings his heart and
life into conformity to the will of God as revealed through
Jesus Christ. "For in Christ Jesus neither circumcision
availeth anything, nor uncircumcision; but faith working
through love." (Gal. 5: 6.) "Faith working through love"
and "keeping the commandments of God" are the same thing.
They express the idea of devotion of heart and life under different aspects.]

20 **Let each man abide in that calling wherein he was
called.**—He enlarges the thought by commanding every one to
remain in the calling or in the relationship in which he was
when he was called. Coming to Christ makes him faithful in
the calling. [This is not intended to prohibit a man's endeavor to better his condition; but that there are certain conditions of life that to the Christian call there is a special form.
Such as the great distinctions—national, social, and natural—
on the maintenance of which in any particular age or country
the preservation of the principles of liberty and order and
their legitimate development in human history mainly depend.
Paul says: "There can be neither Jew nor Greek, there can be
neither bond nor free, there can be no male and female; for ye
all are one man in Christ Jesus." (Gal. 3: 28.) This enumer-

he was called. 21 Wast thou called being a bondservant? care not for it:

---

ation sets before us the three great fundamental conceptions that at once divide and unite the race—that of Jew and Greek, or the national distinction; that of slave and free, or the social distinction; and that of male and female, or the physical distinction. No one should desire to change the status of life on becoming a Christian. Paul was endeavoring to convince his readers that their relation to Christ was compatible with any of the conditions of life enumerated. The gospel is just as well suited to people in one condition as another, and its blessings can be enjoyed in all their fullness equally in any condition of life. They were to continue to be Christians of the kind which God's call made them. If they were circumcised—and so God's call into Christ made them circumcised Christians—continue so. They were to do nothing which would seem to imply that some other change in addition to their becoming obedient to the gospel was necessary to complete their admission into the fullness of the blessings in Christ.]

21 Wast thou called being a bondservant? care not for it: —Bond servants that are called owe their service to their earthly masters. In serving them they cannot devote their whole time and means to the service of God that they would were they free. [But the fact of their being in slavery did not affect the reality or completeness of their relation to Christ, and their anxiety to escape from bondage was needless.]

nay, even if thou canst become free, use it rather.—Some expositors claim that this teaches that if a slave could obtain his liberty he was to avail himself of the opportunity to do so. But such an interpretation is at variance with the whole drift of the argument, which is, that he is not to seek such a change. What Paul does say is that if the Christian slave could be free, he should prefer his condition as a converted slave. Slavery, as well as other positions of life, can be used to the glory of God. This interpretation is in perfect harmony, not only with the rest of the passage, but with all Paul's teaching and his universal practice on the subject.

[One point which should certainly be well pondered in con-

³nay, even if thou canst become free, use *it* rather.　22 For he that was
called in the Lord being a bondservant, is the Lord's freedman: likewise he

³Or, *but if*

sidering this question is, if one word from Christian teaching
could have been quoted at Rome as tending to excite the
slaves to revolt, it would have set the Roman Government in
direct and active hostility to the faith in Christ. Nor would
the danger of preaching the abolition of slavery be confined
to that arising from external violence on the part of the Roman
Government; but it would have been pregnant with danger to
the purity of the church itself. For it is altogether probable
that many would have been led to join a communion which
would have aided them in securing their social freedom. In
these considerations we find ample reasons for the position of
non-interference which Paul maintains in regard to slavery.
Under a particular and exceptional round of circumstances,
the Holy Spirit directed Paul not to interfere with it, but to
teach fearlessly those imperishable principles which led in
after ages to its extinction. He left slavery, therefore, unas-
sailed, as he did civil relations in general, not asking, in his
letter to Philemon, that Onesimus should be set free; but introduced the idea of love, unity, and equality. (13: 13; Gal. 3:
28; Eph. 6: 8; Col. 4: 1; Phile. 16.)]

22 **For he that was called in the Lord being a bondservant,
is the Lord's freedman:**—God does not require so much from
him, so he is the Lord's freedman. [The Lord's freedman
was one set free from service to sin (Rom. 6: 22) by Christ.
These words simply mean that the slave who hears and becomes obedient to "the faith," and is thus brought into union
with Christ as his Master, is thereby made free (John 8: 32,
36) from every kind of bondage; and made free by Christ. So
complete is this freedom that it cannot be destroyed or weak-
ened even in civil bondage. He is even free while serving his
earthly master to earn the highest possible reward; for the
apostle teaches that if slaves do their duty to their earthly
masters as to Christ they will receive the reward of the inheritance, for they "serve the Lord Christ." (Col. 3: 24.)]

likewise he that was called being free, is Christ's bondser-

that was called being free, is Christ's bondservant. 23 Ye were bought with
a price; become not bondservants of men. 24 Brethren, let each man, wherein he was called, therein abide with God.

---

vant.—He is under obligations to devote more of his time and
means to the service of God, so is God's slave. [The distinction between master and slave is obliterated. To be the
Lord's freedman and the Lord's bond servant are the same
thing. The Lord's freedman is the one whom the Lord has
redeemed from Satan and made his own; and the Lord's bond
servant is also one whom "he purchased with his own blood."
(Acts 20: 28.) So that master and slave stand on the same
level before Christ.]

23 **Ye were bought with a price; become not bondservants
of men.**—Inasmuch as Christ had bought them with his
blood, they were his bond servants. Now they were to serve
Christ in continuing in submission to their earthly masters
with the fidelity with which they served God and as service
rendered to God. Paul gives the principle on which the slave
was to serve: "Servants, be obedient unto them that according
to the flesh are your masters, with fear and trembling, in sin-
gleness of your heart, as unto Christ; not in the way of eye-
service, as men-pleasers; but as servants of Christ, doing the
will of God from the heart; with good will doing service, as
unto the Lord, and not unto men: knowing that whatsoever
good things each one doeth, the same shall he receive again
from the Lord, whether he be bond or free." (Eph. 6: 5-8.)
The servant is to do service to the earthly master as to the
Lord, and God will recompense him for the service done, as
though rendered unto him.

24 **Brethren, let each man, wherein he was called, therein
abide with God.**—Here is a summary and reiteration of the
principles underlying the instruction contained in this paragraph. Let the bond servant who has become obedient to the
faith abide, as regards his social state, as he was. His being a
slave came to him without his choice and is powerless to destroy or lessen his Christian liberty or hinder his service to
Christ, and his principle only justifies the exhortation here
given.

4. ADVICE TO THE UNMARRIED IN VIEW OF CIRCUM-
STANCES THEN IN EXISTENCE
7: 25-35

25 Now concerning virgins I have no commandment of the Lord: but I give my judgment, as one that hath obtained mercy of the Lord to be trustworthy. 26 I think therefore that this is good by reason of the distress that is upon us, *namely,* that it is good for a man ⁴to be as he is. 27 Art thou bound unto a wife? seek not to be loosed. Art thou loosed from a wife? seek not a wife. 28 But shouldest thou marry, thou hast not sinned; and if a virgin marry, she hath not sinned. Yet such shall have tribulation in the

⁴Gr. *so to be.*

25 **Now concerning virgins**—Paul here introduces a different, but kindred, subject to that which he has been discussing. He had been discussing the relation of husband and wife. He now turns to that of those not yet given in marriage.

I have no commandment of the Lord: but I give my judgment, as one that hath obtained mercy of the Lord to be trustworthy.—[Paul had no specific word from Jesus on the subject of virgins. They call for special treatment, but he had the command of Jesus concerning divorce to guide him. So he gives no command, but only a judgment, a deliberately formed decision from knowledge (2 Cor. 8: 10), not a mere passing fancy. The language, so far from being a disclaimer of inspiration, is an express claim to help from the Lord in forming this duly considered judgment.] From his familiarity with the teaching of the Lord he gives his judgment as one who has obtained mercy of the Lord to be trustworthy.

26 **I think therefore that this is good by reason of the distress that is upon us, namely, that it is good for a man to be as he is.**—He says again, on account of the present distress, that it is good for every man to remain as he is, whether married or unmarried. (See note on verse 1.)

27 **Art thou bound unto a wife? seek not to be loosed. Art thou loosed from a wife? seek not a wife.**—Neither the married nor the unmarried are to seek for a change. [This is an explanation and reassertion of "to be as he is" in the preceding verse. He dissuades from the spirit of change in consideration of the distress that was pending.]

28 **But shouldest thou marry, thou hast not sinned; and if a**

flesh: and I would spare you. 29 But this I say, brethren, the time ⁵is shortened, that henceforth both those that have wives may be as though they had
none; 30 and those that weep, as though they wept not; and those that rejoice, as though they rejoiced not; and those that buy, as though they possessed not; 31 and those that use the world, as not using it to the full: for the
fashion of this world passeth away. 32 But I would have you to be free from

⁵Or, *is shortened henceforth, that both those &c.*

virgin marry, she hath not sinned.—But if he cannot restrain
himself and he marries, he does not sin. And if a virgin marries, she does not sin. But under persecutions, such will have
trouble in the flesh. Childbearing, family duties, and obligations will increase the troubles that will come upon them.

**Yet such shall have tribulation in the flesh: and I would
spare you.**—He would save them from these added troubles
and afflictions, so he gives this advice as prudential, not as a
command from God. The following or not following the advice does not involve disobedience to God, or sin; but he
would spare them added troubles brought on by marriage.

**29, 30 But this I say, brethren, the time is shortened, that
henceforth both those that have wives may be as though they
had none; and those that weep, as though they wept not; and
those that rejoice, as though they rejoiced not; and those that
buy, as though they possessed not;**—In this Paul breaks off
into one of his characteristic digressions, in which he shows
that time here on earth was so short to them when they would
leave the world, that what they are while here matters but little. [Paul here means that the present epoch will embrace a
greater or less number of years, and its character is its being
contained between precise limits—drawn together into brief
compass which does not admit of its being extended indefi-
nitely. These limits are, on the one side, Christ's coming at
the end of the Jewish dispensation (Acts 2: 17; Heb. 9: 26)
and, on the other, his coming again, which may be expected at
any hour—the time is limited as to what remains (Matt. 24:
42-44; 25: 13; 1 Thess. 5: 1-3; 2 Pet. 3: 8-13).]

31 and those that use the world, as not using it to the full:
—All things mentioned in this series are right things; and the
warning is against eagerly using up all opportunities of gain
or pleasure as if they were the end of life. We are not to try

cares. He that is unmarried is careful for the things of the Lord, how he may please the Lord: 33 but he that is married is careful for the things of the world, how he may please his [1]wife, 34 and is divided. *So* also the woman that is unmarried and the virgin is careful for the things of the Lord, that she may be holy both in body and in spirit: but she that is married is careful for the things of the world, how she may please her husband. 35 And this I

[1]Some ancient authorities read *wife. And there is a difference also between the wife and the virgin. She that is unmarried is careful &c.*

to get all we can out of externals. The man who remembers that he is only a sojourner in the world is likely to remember also that worldly possessions are not everything, and that worldly surroundings cannot be made permanent.

for the fashion of this world passeth away.—[John says: "And the world passeth away, and the lust thereof." (1 John 2: 17.) The fact that their present condition was not to last long, and their participation in its joys and sorrows was to be so short-lived, is the reason which the apostle urges why they should not be wedded to earthly things.] It is probable that raging persecution threatened to burst upon them with such fury as to add force to this exhortation.

32 But I would have you to be free from cares.—When persecutions came upon them, he would like to have them without the additional cares which marriage would impose upon them. [It must be borne in mind that this advice was given solely to guide those under the distress that was then upon them (verse 26), and not to be applied in normal times.]

He that is unmarried is careful for the things of the Lord, how he may please the Lord:—[The unmarried man, having no family to provide for and to protect in times of distress and persecution, is less encumbered with worldly cares than the married man who was compelled to take care of his wife and dependent children; and might be thus kept back from that unswerving courage which in those dark days full loyalty to Christ demanded.]

33, 34 but he that is married is careful for the things of the world, how he may please his wife, and is divided. So also the woman that is unmarried and the virgin is careful for the things of the Lord, that she may be holy both in body and in spirit: but she that is married is careful for the things of the

say for your own profit; not that I may cast a ²snare upon you, but for that which is seemly, and that ye may attend upon the Lord without distraction.

²Or, *constraint* Gr. *noose.*

---

world, how she may please her husband.—Paul here states a truth that is applicable in a general way only to those who live continently and contentedly without marriage, free from the cares that grow with a family both of men and women. Generally unmarried men, and women too, with the sexual desires active, give less care, place their affections less on the Lord, than the married. Paul himself states this truth: "But younger widows refuse: for when they have waxed wanton against Christ, they desire to marry." (1 Tim. 5: 11.) That his language here was only for the time of the distress that was then upon them is seen in this statement: "I desire therefore that the younger widows marry, bear children, rule the household, give no occasion to the adversary for reviling: for already some are turned aside after Satan." (1 Tim. 5: 14, 15.) As a rule among men and women the married state is more promotive of virtue and devotion than that of the unmarried.

35 **And this I say for your own profit;**—[The advice was given that they might avail themselves of all their advantages and privileges, and pursue such a course as would tend to advance their personal piety and spiritual growth. Nothing here was ever designed to be of general application; it concerned the church at Corinth alone; or churches in similar circumstances.]

not that I may cast a snare upon you, but for that which is seemly, and that ye may attend upon the Lord without distraction.—He did not wish to lead them into temptation which they could not withstand, so become ensnared to sin; but he spoke it that they might do that which was for their well-being and what would leave them time to serve the Lord without the care and distractions which a family would impose upon them.

5. INSTRUCTIONS FOR FATHERS AS TO THE MARRIAGE OF THEIR DAUGHTERS UNDER THE CIRCUMSTANCES IN VIEW
7 : 36-38

36 But if any man thinketh that he behaveth himself unseemly toward his [3]virgin *daughter,* if she be past the flower of her age, and if need so requireth, let him do what he will; he sinneth not; let them marry. 37 But he that standeth stedfast in his heart, having no necessity, but hath power as touching his own will, and hath determined this in his own heart, to keep his own [3]virgin *daughter,* shall do well. 38 So then both he that giveth his own

[3]Or, *virgin* (omitting daughter)

36 **But if any man**—In that age and country the father disposed of his daughters in marriage without consulting them, and his will was the law in the matter.

thinketh that he behaveth himself unseemly toward his virgin daughter,—If he thinks he treats her wrong in withholding her from marriage, exposing her to a temptation to sin with her lover, or at least, bringing on her the imputation of it.

if she be past the flower of her age,—Past the usual age of marriage.

and if need so requireth, let him do what he will; he sinneth not; let them marry.—If, then, a man thinks he treats his virgin daughter wrong in witholding her from marriage, he must act according to her requirements. That is, if she cannot live satisfied in the unmarried state, let him give her in marriage, and he need not fear that in doing so he does wrong.

37 **But he that standeth stedfast in his heart,**—Whose judgment is settled and firm, being fully persuaded of the inexpediency of his daughter's marrying.

having no necessity,—Being controlled by no external necessity; nothing, in other words, rendering it necessary for him to act contrary to his own judgment.

but hath power as touching his own will,—Is able to act as he deems best.

and hath determined this in his own heart, to keep his own virgin daughter,—Has fully made up his mind to keep his daughter in those perilous times from marriage and under his own control.

³virgin *daughter* in marriage doeth well; and he that giveth her not in marriage shall do better.   39 A wife is bound for so long time as her husband

shall do well.—In either of these cases he does right.

38 So then both he that giveth his own virgin daughter in marriage doeth well;—He violates no law in so doing, and is not to be censured for it.

and he that giveth her not in marriage shall do better.—He more certainly under the trying circumstances considered her happiness by holding her from entering into the married state than he would by allowing her to enter into it. [And yet, when all is said, Paul leaves the whole problem of getting married an open question to be settled by each individual case.]

6. INSTRUCTIONS AS TO THE MARRIAGE OF WIDOWS
7: 39, 40

liveth; but if the husband be ⁴dead, she is free to be married to whom she will; only in the Lord. 40 But she is happier if she abide as she is, after my

⁴Gr. *fallen asleep.* See Acts 7. 60.

39 A wife is bound for so long time as her husband liveth; —He adds advice concerning widows marrying, probably in answer to a question that had been propounded to him.

but if the husband be dead, she is free to be married to whom she will;—[It is the teaching of the New Testament that marriage is a contract for life, between one man and one woman, indissoluble by the will of the parties or by human law; but that the death of either party leaves the survivor free to contract another marriage. (Rom. 7: 1-3.) Such being the teaching of the Holy Spirit, no civil or ecclesiastical body can rightfully enact a different law. All efforts to change God's law only render men and women worse.]

only in the Lord.—This prohibits the widow marrying one not a Christian. I know no reason why a widow should be more restricted as to whom she marry than a virgin. This restriction however, together with the general principles laid down regulating the association of Christians with unbelievers, indicates that it was not contemplated that Christians should marry those not in the Lord. Under the law of Moses the man was prohibited marrying out of the family of Israel, save when the woman would identify herself with the chosen people. The reason given was, lest they should draw them into idolatry. Solomon violated the law, and, despite his wisdom and power, his wives drew him into idolatry. Influence is frequently more potent for evil than authority or power.

The law of Moses is an earthly type of the law of Christ. The inference would be that the children of God could not marry out of the family of God. "Be not unequally yoked with unbelievers: for 'what fellowship have righteousness and iniquity? or what communion hath light with darkness? And what concord hath Christ with Belial? or what portion hath a believer with an unbeliever? And what agreement hath a temple of God with idols? for we are a temple of the living God; even as God said, I will dwell in them, and walk in them; and will be their God, and they shall be my people. Wherefore come ye out from among them, and be ye separate, saith the Lord, and touch no unclean thing; and I will receive you, and will be to you a Father, and ye shall be to me sons and daughters, saith the Lord Almighty." (2 Cor. 6: 14-18.) To be unequally yoked would be to be so connected with the unbeliever that the Christian would be controlled by the unbeliever.

I know of no relation in which this would be more so than in the marriage relation. The whole drift and tenor of the Scriptures, both of the Old Testament and the New, is that in the close and intimate relations of life the people of God should seek the companionship of servants of God, that they might help and encourage each other in the Christian life. When both are working together, man in his weakness often becomes discouraged; it is greatly worse when the nearest and dearest one pulls away from Christ and duty. Then, too, when people marry, they ought to consider the probability of rearing children. It is the duty of Christian parents to rear their children in the nurture and admonition of the Lord. How can one do this when the other sets the example of unbelief and disobedience to God? I conclude, therefore, that the spirit and teaching of the Bible is against Christians marrying

judgment: and I think that I also have the Spirit of God.

those not members of the body of Christ, and yet there is no direct and specific prohibition of it, other than for widows.

40 But she is happier if she abide as she is, after my judgment:—While Paul gives this permission to the widow, she will be happier according to his judgment, if she remains unmarried. [This was said because she would have the same cares and troubles as those referred to in the preceding verses.]

and I think that I also have the Spirit of God.—[Not that there was any doubt in Paul's mind on this point. The word implies full persuasion that in the advice he had given he was speaking under the direction of the Holy Spirit.]

SECTION FIVE

RELATION OF LIBERTY TO SELF-DENIAL
8: 1 to 11: 1

1. CHRISTIAN LIBERTY AS RELATED TO THE EATING OF MEATS OFFERED TO IDOLS
8: 1-13

1 Now concerning things sacrificed to idols: We know that we all have

---

1 **Now concerning things sacrificed to idols:**—Here Paul introduces eating meats offered to idols, and the treatment of idolaters. The style of introducing the subject indicates that the Corinthians had asked him questions concerning what was right in regard to these matters. The Christians at Corinth and throughout the Gentile countries had been reared in idolatry, and revered and worshiped idols. Idols were worshiped by sacrificing animals to them. [When an animal was offered in sacrifice to an idol, or to a false god represented by an idol, only a small part, such as the legs wrapped in fat, or the intestines, was consumed by the fire on the altar. The remainder was eaten by the sacrificer and his friends, or those who were invited to the sacrificial feast, which took place either in the temple or in the adjoining grove, and to these feasts Christians were invited (verse 10); or the remainder of the flesh, after what was burnt in honor of the idol, as their perquisite by the priests, would be sold by them in the markets, and the heathen would partake of it as meat of peculiar sanctity.]

It became a question at once: How shall Christians regard and treat these idols and meats offered to them? In the consultation, held by the apostles at Jerusalem, in reference to the circumcising of the Gentiles, they wrote to the Gentile Christians to "abstain from things sacrificed to idols." (Acts 15: 29.) When they were first converted to Christ, it seems that they were commanded to abstain from meats offered to them, because while they were yet fresh from the worship of idols, and their consciences were tender in regard to them, the eating of meats offered would tend to revive their reverence for them, and lead them back into idolatry. So they were commanded to abstain from it. As they grew stronger in

Christ, and came to know that an idol was nothing, they might eat without their conscience being defiled by eating. The question arose: Shall those who can eat without defiling their consciences be prohibited in its use?

[At this day we can scarcely realize how closely this question affected the whole life of the early Christians. For not only was the worship of the Gentiles sacrificial, but this worship was not confined to the temple precincts, but extended itself to their social gatherings, and even domestic meals.]

We know that we all have knowledge.—All Christians had knowledge that there is but one God, and that idols are nothing.

Knowledge puffeth up,—Knowledge, without the love of God, puffeth up with pride, makes one conceited, self-sufficient, and disregardful of the rights of others. [As a matter of fact, too well known to be denied, men of keen insight into moral and spiritual truths are sometimes prone to despise the less enlightened that stumble among scruples that constantly come before them. The knowledge that is not guarded by humility and love does harm both to its possessor and to other Christians. It puffs up its possessor with scorn, and it alienates and embitters the less enlightened. Knowledge which does not take into consideration the difficulties and scruples of brethren in Christ cannot be admired or commended, for though in itself a good thing and capable of being used for the advancement of the cause of Christ, divorced from love can do good neither to him who possesses it nor to the cause of Christ. It is too often the case that possessors of such knowledge glory in themselves as the men of deep spiritual insight and valiant soldiers of the cross. It is not by knowledge alone that the church can solidly grow. Such knowledge does sometimes produce an appearance of growth, a puffed up, and unhealthy, mushroom growth.]

but love edifieth.—Love to God makes one strong in faith and Christian character, helpful to others, and leads him to look to the good of others, even at the sacrifice of his own rights. This shows that learning without religion, the only basis of love, is not helpful to the world.

knowledge. Knowledge puffeth up, but love [5]edifieth. 2 If any man thinketh that he knoweth anything, he knoweth not yet as he ought to know; 3 but if any man loveth God, the same is known by him. 4 Concerning therefore the eating of things sacrificed to idols, we know that no idol is *anything* in the

[5]Gr. *buildeth up*.

---

2 **If any man thinketh that he knoweth anything, he knoweth not yet as he ought to know;**—One confident in his own wisdom or knowledge to guide him knows nothing in a loving, helpful way. He does not know anything in its relation to other truths, to man, and to God. The Holy Spirit says: "For seeing that in the wisdom of God the world through its wisdom knew not God, it was God's good pleasure through the foolishness of the preaching to save them that believe." (1: 21.) This knowledge helps a man and leads him to look to the good of others, as well as his own good. Knowledge that stops short of this is selfish, and selfishness brings leanness and poverty of spirit.

3 **but if any man loveth God, the same is known by him.**— To love God is to so honor and serve him as to seek his will that we may do it. If one properly esteems God as the great source and center of all things, honors him, and acts from a sense of duty to him, he is known and approved by God, for "the Lord knoweth them that are his." (2 Tim. 2: 19.) Jesus said: "If any man willeth to do his will, he shall know of the teaching, whether it is of God, or whether I speak from myself." (John 7: 17.) The man who loves God is the one who rightly solves the question about meat offered to idols, for nothing is viewed by him that does not take into consideration the will of God and the good of his fellow men.

4 **Concerning therefore the eating of things sacrificed to idols, we know that no idol is anything in the world,**—All Christians know that an idol is nothing, and that there are no such gods. Hence the things sacrificed to idols are as though they had never been sacrificed.

and that there is no God but one.—This is the foundation truth of the Christian life. Without it no one can live the Christian life or form a godlike character that suffers to help others.

world, and that there is no God but one. 5 For though there be that are called gods, whether in heaven or on earth; as there are gods many, and lords many; 6 yet to us there is one God, the Father, of whom are all things, and we unto him; and one Lord, Jesus Christ, through whom are all things,

5 For though there be that are called gods, whether in heaven or on earth;—The heathen made the distinction of the superior gods who ruled in the heavens, and the inferior ones that dwelt upon earth, presiding over seas, rivers, fountains, forests, and local places.

as there are gods many, and lords many;—In the minds of the heathen there were many of each of these classes. [The heathen mythology, especially in its Greek development, may be regarded as the religious expression of national ideals and civilization. The Greek conception of every conception of the independence of every unit in nature and society was embodied in the mythology. Every city had its guardian deity; every spring was haunted; every crop of corn was under the protection of a goddess; every movement of the elements and every human action might assume a sacred character and become, the one a prayer, the other the answer.]

6 yet to us there is one God, the Father, of whom are all things,—In contrast with these false gods, to the Christian, there is one true and living God, the Originator, Creator, and Founder of the universe; hence possessed of all the wisdom, power, and authority that dwell in the universe.

and we unto him;—This is given as an evidence of his nearness to man, "for in him we live, and move, and have our being." (Acts 17: 28.) From him all blessings come; by his strength and power we live and are upheld by him daily.

and one Lord, Jesus Christ, through whom are all things,— The "all things" in this clause must be co-extensive with the "all things" in the preceding one—that is, the universe. The universe was created through Jesus Christ. The energy of the one God was exercised through the Word, who "became flesh, and dwelt among us." (John 1: 14.) Of him it is said: "In the beginning was the Word, and the Word was with God, and the Word was God. The same was in the beginning with God. All things were made through him; and without him was not anything made that hath been made." (John 1: 1-3.) The following passages teach the same thing: "Through whom also he made the worlds." (Heb. 1: 2.) "For in him were all things created, in the heavens and upon the earth, things visible and things invisible, . . . all things have been created through him, and unto him." (Col. 1: 16.)

and we through him.—Jesus Christ performs the same act of creating in the spiritual world that he did in the material. In this God, the Father, originated and provided the great scheme of redemption. Jesus Christ came into the world. Through his mission; his teaching in precept and example; his suffering, death, burial, his struggle in the grave with the powers of death, and hell (in the grave the battle for man's redemption was fought and the victory won); his resurrection and his ascent to his Father, he created the material for the new spiritual kingdom. The apostles and their fellow disciples constituted this nucleus for the new creation. Christ completed his work and left them with the command: "Tarry ye in the city [Jerusalem], until ye be clothed with power from on high." (Luke 24: 49.) No step could be taken in the procreation of disciples or in the establishment and development of the kingdom of which they constituted the beginning until the Spirit should come to guide them into all the truth.

[The divinity of Christ can no more be denied because the Father is here called the one God, than the dominion of the Father can be denied because the Son is called the one Lord. By this mode of expression it is intimated that Father and Son are one God and one Lord in the unity of the godhead. (Acts 17: 29; Col. 2: 9.)]

[It is consideration of these great truths that makes idolatry ridiculous, and the eating of food sacrificed to idols a matter of indifference. Such was the conclusion of the Corinthians, and such, but for the weaker brethren, would have been Paul's conclusion.]

7 Howbeit there is not in all men that knowledge:—While all men should know that there is but one true and living God,

and we through him. 7 Howbeit there is not in all men that knowledge: but some, being used until now to the idol, eat as *of* a thing sacrificed to an idol; and their conscience being weak is defiled. 8 But food will not [6]commend us to God; neither, if we eat not, [7]are we the worse; nor, if we eat, [8]are we the

[6]Gr. *present.*
[7]Gr. *do we lack.*
[8]Gr. *do we abound.*

even all Christians did not possess the knowledge that enabled them to be independent of these idols.

but some, being used until now to the idol, eat as of a thing sacrificed to an idol;—Some who had been converted to Christ had a lingering reverence for the idols they had long worshiped, [and therefore they regarded the meat as offered to some kind of reality.]

and their conscience being weak is defiled.—While one completely free from reverence for an idol might eat of things sacrificed to it without any feeling of reverence for it, others could not eat of them without having their reverence aroused for the idol, and, their conscience being so weak as to reverence the idol, would be defiled.

8 But food will not commend us to God: neither, if we eat not, are we the worse;—The flesh offered in sacrifice to idols was eaten as food by the people. Some ate it as worship to idols; others, having knowledge of these things, ate it as food. God was willing for them to eat it if they could do so without leading others to sin. The danger was that those not fully taught, seeing others eat it as food, would be encouraged to eat it as worship, and so be defiled.

nor, if we eat, are we the better.—Eating meat is not service to God, and eating or failing to eat would not commend them to God. So far as their relation to God was concerned, eating would not affect their spiritual interests. [By showing that the eating is a matter of indifference, Paul introduces his reason for yielding to the weakness of another. If the weakness involved a matter of our vital relation to God, then to yield would be wrong.]

9 But take heed lest by any means this liberty of yours be-

better. 9 But take heed lest by any means this ⁹liberty of yours become a stumblingblock to the weak. 10 For if a man see thee who hast knowledge sitting at meat in an idol's temple, will not his conscience, if he is weak, ¹⁰be emboldened to eat things sacrificed to idols? 11 For ¹¹through thy knowl-

⁹Or, *power*
¹⁰Gr. *be builded up.*
¹¹Gr. *in.*

---

come a stumblingblock to the weak.—While the eating and the not eating did not affect the one having knowledge, there was danger that, in exercising the liberty to eat, the example might lead a weak brother to eat the flesh as worship to an idol. So the liberty to eat would become the cause of his being led into idolatry and ruin. No Christian can put a stumbling block in his brother's way and be guiltless.

10 For if a man see thee who hast knowledge sitting at meat in an idol's temple, will not his conscience, if he is weak, be emboldened to eat things sacrificed to idols?—Those who have not freed themselves from conscience of the idol, who cannot eat of the meat sacrificed to it, without worshiping it, seeing one who has knowledge sitting at meat in the idol's temple, would suppose that the strong brother was worshiping the idol, and be led by the example to eat in worship to the idol. [The fact of his example being avowedly advanced in the knowledge of the faith would make his example the more dangerous, because more effective.]

11 For through thy knowledge he that is weak perisheth, the brother for whose sake Christ died.—Through their knowledge that they might eat the flesh offered to an idol the weak brother perisheth. This shows that a thing not a sin in itself becomes sin when so done as to lead the weak ones into sin. We are held accountable for leading others into that which, in their ignorance and weakness, will prove their ruin.

Speaking more fully on this same subject, Paul says: "If one of them that believe not biddeth you to a feast, and ye are disposed to go; whatsoever is set before you, eat, asking no question for conscience' sake. But if any man say unto you, This hath been offered in sacrifice, eat not, for his sake that

edge he that is weak perisheth, the brother for whose sake Christ died. 12 And thus, sinning against the brethren, and wounding their conscience when it is weak, ye sin against Christ. 13 Wherefore, if meat causeth my brother to stumble, I will eat no flesh for evermore, that I cause not my brother to stumble.

showed it, and for conscience' sake: conscience, I say, not thine own, but the other's; for why is my liberty judged by another conscience? If I partake with thankfulness, why am I evil spoken of for that for which I give thanks? Whether therefore ye eat, or drink, or whatsoever ye do, do all to the glory of God. Give no occasion of stumbling, either to Jews, or to Greeks, or to the church of God: even as I also please all men in all things, not seeking mine own profit, but the profit of the many, that they may be saved." (10: 27-33.) We are to do nothing that will lead others into sin; we are to do nothing that will defile the conscience of others; we are not to assert our rights when to do so will injure others; and we must deny ourselves things that would please us, to profit and save others. This is an important principle, far-reaching in its results, and embodies the essential principle of the Christian religion.

12 **And thus, sinning against the brethren, and wounding their conscience when it is weak, ye sin against Christ.**—To sin against the weakest of the brethren in Christ, and wound the weakest conscience by drawing it into sin, is to sin against Christ, for he said: "Verily I say unto you, Inasmuch as ye did it unto one of these my brethren, even these least, ye did it unto me." (Matt. 25: 40.) Jesus here personifies himself in the poorest of his brethren in want, so that what is done to them is done to him. Here Paul tells us that he who causes that brother to stumble sins against Christ.

13 **Wherefore, if meat causeth my brother to stumble, I will eat no flesh for evermore,**—Paul's own welfare for the good of his brethren was such that he would forego many privileges and lay aside many liberties to save them from temptation to do wrong.

that I cause not my brother to stumble.—To cause a brother to sin is a fearful wrong to the brother and a sin against Christ. So in this our conscience is ruled by the conscience of the weak brother. In all the relations of life we should act on this principle and seek the good of others as we seek our own good. This is to love others as we do ourselves. This should be our aim in all that we do and say. Paul says: "It is good not to eat flesh, nor to drink wine, nor to do anything whereby thy brother stumbleth." (Rom. 14: 21.) "Now we that are strong ought to bear the infirmities of the weak, and not to please ourselves." (Rom. 15: 1.) This is the true spirit of Christ, ruling the life of a Christian.

When we sin against a weak brother, we sin against Christ who died for him. Christ denied himself all the honors and all the enjoyments of the Father's throne and his glories in order to help and bless man. If we are God's children, we are to drink into the same spirit, so as to make us forego pleasures, honors, privileges, and enjoyments in order to help and benefit the weak brethren. The weaker they are, the more they are entitled to consideration and help at our hands. Jesus Christ is our perfect example.

2. THE RIGHTS AND PRIVILEGES WHICH THE APOSTLE HAD WAIVED IN THE INTEREST OF OTHERS
9: 1-14

1 Am I not free? am I not an apostle? have I not seen Jesus our

1 **Am I not free?**—He had just said that those who had "knowledge" should be ready to surrender their rights for the good of the "weak." He now shows them that in matters which affected his whole life he had himself been governed by this rule. He was free and could have claimed that those to whom he preached should support him, but he deemed it wise to waive that right, and in so doing he subjected himself to great hardships and privations. (See Acts 20: 34; 1 Thess. 2: 9.)

am I not an apostle?—Some one had gained an influence in the church at Corinth, who, in seeking to destroy Paul's influence, denied that he was an apostle. As he had refused to receive help of the church at Corinth while among them, this question indicates that they had made the facts—that he was

Lord? are not ye my work in the Lord? 2 If to others I am not an apostle, yet at least I am to you; for the seal of mine apostleship are ye in the

not married and would not receive support—reasons for saying he was not an apostle. He had performed works in their midst which none but the apostles did. He says: "Truly the signs of an apostle were wrought among you in all patience, by signs and wonders and mighty works." (2 Cor. 12: 12.) These signs have been wrought in their midst and he refers to them as evidence of his claims.

An idea has prevailed that Apollos was at the head of the opposition to Paul; that some of the parties at Corinth claimed to be "of Apollos" is made the ground of this conclusion. But this is incorrect, for the relations between Paul and Apollos were cordial. (16: 12.)

have I not seen Jesus our Lord?—Paul had not seen and learned of Jesus when in the flesh as the other apostles had. This difference he himself recognized and made mention of it on several occasions. But he had seen Jesus even as he appeared to the twelve after his resurrection. After having recounted these appearances, he specifies with solemn emphasis, "And last of all, as to the child untimely born, he appeared to me also." (15: 5-8.) [This manifestation of the risen and glorified Lord, which was vouchsafed to him on the way to Damascus (Acts 9: 17), placed him on a level, in regard to this important particular, with the twelve.]

are not ye my work in the Lord?—He had been instrumental in converting them to Christ. He says: "For though ye have ten thousand tutors in Christ, yet have ye not many fathers; for in Christ Jesus I begat you through the gospel." (4: 15.)

2 If to others I am not an apostle, yet at least I am to you; —If others should reject him as an apostle, how could they, since they were the fruit of his labor as an apostle? They were the seal of his apostleship. "He dwelt there a year and six months, teaching the word of God among them" (Acts 18: 11), and he built a larger church there than he had built at any other place. His claims to be an apostle had been accom-

Lord. 3 My defence to them that examine me is this. 4 Have we no right to eat and to drink? 5 Have we no right to lead about a wife that is a ¹believer, even as the rest of the apostles, and the brethren of the Lord, and

¹Gr. *sister.*

panied by miracles, and they had believed on the evidence given through these of God's presence with him. Now to deny that he was an apostle would be to say that God had enabled one to work miracles and wonders who made false claims, or to admit that the miracles and wonders on which their faith rested had not been performed. They above all others could not question his apostleship.

for the seal of mine apostleship are ye in the Lord.—[A seal is that which is affixed to a deed, or other instrument to make it sure and indisputable. The Corinthian church itself is represented as such a seal of his apostleship. After their conversion he had bestowed on many of them gifts of the Holy Spirit in such abundance that they were inferior to no church whatever. (1: 5-7; 2 Cor. 12: 13.)]

3 **My defence to them that examine me is this.**—When any of his opponents undertook to question him as to his apostleship, he answered that he had seen the Lord Jesus, and that he had set his seal upon his commission by the success which had crowned his labors. This answer satisfied Peter, James, and John, who gave to him the right hands of fellowship, seeing to him had been committed the apostleship to the Gentiles. (Gal. 2: 8, 9.)

4 **Have we no right to eat and to drink?**—[Having proved his apostleship, he now proves his right to be maintained by those among whom he labored.]

5 **Have we no right to lead about a wife that is a believer,** —[He answered those who called in question his apostleship, on the ground that he had no wife neither did he receive a support from those among whom he labored, by informing them that, while he and Barnabas had the right to do so, they did not avail themselves of these privileges as a matter of choice.]

even as the rest of the apostles,—These had wives who accompanied them in their work, and he and Barnabas had the

Cephas? 6 Or I only and Barnabas, have we not a right to forbear working?
7 What soldier ever serveth at his own charges? who planteth a vineyard,

---

same right. [This passage certainly leads to the conclusion
that most of the apostles, if not all, were married men; that all
had the privilege of having themselves and their wives maintained by the churches.]

and the brethren of the Lord,—[The brethren of the Lord
were "James, and Joseph, and Simon, and Judas." (Matt. 13:
55.) Various and ingenious suppositions have been made as
to who these were. Some have endeavored to prove that they
were the cousins of Jesus; others that they were the sons of
Joseph by a former marriage. These views have been fos-
tered by those who have endeavored to establish the perpetual
virginity of Mary. But the natural conclusion from a study of
what is said in the Gospels, without preconceived prejudice,
would be that Joseph and Mary lived together as husband and
wife after the miraculous conception and birth of Jesus, and
that these sons were born unto them. This conclusion is supported by the use of the words: "She brought forth her first-
born son" (Luke 2: 7); "And knew her not till she had
brought forth a son" (Matt. 1: 25); "before they came together" (Matt. 1: 18); and the repeated mention of them in
connection with his mother Mary (Matt. 12: 46; 13: 55; Mark
6: 3).]

and Cephas?—[This statement and the account of Jesus
healing Peter's mother-in-law (Matt. 8: 14; Mark 1: 30; Luke
4: 38) is conclusive proof that he was a married man.]

6 Or I only and Barnabas, have we not a right to forbear
working?—Not only had they the right to marry if they saw
fit, but they had a right to forbear laboring with their hands
for support and to call on the brethren to support them in the
work to which they were called. [The word "only" here implies that the other apostles and the brethren of the Lord exercised their right to be maintained by the church.]

7 What soldier ever serveth at his own charges?—The soldier had a right to receive support from those whom he
served. This was a matter of common equity; and on this

and eateth not the fruit thereof? or who feedeth a flock, and eateth not of the milk of the flock? 8 Do I speak these things after the manner of men? or saith not the law also the same? 9 For it is written in the law of Moses, ²Thou shalt not muzzle the ox when he treadeth out the corn. Is it for the oxen that God careth, 10 or saith he it ³assuredly for our sake? Yea, for

²Dt. xxv. 4.
³Or, *altogether*

principle all acted who enlisted as soldiers. So then any man who goes into the world to fight for Jesus is entitled to his support from those to whom he renders service.

who planteth a vineyard, and eateth not the fruit thereof? —Any man that plants a vineyard is entitled to the fruit of the vineyard he planted.

or who feedeth a flock, and eateth not of the milk of the flock?—Any man that feeds a flock is entitled to the milk of that flock. In all this he asserts the right of those who labor for the church of God to live by that labor. He is entitled to a living for the work he does. If he does not labor in his calling, he is not entitled to it, for "if any will not work, neither let him eat." (2 Thess. 3: 10.)

8 Do I speak these things after the manner of men? or saith not the law also the same?—It is not merely in accordance with human judgment of what is fitting that he lays down the principle that the laborer has a right to a living wage. There is a higher authority than that, for God had ordained it in the law.

9 For it is written in the law of Moses, Thou shalt not muzzle the ox when he treadeth out the corn.—The ox when treading out the grain was allowed to eat what he needed while so doing.

Is it for the oxen that God careth,—[Certainly God cares for the ox. He had commanded the Israelites that when the harvest came, the ox, while treading out the corn which it had contributed to produce by the painful labor of plowing, should not be muzzled, and thereby prevented from enjoying, conjointly with man, the fruit of its toil. God's object in acting thus was evidently to cultivate in the hearts of his people feelings of justice and equity. This moral object appears not only from the prohibition itself, but also from all the other in-

our sake it was written: because he that ploweth ought to plow in hope, and he that thresheth, *to thresh* in hope of partaking. 11 If we sowed unto you spiritual things, is it a great matter if we shall reap your carnal things? 12 If others partake of *this* right over you, do not we yet more? Nevertheless

junctions which accompany it—pay to the poor laborer his wages on the same evening; not to put the child to death with the guilty father; always to leave, when gathering the harvest, a gleaning for widows and strangers; not to subject the criminal to more than forty stripes. (Deut. 24: 10 to 25: 4.) This whole context shows clearly enough what the object of the prohibition was. It was not from solicitude for the ox that God made this prohibition; there were other ways for providing for his nourishment. By calling on the Israelites to exercise gentleness and gratitude, even to a poor animal, it is clear that God desired to impress on them, with stronger reason, the same way of acting toward the human workmen whose help they engaged in their labor. It was the duties of moral beings to one another that God wished to impress by this precept.]

10 **or saith he it assuredly for your sake? Yea, for our sake it was written: because he that ploweth ought to plow in hope, and he that thresheth, to thresh in hope of partaking.**— This was written to teach that those laboring in the service of the Lord were entitled to a living from those for whom they labored, whatever their labor might be. [So the good which such a provision as the law achieved for the oxen was nothing compared to the good which it accomplished for man. God did not do this simply as a provision for the ox, but to teach us that it is a divine principle that the laborer should have his reward.]

11 **If we sowed unto you spiritual things, is it a great matter if we shall reap your carnal things?**—If Paul and Barnabas had preached to them, fed their souls with spiritual food, it was not unreasonable that they should minister to their fleshly necessities.

12 **If others partake of this right over you, do not we yet more?**—These opponents of Paul had received support from them. Certainly if any one had the right to receive their sup-

we did not use this right; but we bear all things, that we may cause no
hindrance to the 4gospel of Christ. 13 Know ye not that they that minister

4See marginal note on ch. 4. 15.

port, Paul, who had labored to support himself and suffered to
plan and build up the church in its weakness, was entitled to
it.

Nevertheless we did not use this right;—He had not demanded this of them, preferring to hold himself above suspicion as to his motives. It is common even yet that an earnest,
faithful worker denies himself, plants the truth through self-
denial, builds up a church, and then the church wishes a popular man to entertain them, and they forget the self-sacrificing
father, wound his feelings, and support in abundance a popular young man, who perverts the truth their father in the gospel taught. Paul's rebuke here applies to all such churches;
but the men who allow themselves to be so used ought to be
regarded as unworthy of countenance or support. Many
young men ought to drink into Paul's spirit—that he would
not build on another man's foundation—and seek destitute
fields in which they can plant vineyards and live of their own
planting, drink the milk of the flock they themselves have watered and cared for.

**but we bear all things, that we may cause no hindrance to
the gospel of Christ.**—While Paul had the right to this support, he refused to accept it lest he should be suspected of
seeking gain. He preferred to suffer and labor with his own
hands, lest the gospel should be hindered by such suspicions
against his character. [From this we should learn that our
right to anything is of itself no sufficient reason for claiming
it. We are bound by our relation to Christ to consider
whether we shall most advance his cause by claiming or waiv-
ing our rights.]

**13 Know ye not that they that minister about sacred things
eat of the things of the temple,**—God ordained in the temple
service that those who administered in the temple should live
from the offerings in the temple.

and they that wait upon the altar have their portion with

about sacred things eat *of* the things of the temple, *and* they that wait upon the altar have their portion with the altar? 14 Even so did the Lord ordain that they that proclaim the ⁴gospel should live of the ⁴gospel. 15 But I have

---

the altar?—Of the offerings and sacrifices brought to the temple, certain portions were set apart for the priests and their helpers around the altar, and for their families. While serving at the altar they must live of the offerings made.

14 Even so did the Lord ordain that they that proclaim the gospel should live of the gospel.—As the priests who ministered about the holy things lived of the gifts made at the altar, so those who preach the gospel should receive their support out of the offerings made by the church, not of special donations made to them while other work of the church suffers, as God ordained it. A failure to support the work of the church left the teacher to suffer.

3. THE APOSTLE'S TESTIMONY AS TO HIS SELF-DENIAL IN RELATION TO THESE RIGHTS
9: 15-23

used none of these things: and I write not these things that it may be so done in my case; for *it were* good for me rather to die, than that any man should make my glorying void. 16 For if I ⁵preach the gospel, I have nothing to glory of; for necessity is laid upon me; for woe is unto me, if I

⁵See marginal note on ch. 1. 17.

---

15 But I have used none of these things:—Paul chose to use none of these privileges of a support to which he was entitled, lest by it he should hinder the gospel of Christ.

and I write not these things that it may be so done in my case;—Neither did he write this to them that they should do so to him.

for it were good for me rather to die, than that any man should make my glorying void.—His glorying was that he might preach the gospel without receiving help from those to whom he preached.

16 For if I preach the gospel, I have nothing to glory of; for necessity is laid upon me;—He had been a sinner in persecuting the church. God chooses men to do work because of their fitness to do it. Paul's persecution of the church continually

⁵preach not the gospel. 17 For if I do this of mine own will, I have a reward: but if not of mine own will, I have a stewardship intrusted to me. 18 What then is my reward? That, when I ⁵preach the gospel, I may make the ⁴gospel without charge, so as not to use to the full my right in the ⁴gospel.

---

reminded him how he should as much as he could compensate for the injury he had done to it. So he felt in preaching and suffering all he could preach and suffer only what he ought to do to undo the former evil work. As he had made others suffer for it, he felt that he ought to bear and suffer to convert the world. Paul's conscience was always tender, quick, alert to lead him to suffer as he had made others suffer.

for woe is unto me, if I preach not the gospel.—As he had received mercy from God, he must proclaim the terms of mercy to others; hence he felt that woe would be unto him, if, after receiving so great mercy, he did not preach the mercy to others.

17 For if I do this of mine own will, I have a reward:—If he preached cheerfully and willingly without support, a reward would be given him.

but if not of mine own will, I have a stewardship intrusted to me.—The stewardship was the responsibility of being an apostle to the Gentiles. And if he should fail to fill it, the responsibility of the Gentiles dying without having the gospel preached to them would be his. And what a woe would have rested upon him had he failed in the discharge of his duty. [Since a steward was a slave, there is a great difference between what he did in obedience to a command and what a man volunteers to do of his own accord. And this is the difference to which Paul refers. The slave may feel honored by the command of his master, and obey him gladly, still it is but service. So "Paul, a servant of Jesus Christ" (Rom. 1: 1), was commanded to preach the gospel (Acts 26: 16-21), and he did it with his whole heart; but he was not commanded to refuse support from those to whom he ministered while so doing.]

18 What then is my reward? That, when I preach the gospel, I may make the gospel without charge,—His reward or

19 For though I was free from all *men*, I brought myself under bondage to
all, that I might gain the more. 20 And to the Jews I became as a Jew, that
I might gain Jews; to them that are under the law, as under the law, not
being myself under the law, that I might gain them that are under the law;

that which brought the reward was that he should preach the
gospel without charge.

so as not to use to the full my right in the gospel.—He was
sensitive lest he should transcend and abuse his right of support while preaching. So he refused it from those to whom he
preached. His own persecution of the church in days past no
doubt wrought upon his conscience and demanded that he
should suffer for the gospel.

19 **For though I was free from all men, I brought myself
under bondage to all, that I might gain the more.**—[None had
any claim on him because they maintained him; yet he re-
duced himself to the condition of a servant, both by serving
all men without requiring even maintenance from them and
by complying with their prejudices in all cases where he could
without violating God's will. How he did this is explained in
the following verses.]

20 **And to the Jews I became as a Jew, that I might gain
Jews;**—To the Jews when he circumcised Timothy, for it is
expressly said: "Him would Paul have to go forth with him;
and he took and circumcised him because of the Jews that
were in those parts." (Acts 16: 3.) Also when he consented
to purify himself and to be at charges with the four men who
had a vow (Acts 21: 20-26); and when he said: "I am a Phari-
see, a son of Pharisees" (Acts 23: 6, 7). He conformed to
their usages, observed the law, avowing at the same time that
he did it as a matter of conciliation. But whenever the fair
inference from his course would have been that he regarded
the Mosaic law and observances as binding on the Christian
he strenuously refused compliance.

His action in relation to Timothy and Titus shows the principle which governed him. Timothy, whose mother was a
Jewess, he circumcised, because it was regarded as a concession. Titus he refused to circumcise, because it was de-

21 to them that are without law, as without law, not being without law to
God, but under law to Christ, that I might gain them that are without law.

manded as a matter of obedience to the Mosaic law. (Gal. 2:
3-5.) Two things are, therefore, to be considered in all cases
in the opinions and practices of others: (1) That the point
conceded be a matter of indifference; for Paul never yielded to
anything which was in itself wrong. In this respect his conduct was directly opposite to that of those who accommodate
themselves to the sins of men or to the religious errors of others. (2) That the concession does not involve any admission
other than what is, in fact, indifferent in a matter of moral or
spiritual obligation.

**to them that are under the law, as under the law, not being
myself under the law, that I might gain them that are under
the law;**—[Expositors generally take the position that this
clause is only explanatory of the expression, "to the Jews,"
that is, to those under the law, I became a Jew, that is, as one
under the law.]

21 to them that are without law,—All peoples and things in
the universe are under the general government and rule of
God. God gives men the privilege of obeying him and being
saved, or of rejecting him as ruler and being condemned and
punished for rebelling against him. If they were not under
the dominion and rule of God, he could not punish them.
Satan himself is under the dominion of God. God is the sole
ruler of the universe. He permits men to rebel, to refuse to
submit, for a time; but if they do not repent, God, as the ruler
of all, will punish them. All men now living ought to be
under "the law of the Spirit of life in Christ Jesus." The reason they are not is because they are unwilling to obey him.
God allows them to live a while in the state of rebellion; then
if they refuse to repent and obey him, in the execution of the
laws of the universe, he will punish them in hell. God for-
bears with them for a time, giving them time and opportunity
to repent. He gives laws only to those willing to obey him.
Those unwilling to serve him he leaves without law, not that
they are not accountable, but because they reject him as ruler.
God gave laws to the Israelites because they were willing at

22 To the weak I became weak, that I might gain the weak: I am become
all things to all men, that I may by all means save some. 23 and I do all

times to obey and serve him. The Gentiles were not willing
to serve him, and he left them without law. When any Gentile was willing to obey God, he entered into the Jewish family and came under the Mosaic law. Just so now; any soul
that is willing to obey God comes into the church of God and
under his law. If a man is not under law it is because he is
not willing to obey God. The Gentiles, who were without law
in the days of Judaism, became willing to obey God under
Christ; hence they were said to be without law, were not
under the law of Moses.

as without law,—[Paul adapted himself to the habits and
modes of thought of the Gentiles; quoted their poets (Acts
17: 23); ate with them, and rebuked Peter when he ceased to
do so (Gal. 2: 11-16); based an argument on the inscriptions
on their altars (Acts 17: 23); and did not urge on them the
ceremonies and "works of the law"; but "by the hearing of
faith" (Gal. 3: 9).]

not being without law to God, but under law to Christ, that
I might gain them that are without law.—This parenthesis ex-
plains in what sense only Paul was "without law." The death
of Jesus on the cross had made him free from the law of
Moses (Col. 2: 14), and brought him under the "law of the
Spirit of life in Christ Jesus" (Rom. 8: 2).

22 To the weak I became weak, that I might gain the weak:
I am become all things to all men, that I may by all means
save some.—Paul's own example is instructive, as showing
how far this method of action may be rightly carried. He ac-
commodated himself to the prejudices and preferences of men
so far as he could without sacrificing truth and righteousness,
in order to win them to Christ. In other words, he sacrificed
personal rights and personal liberty of action rather than to
insist upon them when they stood in the way of winning any
man, or set of men, to the Lord. As an example he earnestly
contended that the law of Moses was no longer binding; yet
he observed it as fully as he could, consistently with the law

things for the ⁴gospel's sake, that I may be a joint partaker thereof. 24

of Christ, for the purpose of conciliating the Jews and obtaining from them a favorable hearing of the gospel. He did this not that he might be personally popular with any man, but that by doing so he might throw no obstacle in the way of their giving the gospel a favorable hearing.

23 And I do all things for the gospel's sake, that I may be a joint partaker thereof.—[Hitherto Paul has dwelt on the duty of self-denial for the good of others; now, however, he rises higher—to the absolute necessity of it to eternal salvation even of himself, as an indispensable feature of Christian character. So we see that in work for the good of others we must not be unmindful of our own good; and there is nothing more conducive to our spiritual benefit than faithful, self-denying service for Christ. "Continue in these things; for in doing this thou shalt save both thyself and them that hear thee." (1 Tim. 4: 16.)]

4. ENFORCEMENT OF THE DUTY OF SELF-DENIAL BY REFERENCE TO THE GRECIAN GAMES
9: 24-27

Know ye not that they that run in a ⁶race run all, but one receiveth the

⁶Gr. *race course.*

24 Know ye not that they that run in a race run all,—There is here an allusion to the Isthmian games, which took place every second year, at a place on the seacoast about nine miles from Corinth. These games had been one of the chief means of fostering the feeling of brotherhood in the Hellenic race. They were the greatest of the national gatherings; and even when one State was at war with another, hostilities were suspended during the celebration of the games. All competitors in the games had ten months' training, under the directions of competent teachers and under various restrictions of diet. For thirty days previous to the contest the candidates had to attend the exercises at the gymnasium. At the beginning of the festival, they were required to prove to the judges that they were of pure Greek blood, and had not forfeited by mis-

conduct the right of citizenship, and had undergone the necessary training.

Only after the fulfillment of these conditions were they allowed, and when the time arrived, to contend in the sight of
assembled Greece. The race was not merely an exhibition of
bodily strength, but solemn trials of the excellence of the competitors in the gymnastic art, and was to the Greeks one-half
of the human education. Proclamation was made of the name
of each competitor by a herald.

but one receiveth the prize?—Of the multitude of competitors one only received the prize. They ran with all their
might—each exerted himself to the utmost. The desire to
succeed was so intense that the contestants suffered great
agony. The issue of the contest was watched by his relatives
and friends with breathless interest. His success depended on
his passing all rivals, so thy cheered him to greater exertion.

[The prize was a wreath of pine leaves, conferred on the
successful contestant on the last day of the games. "Every
one thronged to see and congratulate him; his relatives,
friends, and countrymen shedding tears of tenderness and joy,
lifted him on their shoulders to show him to the crowd, and
held him up to the applause of the whole assembly, who
strewed handfuls of flowers over him." His family was
greatly honored by his victory, and when he returned to his
home, he rode in a triumphal chariot through a breach in the
wall which enclosed the city, the object of this being to sym-
bolize that for a city which was honored by such a citizen no
walls of defense were needful. His name was sung in triumphal odes and his likeness was placed in the long line of stat-
ues which formed the approach to the adjacent temple. Such
was the imagery before Paul's mind when he wrote these
words.]

Even so run; that ye may attain.—That is, run as the victor
runs, in order to attain. We have seen that the victor's success depended on great self-denial in preparation, and the
greatest possible effort in the contest. In the Christian race
he who crowns is willing to crown not the first only but the
last. Yet all must run in a certain way. What this so run-

prize? Even so run; that ye may attain. 25 And every man that striveth in
the games exerciseth self-control in all things. Now they *do it* to receive a
corruptible crown; but we an incorruptible. 26 I therefore so run, as not

ning is, we learn from the following: "Therefore let us also,
seeing we are compassed about with so great a cloud of witnesses, lay aside every weight, and the sin which doth so easily beset us, and let us run with patience the race that is set
before us, looking unto Jesus the author and perfecter of our
faith, who for the joy that was set before him endured the
cross, despising shame, and hath sat down at the right hand of
the throne of God." (Heb. 12: 1, 2.) This gives special
prominence to the immense concourse which the Greek spectacle called together, as well as the necessity of being free
from every hindrance and of straining to the utmost every
nerve, in order to attain the heavenly runner's prize.

25 **And every man that striveth in the games exerciseth
self-control in all things.**—Contentedly and without a murmur
he submits himself to the rules and restrictions of his ten
months' training, without which he may as well not compete.
The indulgences which other men allow themselves he must
forego. Not once will he break the trainer's rules, for he
knows that some competitor will refrain even from that
once and gain the strength while he is losing it. He glories in
his hardships and fatigues and privation, and counts it a point
of honor scrupulously to abstain from anything which might
in the slightest degree diminish his chance of success, because
his heart is set on the prize, and severe training is indispensable. He knows that his chances are gone if in any point or on
any occasion he relaxes the rigor of the discipline.

Now they do it to receive a corruptible crown;—A crown of
pine leaves. The victor, it is true, won a crown of glory; but
the glory faded almost as fast as the wreath. No permanent
satisfaction could result from being victorious in a contest of
physical strength, activity, and skill.

but we an incorruptible.—An incorruptible, an unfading,
and eternal crown. It is called "the crown of righteousness"
(2 Tim. 4: 8); "the crown of life" (James 1: 12; Rev. 2: 10);
and "the crown of glory" (1 Pet. 5: 4). It is possible for

uncertainly; so [7]fight I, as not beating the air: 27 but I [8]buffet my body, and
bring it into bondage: lest by any means, after that I [9]have preached to

[7]Gr. *box.*
[8]Gr. *bruise.* Lk. 18. 5.
[9]Or, *have been a herald*

---

every one who runs the Christian race to receive this crown,
which shall forever be unto him a joy as thrilling as at the
moment of receiving it. [It is worthy of the determined and
sustained effort of a lifetime. As victory in the games was
the actual incentive which stimulated the Grecian youth to
strive for the physical strength and development, so there is
laid before the Christian an incentive which, when fully appre-
hended, is sufficient to carry him to great spiritual attain-
ments. To have righteousness and life in perfection is his
true glory, and this is the very crown of his being. And such
a crown cannot fade away.]

26 **I therefore so run, as not uncertainly;**—Here Paul appeals to his own conduct as an illustration of the lesson which
he is teaching, and by means of it reminds the reader that the
whole of this chapter has been a vindication of his own self-
denial, and that he has a clear and definite object in view. No
man can run as Paul did who has no definite object to be
gained. [We must be resolved to win and have no thought of
defeat, of failure, or of doing something better. It is the absence of deliberate choice and a strong determination which
causes such uncertain running on the part of many who claim
to be in the race. Their faces are as often turned from the
goals as towards it. They fail to understand that all strength
spent in any other direction than towards the goal is lost.
They act as though they do not know what they wish to make
of life.]

so fight I, as not beating the air:—The illustration is
changed from running to fighting, both being included in
"striveth." He had an adversary to contend against, and did
not strive with uncertain blows; but all his efforts were directed, with good account, to the great purpose of subjecting
his enemy, and bringing every thought into captivity to God.

27 **but I buffet my body,**—By this he plainly means his
whole embodied self, as acting and acting on through the

body. So viewed he expressed his determination to beat down relentlessly all those unholy inclinations of which the body is the essential organ. [Every man's body is his enemy when, instead of being his servant, it becomes his master. The proper function of the body is to serve the will, to bring the inner man into contact with the outer world and enable him to influence it. When the body refuses to obey the will, when it usurps the authority and compels the man to do its bidding, it becomes his dangerous enemy.]

and bring it into bondage:—He brought all its desires under subjection, that it might serve, not rule, the spirit. "For the flesh lusteth against the Spirit, and the Spirit against the flesh; for these are contrary the one to the other" (Gal. 5: 17), "because the mind of the flesh is enmity against God" (Rom. 8: 7). God is Spirit; so the flesh opposes God. Paul kept under his body, and brought it, with all its lusts and desires, into subjection to the Spirit. He also says: "For though we walk in the flesh, we do not war according to the flesh (for the weapons of our warfare are not of the flesh, but mighty before God to the casting down of strongholds); casting down imaginations, and every high thing that is exalted against the knowledge of God, and bringing every thought into captivity to the obedience of Christ." (2 Cor. 10: 3-5.)

[It is difficult to control the thoughts. Evil thoughts will rise in the mind, excited by fleshly lusts. To bring into subjection to the will of God is the triumph of the Spirit, yet by constant prayer and watchfulness it can be done. By devotion to the Lord and persevering effort the thoughts that spring from the heart can be brought into subjection to the will of Christ. The heart can be so trained that the thoughts that arise will be of God, of our duties, and obligations to him, and of the high and exalted privileges and blessings that are bestowed on us as his children. This state is gained only by the constant study of God's word, a drinking into the Spirit, a cultivation of the devotional feelings, and a constant effort to conform the life to the will of God. This is the only way to fit the soul for companionship with God and "the spirits of just men made perfect." The church is the training school to fit

others, I myself should be rejected.

---

man for the eternal home, and the will of Christ is for disciplining and training for the blessed companionship with the redeemed in the heavenly home.]

lest by any means, after that I have preached to others,— [The image is carried on, and Paul says that he has a further motive to live a life of self-denial—that having acted as a herald, proclaiming the conditions of the contest, and the requisite preliminaries for it, should not be found to have himself fulfilled them. It is the same image kept up still of this race, and of the herald who announced the name of the victor, and the fact that he had fulfilled the necessary conditions. It was not the custom for the herald to join in the contest, but the apostle was himself both a runner in the Christian race and a herald of the conditions of that race to others. Hence, naturally, he speaks of the two characters, which in the actual illustration would be distinct, as united in one when applied spiritually to himself.]

I myself should be rejected.—[Lest he should fail utterly of the prize. If such earnest, self-denying watchfulness was needed on the part of Paul, with all his labors for others, to make his own calling and election sure, we should learn that not to do our utmost to save, at any personal sacrifice, the souls of others is to imperil our own salvation. For such effort and sacrifice strengthen the spiritual life. And so serious is our conflict and so tremendous are its issues that we dare not leave unused any means of spiritual strength. In seeking to save others, we are working out our own salvation.]

5. EXHORTATION TO SELF-DENIAL BASED ON JEWISH HISTORY
10: 1-13

1 For I would not, brethren, have you ignorant, that our fathers were all

---

1 **For**—Paul had just shown them, by his own example, the necessity for watchfulness and untiring effort, lest they should be unapproved, and now he continues this same thought by reference to the history of Israel that the possession of great

privileges is no safeguard, and that the seductions of idolatry must not be consciously despised.

I would not, brethren, have you ignorant,—By this he does not mean their being ignorant of the bare facts of the narrative, for they were the most striking in the Old Testament, but of their spiritual significance. This practical application is found in the fact that the fleshly kingdom of Israel was the type of the spiritual kingdom, the church of Jesus Christ. The earthly Canaan, the type of the heavenly. The rewards, the conflicts, the weapons of the one were earthly and carnal; in the other, heavenly and spiritual. The conduct of the people under the law of God and his dealings with them were recorded for our instruction and warning. Paul introduces the dealing of God with them here for the instruction and warning of the church at Corinth and for all Christians, as the letter is addressed "unto the church of God which is at Corinth, even them that are sanctified in Christ Jesus, called to be saints, with all that call upon the name of our Lord Jesus Christ in every place, their Lord and ours." (1:2.) So after telling them in the preceding paragraph how he labored to keep under his body lest he should be rejected, he pleads with them to be guarded and careful, and introduces these dealings of God with Israel to warn and help them by these examples.

that our fathers were all under the cloud, and all passed through the sea;—[The cloud betokened the immediate presence of the angel of God; "And the angel of God, who went before the camp of Israel, removed and went behind them; and the pillar of cloud removed from before them, and stood behind them: and it came between the camp of Egypt and the camp of Israel; and there was the cloud and the darkness, yet gave it light by night: and the one came not near the other all the night." (Ex. 14: 19, 20.) And immediately after this, trusting themselves to Moses as a medium of God's power, they passed through the dried-up bed of the sea so that] the cloud was over them and the sea stood as a wall on each side of them, thus were they covered and overwhelmed with the two.

under the cloud, and all passed through the sea; 2 and were all baptized.
[10]unto Moses in the cloud and in the sea; 3 and did all eat the same spiritual

[10]Gr. *into.*

---

2 and were all baptized unto Moses—It brought them into a
relationship to Moses they had never sustained before. That
is, into his undisputed control over their movements. Up to
the very moment of that baptism this control was still dis-
puted by Pharaoh. They were saved by that baptism from his
hands and passed under the leadership of Moses. True they
were baptized figuratively in the cloud and in the sea; yet at
the same time, by a like figure, passed out of Pharaoh into
Moses. They were committed to his leadership as men now by
baptism are consecrated to the leadership of Jesus Christ, and
this transition into Moses by an act quite similar to baptism.

in the cloud and in the sea;—Those who passed through the
sea did not have water sprinkled or poured upon them. The
cloud was not a rain cloud, but one of smoke, that presented
at night an appearance of fire and by day a cloud to guide
them. (see Ex. 13: 21-25.) The water from the sea did not wet
them, for a strong east wind blew the waters back and con-
gealed them, and they went over on dry land. (Ex. 15: 8.) In
this passage the whole body of people were hidden, enclosed,
covered by the sea and the cloud, [prefiguring the double process of submersion and emersion in baptism]. They were
baptized in these. "The waters were a wall unto them on
their right hand, and on their left. Thus Jehovah saved Israel
that day out of the hand of the Egyptians." (Ex. 14: 29, 30.)

3 and did all eat the same spiritual food;—They ate of
the food that God gave them—the manna and the quails.
[Spiritual is to be taken in contrast with natural, not as regards the nature of the food, but of its source, which was supernatural and miraculous.] The manna given by God is contrasted by Jesus with himself as the true bread that came
down from heaven. (See John 6: 31-35.) As the Israelites ate
of the manna and were preserved alive, so the disciples ate of
the true bread, Jesus Christ. The disciples ate of him by making him their Lord and doing his will. Jesus said: "My meat

food; 4 and did all drink the same spiritual drink: for they drank of a spiritual rock that followed them: and the rock was [11]Christ. 5 Howbeit with

[11]Or, *the Christ* Comp. Heb. 11. 26.

is to do the will of him that sent me, and to accomplish his work." (John 4: 34.) So it is the meat of his disciples to do the will of Jesus and to finish the work he has given them to do. To do his will strengthens the soul as bread does the body.

4 and did all drink the same spiritual drink:—When they were in the wilderness they were thirsty; Jehovah told Moses to smite the rock; he did so; the water gushed out; they drank of it, and were refreshed. Jesus compares the life he gives to living water, of which if a man drinks, he shall never die: "Whosoever drinketh of the water that I shall give him shall never thirst; but the water that I shall give him shall become in him a well of water springing up unto eternal life." (John 4: 14.)

for they drank of a spiritual rock that followed them:— [They habitually made use of the source which was always at hand. In drinking from the smitten rock the Israelites were drinking at the same time of a "spiritual rock"—and not supplying them once alone, but following them throughout their history. So that looking back on the entire journey, it might very naturally be said that the rock had followed them, not meaning that wherever they went they had the same source to draw from, but that throughout their journey they were supplied with water in places and ways as unexpectedly and unlikely.]

and the rock was Christ.—The object of the two epithets— "followed" and "spiritual"—is certainly to distinguish exactly the invisible and spiritual rock, of which he himself speaks, from the material rock spoken of in Exodus, that of which Jehovah said to Moses the first time: "Behold, I will stand before thee there upon the rock in Horeb; and thou shalt smite the rock, and there shall come water out of it, that the people may drink" (Ex. 17: 6), and the second time in the Wilderness of Sin: "Take the rod, and assemble the congregation, thou,

most of them God was not well pleased: for they were overthrown in the

and Aaron thy brother, and speak ye unto the rock before their eyes, that it give forth its water; and thou shalt bring forth to them water out of the rock" (Num. 20: 8). These two rocks already stood there when Israel arrived in these two localities, and remained there when Israel left them. Paul, therefore, can only mean that, behind these material, immovable rocks, there was one invisible and movable, the true giver of the water, to wit, the Christ himself.

[This is plainly the meaning of the passage in the light of the numerous sayings of Moses in which the Lord is called the Rock of Israel: "The Rock, his work is perfect." "And lightly esteemed the Rock of his salvation." "Of the Rock that begat thee thou art unmindful." (Deut. 32: 4, 15, 18.) And by similar ones in Isaiah: "For thou hast forgotten the God of thy salvation, and hast not been mindful of the rock of thy strength." (17: 10.) "Trust ye in Jehovah for ever; for in Jehovah, even Jehovah, is an everlasting rock." (26: 4.) Only what is special in the passage under consideration is that this title "Rock" during the journey through the wilderness is ascribed here, not to Jehovah, but to Christ. The passage forms an analogy to the words in John 12: 41, where the apostle applies to Jesus the vision in which Isaiah beholds Jehovah in the temple of his glory. (Isa. 6: 1-13.) Christ is represented in the passages by Paul and John as pre-existent before coming to the earth, and presiding over the Israelites in their journey through the wilderness. In chapter 8: 6, Paul had spoken of Christ as the one "through whom are all things." Here he designates him as the one who accompanied Israel in the cloud through the wilderness, and gave them deliverances when they needed.]

5 Howbeit with most of them God was not well pleased:— [In the course of these opening verses the emphatic word *all* occurs five times, the more emphatically to make the sad contrast between the commencement and the close of the journey. They all without exception stood on the same level of divine favor. In his marvelous dealings with them he was one and

wilderness. 6 Now ¹these things were our examples, to the intent we should
not lust after evil things, as they also lusted. 7 Neither be ye idolaters, as

¹Or, *in these things they became figures of us*

the same to them all: to the standing and the falling he was
gracious alike, for as "all were baptized unto Moses in the
cloud and in the sea," so in the wilderness the same food was
common to them all and the same drink to all, both of divine
origin, and had they but remained steadfast in the covenant,
the same prospect of reaching Canaan was before them all.]
But notwithstanding the deliverance he had given them from
bondage, and the many works he did in their behalf, most of
them forgot his goodness, turned from following Moses, and
with them God was not well pleased.

for they were overthrown in the wilderness.—All of the
generation that left Egypt, except Joshua and Caleb, were dis-
qualified by their misconduct. They were overthrown by the
pestilence, by wars, or by natural and unusual diseases, so
that they did not reach the land of Canaan. [So now notwithstanding Jesus has delivered us from the slavery of sin, he has
provided blessings and favors at every step of the way, we
murmur and complain at his dealings and rebel against his
law and displease him, and as the Israelites were overthrown
in the wilderness, so we fall from our steadfastness and are
overthrown by the way, fail to reach the promised land.]

6 Now these things were our examples, to the intent we
should not lust after evil things, as they also lusted.—The Israelites and the facts of their history are examples to us. The
same Lord directs our affairs that ordered theirs; and if we
sin as they did, we also must expect to be punished and excluded from his favors and from heaven. [In the case of Israel, the punishment was directly and visibly connected with
the sin, and it is recorded so that their history might be used
to instruct future generations; for in this life punishment is
not, as a rule, summarily and immediately meted out to sinners. In fact, if we judge by appearances only, we might
sometimes even think that God rewarded crime and set a pre-
mium on sin. The Scripture records show that such appearances are deceptive, and that God's punishments are sure,

were some of them; as it is written, ²The people sat down to eat and drink, and rose up to play. 8 Neither let us commit fornication, as some of them committed, and fell in one day three and twenty thousand. 9 Neither let us

²Ex. xxxii. 6.

though they may be long delayed. Israel lusted after flesh, and God granted them their desires, and the consequence was a plague, and the destruction of multitudes. (Num. 11: 4, 33, 34.) This is a perpetual warning against the indulgence of inordinate desires for forbidden things. It was especially appropriate as a warning to the Corinthians not to desire participation in the sacrificial feasts of the heathen in which they had been accustomed to indulge.]

7 Neither be ye idolaters, as were some of them;—Some of them had a fondness for idolatry and were drawn into it. When Moses went up into the mountain to receive the law, the people induced Aaron to make them the golden calf, "and they said, These are thy gods, O Israel, which brought thee out of the land of Egypt." (Ex. 32: 4.)

as it is written, The people sat down to eat and drink, and rose up to play.—[To play here refers to those lively dances which occurred at heathen festivals (Ex. 32: 3-6, 18, 19, 25), in which the Corinthians, who, before they became Christians, had indulged. Here lay their peril. They had been released from the superstitions of idolatry (8: 4), and were still attracted by the feasting and gaiety, which were directly designed to provoke the most licentious passions—dances of which those now practiced are the direct lineal descendants. Hence the close connection between idolatry and fornication, which appears all through this epistle.]

8 Neither let us commit fornication, as some of them committed,—They were guilty of fornication with the daughters of Moab, and by them led into idolatry and three and twenty thousand were destroyed. This is held up as a warning to Christians to avoid associations that lead to idolatry. [The danger of fornication was always connected with idolatry. At Corinth, therefore, it might easily follow participation in sacrificial feasts.]

make trial of the [3]Lord, as some of them made trial, and perished by the

[3]Some ancient authorities read *Christ*.

---

and fell in one day three and twenty thousand.—In Num.
25: 1-9, it is said that there were four and twenty thousand.
Why this discrepancy I am not able to explain.

**9 Neither, let us make trial of the Lord, as some of them
made trial,**—When difficulties presented themselves in the
way, the Israelites often tried the Lord by their distrust of
him and readiness to turn back and follow him no more.

[The word, try, when applied to man, means to present motives or inducements to sin; when used in reference to the
Lord, it means to try his patience, to provoke his anger to act
in such a way as to see how much he will bear and how long
he will endure the wickedness of men. The Israelites tried
his patience by rebellion, by murmuring, by impatience, and
dissatisfaction with his dealings. The Corinthians tried him
when they exposed themselves to temptations in idol temples,
and thus needlessly trying the strength of his religion, and
making the experiment on the grace of the Lord, as if he were
bound to keep them even in the midst of danger into which
they needlessly ran. They had the promise of grace to keep
them only when they were in the way of duty, and were using
all proper precautions against sin. To go beyond this would
be to try him, and to provoke him to leave them.]

and perished by the serpents.—"And they journeyed from
mount Hor by the way to the Red Sea, to compass the land of
Edom: and the soul of the people was much discouraged because of the way. And the people spake against God, and
against Moses, Wherefore have ye brought us up out of Egypt
to die in the wilderness? for there is no bread, and there is no
water; and our soul loatheth this light bread. And Jehovah
sent fiery serpents among the people, and they bit the people;
and much people of Israel died. And the people came to
Moses, and said, We have sinned, because we have spoken
against Jehovah, and against thee; pray unto Jehovah, that he
take away the serpents from us. And Moses prayed for the
people. And Jehovah said unto Moses, Make thee a fiery ser-

serpents. 10 Neither murmur ye, as some of them murmured, and perished
by the destroyer. 11 Now these things happened unto them ⁴by way of example; and they were written for our admonition upon whom the ends of the

⁴Gr. *by way of figure.*

---

pent, and set it upon a standard: and it shall come to pass,
that every one that is bitten, when he seeth it, shall live. And
Moses made a serpent of brass, and set it upon the standard:
and it came to pass, that if a serpent had bitten any man,
when he looked unto the serpent of brass, he lived." (Num.
21: 4-9.)

10 **Neither murmur ye,**—To murmur is to complain in a dis-
contented rebellious spirit.

as some of them murmured,—The fact here recited is that
of the revolt of Korah, Dathan, and Abiram who murdered because they were not permitted to serve in the priestly office.
They envied others who were entrusted with higher trusts
than they. [In quoting this example, Paul possibly had in
view the irritation felt by a party among the Corinthians
against himself and his fellow laborers who disapproved of
their taking part in heathen rejoicings. This party chafed at
their severity, which gave rise to so painful a situation for
Christians in relation to their idolatrous friends.]

and perished by the destroyer.—Korah, Dathan, and Abiram were swallowed up by the earth. (Num. 16: 1-35.) [The
destroyer means the pestilence which destroyed fourteen thousand and seven hundred persons. (Num. 16: 49.) The
pestilence in David's day was administered by a destroying
angel. (2 Sam. 24: 16, 17.) The angel in Ex. 12: 23 is called
the destroyer. It should be noted, (1) that in all the sins
specified in the foregoing, Paul says, "some of them," showing
that it was not true of all the Israelites of that day; (2) that
he regards all these sins as connected with and growing out of
lusting. (Compare James 1: 14, 15; 1 John 2: 16, 17.)]

11 **Now these things happened unto them by way of example;**—In the days of the patriarchs and of Moses, God gave
the law, and then applied the law to the facts and conditions
as they arose in the workings of human affairs.

ages are come. 12 Wherefore let him that thinketh he standeth take heed
lest he fall.　13 There hath no temptation taken you but such as man can

and they were written for our admonition,—They were
written for examples and instruction to the world for all succeeding time, to teach how God deals with man and how he
applies his own law.　No man can have a clear knowledge of
how God will apply his law without studying the lessons he
has given in the Old Testament Scriptures.　All his dealings
with men are instructive to us, and help in learning our duty
and how God will regard our actions under his law.　God's
dealings with the unfaithful are just as much for our good as
his dealings with the righteous.　With both it has been impossible to keep man long in the strait and narrow way.　So it
behooves us in questions of God's dealings with men to go to
these examples in which God applies his law to learn the conditions required.

upon whom the ends of the ages are come.—[The ages are
the ages of the world's history, and the apostle means that we
belong to the last dispensation, or the gospel era.　In Heb. 9:
26, Christ's manifestation as the Messiah is said to mark the
end or completion of the ages.　The Christian dispensation is
called "the end of the ages" because it is the last and final dispensation.　(1 John 2: 18; 1 Pet. 4: 7.)　The church is the heir
of all the past—history culminates in it, and the lessons
taught by the past are for its admonition.]

**12 Wherefore let him that thinketh he standeth take heed
lest he fall.**—When one feels most confidence in himself, then
there is the greatest danger that he will be presumptuous and
commit the greatest sin.　Poor in spirit, contrite and humble
in heart are qualities that God loves in man.　[Distrust of self
leads to trust in God, and God loves not him who thanked
God that he was not as other men are, and felt that his good
deeds and holy life entitled him to the high privileges of divine favor; but loved him who in humility smote upon his
breast and cried, "Be merciful to me a sinner."　Self-
confidence leads to reliance on self instead of God.]

bear but God is faithful, who will not suffer you to be tempted above that ye
are able; but will with the temptation make also the way of escape, that ye
may be able to endure it.

13 **There hath no temptation taken you**—[Seized upon you,
or assailed you, as when an enemy grasps one and attempts
to hold him fast.]

but such as man can bear:—Temptations come to all men to
test, prove them, and show their fitness to enter the kingdom
of heaven, and their worthiness to stand before God in the immortal state. [In verse 10 was a warning; this is an encouragement. Having just heard what efforts even Paul had to
make in order to run successfully the Christian race, and how
terribly the Israelites in the wilderness had failed, they might
be inclined to throw up every effort in despair. Paul, therefore, reminds them that these temptations were not superhu-
man, but such as man had resisted, and such as they could
resist.]

**but God is faithful, who will not suffer you to be tempted
above that ye are able;**—[This was the only source of security, and this was enough. If they looked only to themselves,
they would fall. If they depended on the faithfulness of God,
they would be secure. Not that God would keep them without any effort of their own; not that he would secure them if
they plunged voluntarily into the temptation, but if they used
the proper precautions to avoid it, if they resisted temptation,
if they sought his aid, and depended upon his promises, then
he would certainly perform his part of the covenant. This is
everywhere implied in the Scriptures; and to depend on the
faithfulness of God otherwise than in the proper use of the
means, and avoiding the places of temptation, is to tempt him,
and provoke him to wrath.]

**but will with the temptation make also the way of escape,
that ye may be able to endure it.**—God permits those whom
he loves to be tempted to test, prove them, and show their
worthiness to stand before him in the immortal state. If we
do not escape, pass through the temptation without sin, we
may know that we are not true to God as we should be. God
is faithful and never fails to provide the way of escape if we

have the fidelity to resist and escape. Men are given to excuse themselves for their wrongs because they are not able to
bear temptations. [As temptations vary, so the means of escape also vary. We have in this verse, perhaps, the most
practical and therefore the clearest exposition in the scriptures of free will in relation to God's overruling power. God
makes an open road, but then man must walk in it: God con-
trols circumstances, but man must use them. This is where
man's responsibility lies.]

6. THE EATING OF SACRIFICIAL MEAT AT AN IDOL'S TABLE OR IN IDOLATROUS FEASTS PROHIBITED
10: 14-22

14 Wherefore, my beloved, flee from idolatry. 15 I speak as to wise men;
judge ye what I say. 16 The cup of blessing which we bless, is it not a

14 **Wherefore,**—[This appeal is made in view of all that has
been said of the severe judgments that came upon the idolatrous Israelites, and the danger that Christians may fall into
the same sins and thus incur God's displeasure.]

my beloved,—While Paul reproves them very sharply, he
speaks to them in much love and tenderness.

flee from idolatry.—Avoid idolatry by fleeing from it.
This is the only safe method of escaping its coils. We are
subject to idolatry, not so gross in form, but more insidious
and deceptive. We serve what we worship. [We should
avoid all that approaches the confines of sin, and keep at a distance from everything which excites evil passions or which
tends to ensnare the soul.]

15 **I speak as to wise men; judge ye what I say.**—[It is a
matter requiring judgment and discrimination. They were
wise men, and could, out of an abundant personal knowledge,
judge as to the wisdom of his counsel when he thus told them
to shun all that pertained to idolatry. For idolatry was so interwoven with drunkenness, revelling, and licentiousness that
it practically included them, and was not to be dallied with.]

16 **The cup of blessing**—He now directs their attention to
the Lord's Supper which they had greatly perverted. The
cup of blessing is the cup that was blessed (Matt. 26: 26, 27)

⁵communion of the blood of Christ? The ⁶bread which we break, is it not a
⁵communion of the body of Christ? 17 ⁷Seeing that we, who are many, are
one ⁶bread, one body: for we all partake ⁸of the one ⁶bread. 18 Behold Israel

⁵Or, *participation in*
⁶Or, *loaf*
⁷Or, *seeing that there is one bread, we, who are many, are one body*
⁸Gr. *from.*

and consecrated as a means of blessings to those who properly
observed it. [The word "blessing" is used interchangeably
with "gave thanks." That is, the same act is sometimes expressed by the one form and sometimes by the other. In
Matt. 26: 26, Mark 14: 22, what is expressed by "blessed" and
"had blessed" in Luke 22: 17, 19; 1 Cor. 11: 24 is expressed by
saying, "had given thanks." And in the account of the Lord's
Supper as given by Matthew and Mark, the one expression is
used in reference to the bread, and the other in reference to
the cup. They therefore mean the same thing, or rather express the same act, for that act was both a benediction and
thanksgiving; that is, it is addressed to God, acknowledging
his mercy and imploring his blessing, and therefore may be
expressed either by the words "had blessed" or "had given
thanks."]

which we bless,—[This is the explanation of the preceding
clause. The cup of blessing is the cup which we bless; which
can only mean the cup on which we implore a blessing; that is,
which we pray may be a blessing to the end for which it was
appointed.]

is it not a communion of the blood of Christ?—In partaking
of it we become partakers of the benefits of the blood of
Christ. The blood is the life, and in partaking of it, we declare that we partake of the life of Christ, we live the life of
Christ.

The bread which we break, is it not a communion of the
body of Christ?—This is but a repetition of the thought contained in the preceding clause. We partake of the benefits of
the blood and body of Christ in the observance of this ordinance.

17 Seeing that we, who are many, are one bread, one body:
for we all partake of the one bread.—[This is in confirmation

after the flesh: have not they that eat the sacrifices communion with the altar? 19 What say I then? that a thing sacrificed to idols is anything, or

of the preceding statement that in the Lord's Supper there is
a fellowship with the body and blood of Christ—with his
death.] We who partake are members individually, but we
constitute one body of Christ, because we all draw our life
from the blood and partake of one bread, the body of Christ.
So we are one body in Christ.

18 **Behold Israel after the flesh:**—This refers to fleshly Israel as distinguished from spiritual Israel, the church. (Rom.
2: 28, 29; Gal. 4: 29; 6: 16.)

**have not they that eat the sacrifices communion with the al-
tar?**—They participate with the altar in partaking of the sacrifice offered. A part of the sacrifice was consumed upon the
altar; the remainder was divided between the priest and the
offerer. (See Lev. 7: 15-19; 8: 31; Deut. 12: 18.) [To eat of
the sacrifices in the way prescribed by the law of Moses was
to take part in the whole sacrificial service. Therefore Paul
says that those who eat the sacrifices are in communion with
the altar. They become worshipers of the God to whom the
altar is dedicated. This is the import and effect of joining in
those sacrificial feasts. The question is not as to the intention
of the actor, but as to the import of the act, and as to the interpretation universally put upon it. To partake of a Jewish
sacrifice as a sacrifice in a holy place was an act of Jewish
worship. Therefore to partake. of a heathen sacrifice as a
sacrifice, and in a holy place, was of necessity an act of heathen worship.]

19 **What say I then? that a thing sacrificed to idols is anything, or that an idol is anything?**—He does not mean to say
that the idol is anything or that which is offered to the idol is
anything. [This however does not alter the case. For although there are no such beings as those whom the heathen
conceive their gods to be, and though their sacrifices are not
what they consider them, still their worship is real idolatry,
and has a destructive influence on the soul.]

that an idol is anything? But I *say*, that the things which the Gentiles sacrifice, they sacrifice to demons, and not to God: and I would not that ye should have communion with demons. 21 Ye cannot drink the cup of the

---

20 But I say, that the things which the Gentiles sacrifice, they sacrifice to demons, and not to God:—The sacrifice made at the altar of the idol is sacrificed to demons, and the demon is a participator in that sacrifice. If Christians partake of that sacrifice they commune with demons to whom the sacrifice is made.

and I would not that ye should have communion with demons.—We are said to be in communion with those between whom and us there is congeniality of mind, community of interest, and friendly intercourse. In this sense we are in communion with our fellow Christians, with God, and with his Son Jesus Christ. And in this sense the worshipers of idols have fellowship with evil spirits. They are united to them so as to form one community, with a common character and a common destiny. Into this state of communion they are brought by sacrificing to them. It was of great importance for the Corinthians to know that it did not depend on their intention whether they came into communion with demons. The heathen did not intend to worship demons, and yet they did it; what would it avail to the reckless Corinthians, who attended the sacrificial feasts of the heathen, to say they did not intend to worship the idols? The question was not what they meant to do, but what was the import and effect of their conduct. A man may not intend to pollute his soul when he frequents the haunts of vice. The effect is altogether independent of his intention.

This principle also applies with all its force to the compliance of professed Christians with the religious services of churches that are using mechanical instruments of music in the worship of God. Whatever their intention may be, by the force of the act they become one with those in whose worship they join. We constitute with them and with the methods of their worship one communion.

21 Ye cannot drink the cup of the Lord,—[The cup of the

Lord, and the cup of demons: ye cannot partake of the table of the Lord,
and of the table of demons. 22 Or do we provoke the Lord to jealousy?
are we stronger than he?

Lord is that cup which brings into communion with the
Lord.]

and the cup of demons:—[The cup of demons is the cup
which brings into communion with demons.]

ye cannot partake of the table of the Lord,—[The table of
the Lord is the Lord's Supper at which the Lord presides and
at which his people are his guests.]

and of the table of demons.—This would be to make them
one. [The table of demons is the table at which demons pre-
side, and at which all present are their guests. Here the apostle teaches that there is not merely an incongruity and incon-
sistency in a man's being the friend and guest of Christ and in
being a guest and friend of demons, but the thing is impossible. A man cannot eat at the table of demons without being
brought under their power and influence; nor can he eat at
the Lord's table, without being brought into contact with him,
either to his salvation or to his condemnation. If he should
come thoughtlessly; without any desire to commune with
Christ, he eats and drinks judgment to himself. But if he
comes in faith with an humble desire to obey his Master and
to seek his presence, he cannot fail to be welcomed and
blessed.]

22 Or do we provoke the Lord to jealousy?—The comparison here is to a wife who would provoke her husband to jealousy by showing her affection for another man. Can we afford thus to treat Christ? [This illustration is the most effective that can be borrowed from human relations, and is often
employed in Scripture to set forth the heinousness of the sin
of idolatry.]

are we stronger than he?—If we arouse his jealousy, he will
destroy us. [As he has threatened to punish such transgressors, it is therefore madness and folly to expose ourselves to
the fury of his indignation.]

7. CHRISTIAN LIBERTY AS REGARDS MEATS OFFERED TO IDOLS WHEN EATEN AT PRIVATE MEALS
10: 23 to 11: 1

23 All things are lawful; but not all things are expedient. All things are lawful; but not all things ⁹edify. 24 Let no man seek his own, but *each* ¹⁰his neighbor's *good.* 25 Whatsoever is sold in the shambles, eat, asking no ques-

⁹Gr. *build up.*
¹⁰Gr. *the other's.* See Rom. 13. 8.

23 **all things are lawful;**—[This is limited to things indifferent, not having a moral quality.] The reference here is to chapter eight, where he insisted that, as the idol was nothing, he who could eat without offense to others was at liberty to do so.

but not all things are expedient.—Here he is referring to the sacrifices made at the altars of the false gods, and as the gods are nothing the altars are nothing, and a man might eat at them without injury to himself; but it was not expedient for Christians to do so, lest weak Christians and the heathen world should be encouraged to worship the idol.

All things are lawful; but not all things edify.—Eating meat at the altar of an idol may be lawful, but will not build up or strengthen the weak, which is the chief concern of the Christian. When we lead a weak brother into sin, or encourage one in sin to remain in it, we sin against Christ who died to save the weak and lost.

24 **Let no man seek his own, but each his neighbor's good.**—Spiritual good is under consideration, and he warns them to let no man seek his own good to the disregard of his neighbor's good. In neglecting his neighbor's good, he destroys his own. Spiritual good is unlike material good, the more we seek the good of others, the more we promote our own. The more we look to our own good to the neglect of others, the more we destroy our own good. The more we divide our blessings with others, the more our own blessings grow.

25 **Whatsoever is sold in the shambles,**—[In the public meat market.] Of the sacrifices made to idols, the part given to the officiating priest was sometimes sold in the meat market; the devotees bought this meat. Sometimes an animal was consecrated to a certain god when slaughtered that it

tion for conscience' sake; 26 for the earth is the Lord's and the fulness thereof. 27 If one of them that believe not biddeth you *to a feast,* and ye are disposed to go; whatsoever is set before you, eat, asking no question for conscience' sake. 28 But if any man say unto you, This hath been offered in sacrifice, eat not, for his sake that showed it, and for conscience' sake: 29

---

might be sold to the devotees of that god. Certain stalls in the market place were consecrated to a certain god, and its devotees patronized that stall. [But with the Christian it was different. If he merely bought his meat in the open market, no one could suspect him of meaning thereby to connive at or show favor to idolatry. It would, therefore, be needless for him to entertain fantastic scruples about matters purely indifferent; for when thus sold it was wholly disassociated from the rites of idolatrous sacrifice, and one so using it could not be suspected of doing so as an act of worship.]

eat, asking no question for conscience' sake;—[He was not to trouble his conscience by scruples arising from needless investigation about the food.]

26 for the earth is the Lord's and the fulness thereof.—"For every creature of God is good, and nothing is to be rejected, if it be received with thanksgiving." (1 Tim. 4: 4.) The intelligent Christian, then, may eat of it as the Lord's.

27 If one of them that believe not biddeth you to a feast,— The Christian was not forbidden to retain his friendship among the heathen, nor was he forbidden association with them.

and ye are disposed to go; whatsoever is set before you, eat, asking no question for conscience' sake.—[If a heathen friend should ask him to a meal in a private house and not in a sacrificial feast in an idol temple, he was not to trouble himself to ask whether the meat that was served was a part of the idol sacrifice, for such a dining was in no sense an act of worship.]

28 But if any man say unto you, This hath been offered in sacrifice, eat not, for his sake that showed it, and for conscience' sake:—If a fellow Christian, one of the weak brethren, being scrupulous himself about such things, thinks that he ought to warn the other of what he chances to know, he is not to eat.

conscience, I say, not thine own, but the other's; for why is my liberty
judged by another conscience? 30 [11]If I partake with thankfulness, why am
I evil spoken of for that for which I give thanks? 31 Whether therefore ye
eat, or drink, or whatsoever ye do, do all to the glory of God. 32 Give no
occasion of stumbling, either to Jews, or to Greeks, or to the church of God:
33 even as I also please all men in all things, not seeking mine own profit,
but the *profit* of the many, that they may be saved. 1 Be ye imitators of me,

[11]Or, *If I by grace partake*

---

29 **conscience, I say, not thine own, but the other's;**—Not
for the sake of his own conscience, which could eat without
injury, knowing that the idol is nothing; but for the sake of
the weak brother or the unbeliever who sits at meat with him.
He is not to eat lest the weak brother be encouraged to eat in
worship to the idol.

for why is my liberty judged by another conscience?—Why
should he make such a use of his liberty as to give offense
when no good end will be served by his eating?

30 **If I partake with thankfulness, why am I evil spoken of
for that for which I give thanks?**—In this Paul seeks to induce the strong to respect the scruples of the weak. They
might eat of sacrificial meat at private tables with freedom, so
far as they themselves were concerned; but why, he asks,
should they do it so as to give offense, and cause the weak to
stumble and speak evil of them?

31 **Whether therefore ye eat, or drink, or whatsoever ye do,
do all to the glory of God.**—All that Christians do should be
done to the glory of God, and his glory is never enhanced by
our destroying his weak children to gratify ourselves. Jesus
pleased not himself, but gave up all to save men and so glorify
God. He is our great exemplar. We must glorify God by
sacrificing self for the good of others.

32 **Give no occasion of stumbling, either to Jews, or to
Greeks, or to the church of God:**—The Christian is to do
nothing that encourages a Jew or Gentile to remain in sin, and
to stay away from God, or that would lead the weakest member of the household of faith to stumble or go into sin. [Love
to God and love to men should govern all our conduct.]

33 **even as I also please all men in all things, not seeking
mine own profit, but the profit of the many,**—As showing how

even as I also am of Christ.

far this method of action may rightly be carried, Paul's own course is given as an example for them to follow. [He sacrificed his personal comfort, and personal liberty of action; but he never sacrificed any important principle, or compromised the liberty of others. (Gal. 2: 5.) With him to please others is what he chose in love to do instead of pleasing himself; he did not sacrifice to it the pleasing of God. We may also be liberal with that which is our own to give. When Peter, in becoming as a Jew to the Jews (Gal. 2: 11-14), abandoned his previous habit of eating with Gentile converts, he both made a serious compromise of principle and went far to impose the burden of the law upon those who were free from it. Hence Paul's rebuke.]

that they may be saved.—The chief consideration with Paul was to save men and honor God. In this he was following in the footsteps of Jesus, who gave up heaven with the glory he had with the Father, and came to earth, and suffered and died to save men. Paul drank of the same spirit, was willing to suffer the loss of all things of earth, and make himself the servant of all if thereby he might save men.

11: 1 **Be ye imitators of me, even as I also am of Christ.**— Having just told them how he himself acted in cases of the kind referred to, Paul bids them to follow his example, and in so doing they would copy that of Christ. [Christ alone is the perfect model; each believer is a model to his brethren only in so far as he is a copy in relation to Christ. In making the exhortation Paul had in mind especially the greatness of the self-denial of the Son of God in taking upon himself "the form of a servant, being made in the likeness of men; and being found in fashion as a man, he humbled himself, becoming obedient even unto death, yea, the death of the cross" (Phil. 2: 7, 8), that he might save men from their sins.] If we are not willing to deny self, and suffer the loss of all earthly things in order to serve and honor God and save men, we have not the spirit of Christ and are none of his.

SECTION SIX

CONCERNING DISORDERS IN WORSHIP IN THE CORINTHIAN CHURCH
11: 2-34

1. DISAPPROVAL OF THE MANNER IN WHICH WOMEN PRAYED AND PROPHESIED
11: 2-16

2 Now I praise you that ye remember me in all things, and hold fast the traditions, even as I delivered them to you. 3 But I would have you know, that the head of every man is Christ; and the head of the woman is the

2 **Now I praise you that ye remember me in all things,—** [This verse is introductory to the whole of this section of the letter which treats of worship. With his usual tact and generosity, Paul before reproving them mentions things which he could honestly and heartily approve.]

and hold fast the traditions, even as I delivered them to you.—By traditions is meant the precepts, ordinances, and doctrine he had taught them orally, and had been given orally from one to another. When Paul was with them he had taught them orally concerning the ordinance of the Supper, and they had kept it up as he had commanded them. They continued the meetings on the first day of the week (16: 1), but corruption had crept in.

3 **But I would have you know,—**He turns now to properly direct the behavior of women in the worship and in their manner of appearing before God, and defines the relationship of man and woman.

that the head of every man is Christ;—Jesus Christ is the head of the man, and man cannot approach God save in subjection to his head, Christ.

and the head of the woman is the man;—Woman cannot approach God save in subjection to her head, man. The duties and bearing of women and men grow out of their respective relations to each other and to God. The same relationship of husband and wife is presented in another place in these words: "Wives, be in subjection unto your own husbands, as unto the Lord. For the husband is the head of the wife, as

man; and the head of Christ is God. 4 Every man praying or prophesying,

Christ also is the head of the church, being himself the savior
of the body. But as the church is subject to Christ, so let the
wives also be to their husbands in everything." (Eph. 5: 22-
24.) In the Lord is here implied, as all are to obey him above
every one else. [Let it here be distinctly understood that the
subordination thus expressed involves no degradation. As the
church is not dishonored by being subject to Christ, so neither
is woman dishonored by being subject to man.]

and the head of Christ is God.—Considered as the Father's
servant (Isa. 42: 1; 52: 13), in which capacity he spoke when
he said: "I glorified thee on the earth, having accomplished
the work which thou hast given me to do" (John 17: 4).
"Though he was a Son, yet learned obedience by the things
which he suffered" (Heb. 5: 8), "becoming obedient even unto
death, yea, the death of the cross" (Phil. 2: 8). It is in this
aspect of mutual relation in the work of redemption that "the
head of Christ is God."

4 **Every man praying or prophesying,**—Praying and prophesying are the two exercises in which the churches engage
in the assembly. All pray, or should pray; one.leads, the others pray as sincerely as does the leader. The purpose is to
show how the women should appear before God in the assembly, not that she should lead in the service. Most assuredly
the apostle does not here tell the women how to lead in the
prayer and teaching in the assembly, and in chapter 14: 34, 1
Tim. 2: 11, 12, gives specific directions for her to keep silent.
The very fact that in all the history of Christ and the apostles
no example is found of women speaking publicly or leading in
public prayer, although they were endowed with miraculous
gifts, and did prophesy and teach in private and in the family
circle, ought to satisfy all as to the will of God in that matter.

having his head covered, dishonoreth his head.—Then a
man must not have his head covered when he comes before
God, either with long hair or with hat, veil, or cloth of any
kind. This would be a shame to him. He may have it covered at other times, but not when he approaches God to pray
or prophesy in his name. [Such conduct dishonors his head

having his head covered, dishonoreth his head. 5 But every woman praying or prophesying with her head unveiled dishonoreth her head; for it is one and the same thing as if she were shaven. 6 For if a woman is not veiled, let her also be shorn: but if it is a shame to a woman to be shorn or shaven,

because covering it is a usage which symbolizes subjection to some visible superior, and in the worship man has none. Those who are visibly present are either his equals or his inferiors. Every man, therefore, who in praying or prophesying covers his head, thereby acknowledges himself dependent on some earthly head other than his heavenly head, and thereby takes from the latter the honor which is due to him as the head of man.]

5 **But every woman praying or prophesying with her head unveiled dishonored her head;**—The woman is under subjection to the man. Because of this, any approach to God with head uncovered is not permitted. It is a dishonor to her head. Man cannot come to God save through and in the name of Christ his head, so woman cannot come to Christ save with the tokens of subjection to man on her head.

for it is one and the same thing as if she were shaven.—To have her head uncovered is the same as to have her head shaven.

6 **For if a woman is not veiled, let her also be shorn:**—[The word "also" in this verse plainly shows that the two veils— the natural hair and the veil with which the head was covered —are under consideration. If her head be not covered with a veil, let her hair be shorn. Let her be consistent by laying aside all the usual and proper indications of her sex. If it be done in one respect, it might with the same propriety be done in all. In verse 13, he says: "Judge ye in yourselves: is it seemly that a woman pray unto God unveiled?" The impropriety of it, he seems to take for granted as apparent to all.]

but if it is a shame to a woman to be shorn or shaven, let her be veiled.—[It is a shame for a woman to be shorn or shaven because it fashions her, to that extent, as a man, and it is God's will, distinctly revealed in the Scriptures, to keep the sexes distinguishable. For a woman to remove her hair is in part to obliterate this outward distinction, and is therefore a

let her be veiled. 7 For a man indeed ought not to have his head veiled, forasmuch as he is the image and glory of God: but the woman is the glory of the man. 8 For the man is not of the woman; but the woman of the

---

trampling under foot God's will. And as further defense of womanly modesty and morality, God forbids the sexes wearing each other's clothes: "A woman shall not wear that which pertaineth unto a man, neither shall a man put on a woman's garment; for whosoever doeth these things is an abomination unto Jehovah thy God." (Deut. 22: 5.)]

7 **For a man indeed ought not to have his head veiled, forasmuch as he is the image and glory of God:**—The man is the image of his maker, was created for him, and to add to his glory. [Man is the glory of God as the crown of creation and as endowed with sovereignty like God himself, naming all creatures and having dominion over all the earth, and over everything that moveth upon the earth. (Gen. 1: 26-28.) He is also the glory of God as showing forth the glory of his Creator, and being his masterwork. The man existing in this double character, as the image and glory of God, must not have his head covered when he comes before God, either with long hair, or with hat, veil, or cloth of any kind. This would be a shame to him. He may have it covered at other times, but not when he approaches God to pray or prophesy in his name.]

but the woman is the glory of the man.—The woman was created of and for the man. [That God provided for man a companion and helper so noble as woman proves the worth of man in God's sight, and thus adds dignity to him; she shares and manifests his superiority; reflects it, as the moon does the light of the sun.]

8 **For the man is not of the woman; but the woman of the man:**—The woman was not first, but the man, and out of the man was the woman made. She was taken out of him, and was created as a separate being for the good and happiness of man. "And Jehovah God said, It is not good that the man should be alone; I will make him a help meet for him. . . . And Jehovah God caused a deep sleep to fall upon the man,

man: 9 for neither was the man created for the woman; but the woman for
the man: 10 for this cause ought the woman to have *a sign of* authority on
her head, because of the angels. 11 Nevertheless, neither is the woman with-

and he slept; and he took one of his ribs, and closed up the
flesh instead thereof: and the rib, which Jehovah God had
taken from the man, made he a woman, and brought her unto
the man. And the man said, This is now bone of my bones,
and flesh of my flesh: she shall be called Woman, because she
was taken out of Man." (Gen. 2: 18-23.) What was in woman
was taken out of man. It takes both man and woman to make
one reproductive being. Both sets of organs necessary to re-
production were originally in man. God separated them into
two beings, counterparts and complements of each other, but
the woman was taken out of and from man, and for his good.
The twain are one, but one in man. Hence the world over she
takes his name.

9 **for neither was the man created for the woman; but the
woman for the man:**—The man was first and the woman was
created for him. Man's priority and consequent leadership
over woman are here affirmed.

10 **for this cause ought the woman to have a sign of authority on her head,**—On account of this priority and supremacy
of man, woman, as subject to man, should always approach
God with the tokens of her subjection on her head. The sign
of authority means the sign or token on her head that she acknowledges the authority of man over her.

because of the angels.—Much diversity exists as to who the
angels are. Many think they were the messengers of the
churches. But the apostle nowhere presents a thought as to
how woman shall appear before men; the question is, How
shall she appear before God? How shall she approach God in
prophecy or prayer? The direction applies to her, whether in
public or private. It is necessary for a woman to approach
God with the tokens of her subjection to man in secret prayer,
or private teaching as in public, just as it is necessary for man
to approach God as a servant of Christ in private or in public.
Not a word is said here as to how woman should appear be-

out the man, nor the man without the woman, in the Lord. 12 For as the
woman is of the man, so is the man also by the woman; but all things are of

fore man when she prayed or taught. The presence or absence
of men, friends or strangers, has nothing to do with how she
shall appear before God. Neither does the question whether
she leads in public prayer or in prayer follows others who lead.
These questions are not here touched. I think the angels in
heaven who see and rejoice or sorrow over what men do here
will rejoice or sorrow over her coming properly or improperly
before God, or in the place to which God assigned her.
Whether the woman prays in the closet at home, or in the assembly, she should approach God with the tokens of her subjection to man on her head. The reason of this we may not
know. That God requires it, the Bible plainly teaches, and
that should suffice. The meaning is, when she comes to worship in prayer or praise, no matter whether she leads or not,
she should be veiled.

11 **Nevertheless, neither is the woman without the man, nor
the man without the woman,**—Although by original constitu-
tion woman is dependent upon man, they are mutually dependent upon each other—the one cannot exist without the other.

in the Lord.—By divine arrangement and direction the
twain are one in the Lord.

12 **For as the woman is of the man, so is the man also by
the woman;**—Since the woman was taken from the man, she
is of him, yet man is born, or comes into the world through
the woman. That man had the priority in time and position,
yet no man can be born without woman. They mutually depend for existence upon each other. So the two constitute but
one real self-propagating being.

but all things are of God.—The twain are one, and both are
of God, and live, move, and have their being in him. [This
expression seems designed to suppress any spirit of complaint
or dissatisfaction with this arrangement; to make the woman
contented in her subordinate station, and to make the man
humble by the consideration that it is all owing to the appointment of God. The woman should therefore be contented

God. 13 Judge ye ¹in yourselves: is it seemly that a woman pray unto God unveiled? 14 Doth not even nature itself teach you, that, if a man have long hair, it is a dishonor to him? 15 But if a woman have long hair, it is a glory to her: for her hair is given her for a covering. 16 But if any man

¹Or, *among*

---

and the man should not assume any important superiority since the whole arrangement is of God.]

13 **Judge ye in yourselves: is it seemly that a woman pray unto God unveiled?**—The impropriety of it he takes for granted as apparent to all. How should she approach God is the question. Man should do it with uncovered head, woman with covered head; and all distinction between public or private prayer is man's imagination. It is as wrong for a man to approach God with covered head in the closet as it is to do it in the public assembly. So also of woman, God makes no difference as to how he shall be approached in public or in private.

14 **Doth not even nature itself teach you, that, if a man have long hair, it is a dishonor to him?**—While in all nations in the world, women wear long hair, and men short hair, is it nature that suggests it? It does not mean custom. The fact so universal, and the declaration of the apostle, seems to settle this. Sometimes nature suggests a custom. A practice prompted by nature becomes a custom, and is said to be from or by nature. How came the custom to be universal among all nations and in all parts of the world, if there is not something in nature to suggest it?

15 **But if a woman have long hair, it is a glory to her: for her hair is given her for a covering.**—[From the creation God intended that woman should wear a veil as a symbol of her subjection to man, but instead of an artificial covering he gave her a covering of long hair, a covering of glory, in which she could take pride. When woman sinned he gave her a second veil of covering, which is a sign of authority to which she must submit as a memorial of her transgression. The reason for the two veils or coverings becomes apparent when we get before us woman's relation to man and God's will concerning them. Paul directed woman to "learn in quietness with all

seemeth to be contentious, we have no such custom, neither the churches of God.

---

subjection" for two reasons: (1) "Adam was first formed, then Eve"; (2) "Adam was not beguiled, but the woman being beguiled hath fallen into transgression" (1 Tim. 2: 11-14); that is, when woman was created, she was created for man (11: 8, 9), and was subjected to him (Eph. 5: 22-24), not as a slave, but as the weaker vessel (1 Pet. 3: 7). Then when Eve transgressed, God placed her under a curse and said: "I will greatly multiply thy pain and thy conception; in pain thou shalt bring forth children; and thy desire shall be to thy husband, and he shall rule over thee." (Gen. 3: 16.) Thus twice was woman subjected to man. Hence the argument is: Since it is a glory for woman to wear a covering of hair which God gave her at creation instead of an artificial covering, she should wear also an artificial covering when she approaches God in prayer.]

16 **But if any man seemeth to be contentious, we have no such custom, neither the churches of God.**—The custom referred to must be women wearing short hair and approaching God in prayer with uncovered heads. He reasoned on the subject to show the impropriety, but adds in an authoritative manner, if any are disposed to be contentious over it, neither we nor the churches of God have any such custom. [With such disturbers of the peace of the church all argument is useless. Authority is the only thing that will silence them. The authority here adduced is that of the inspired apostles, which was decisive, because they were invested with the authority not only to preach the gospel, but to instruct the church and to decide everything relating to the worship.]

2. REPROOF ON ACCOUNT OF THEIR GROSS PERVERSION OF THE LORD'S SUPPER
11: 17-34

17 But in giving you this charge, I praise you not, that ye come together

---

17 **But in giving you this charge, I praise you not, that ye come together not for the better but for the worse.**—The ob-

not for the better but for the worse. 18 For first of all, when ye come together ²in the church, I hear that ³divisions exist among you; and I partly
believe it. 19 For there must be also ⁴factions among you, that they that are

²Or, *in congregation*
³Gr. *schisms.*
⁴Gr. *heresies.*

ject of the weekly meeting was to unite them more closely to
the Lord, and in doing this, to draw them into closer union
with each other; but their services were so perverted that
they produced strife and separation instead of unity.

18 **For first of all, when ye come together in the church, I
hear that divisions exist among you;**—The parties, in following the different leaders, which had been reported to him by
the house of Chloe, were accompanied by divisions when they
met for worship.

and I partly believe it.—The facts had possibly been exag-
gerated by others, [but he was forced to believe enough to
excite his strong disapproval.]

19 **For there must be also factions among you,**—It is a part
of the policy of God in governing the world to test those
serving him, and to that end he allows evil men to come into
their midst.

**that they that are approved may be made manifest among
you.**—The church of God, like the Jewish nation, will continually fall away from steadfastness in the faith. Those who
cannot be faithful to God under temptations to disobey him
are not worthy of his kingdom. So God allows evil men to
come among his people who would lead away from God and
his order, to try and test who among them are faithful and
true to him. Paul said to the elders of the Ephesian church:
"Take heed unto yourselves, and to all the flock, in which the
Holy Spirit hath made you bishops, to feed the church of the
Lord which he purchased with his own blood. I know that
after my departing grievous wolves shall enter in among you,
not sparing the flock; and from among your own selves shall
men arise, speaking perverse things, to draw away the disciples after them." (Acts 20: 28-30.) This was permitted to
prove and to show who could stand firm and steadfast under
temptations to turn away from God.

approved may be made manifest among you. 20 When therefore ye assemble
yourselves together, it is not possible to eat the Lord's supper: 21 for in your
eating each one taketh before *other* his own supper; and one is hungry, and

---

God tests them on the points of fidelity to him in faith and
doctrine as well as love of the world, lusts of the flesh, and
pleasures of life. One who cannot resist these and give them
up for the Lord is rejected by him as unworthy to be his disciple; so every one who cannot stand fast for the truth despite
the divisions and the popular currents that sweep through the
churches to carry them away from their steadfastness is unworthy of Christ. These are God's tests to purify the
churches. He desires only true and tried and faithful subjects
in his kingdom. Those who cannot stand the test must be
purged out. So divisions come to every church to make manifest those who are approved. It is God bringing the churches
to judgment in this world, that those who are approved and
true may be made manifest. All we have to do is to stand
true and firm to God and his word, and leave the results with
him.

20 **When therefore ye assemble yourselves together, it is
not possible to eat the Lord's supper:**—Their meeting together did not result in their eating the Lord's Supper. That
was the occasion of their coming together, but they so perverted it that it made it impossible for them to do so.

21 **for in your eating each one taketh before other his own
supper; and one is hungry, and another is drunken.**—The eating of a feast with its attendant gluttony and drinking led
many to attend. Each family brought its own portion and
each partook of his own. The rich eating and drinking to satiety of their abundance. The poor were shamed by the
scantiness of their food and went hungry. This was all
wrong. It is thought by some that this feasting preceded the
Lord's Supper, so that some were filled to satiety, while others were hungry when they partook of the emblems of the
Lord's body and blood.

22 **What, have ye not houses to eat and to drink in? or despise ye the church of God, and put them to shame that have**

another is drunken. 22 What, have ye not houses to eat and to drink in? or despise ye the [5]church of God, and put them to shame that [6]have not? What shall I say to you? [7]shall I praise you? In this I praise you not. 23 For I received of the Lord that which also I delivered unto you, that the Lord Jesus in the night in which he was [8]betrayed took bread; 24 and when he

[5]Or, *congregation*
[6]Or, *have nothing*
[7]Or, *shall I praise you in this? I praise you not.*
[8]Or, *delivered up*

not? What shall I say to you? shall I praise you?—He shames them with these questions. If they had a feast in public, brotherly love for each other would have suggested a common table at which all would have fared alike, and as a consequence those without food at home would have had their wants supplied. The course pursued caused shame to the poor and left them hungry.

In this I praise you not.—He had told them (verse 1) that he praised them for remembering him and holding fast the traditions, but here was such a perversion that he could not praise them for doing it.

23 For I received of the Lord—[The information of which he treats was what he himself had received from the immediate and personal communication of the Lord himself, and according to the express injunction therein contained was appointed for their observance. It was not therefore of his own devising, not that of any man, but divinely instituted, and consequently imperatively binding on all Christians.]

that which also I delivered unto you,—[He transmitted to them the very thing which he had received from the Lord, so that they were well aware of what ought to have made these disorders impossible.]

that the Lord Jesus in the night in which he was betrayed—[The delivery of Jesus to his enemies had already begun and was going on at the very time when the Lord instituted the Supper. The marginal reading, "delivered up," is better than "was betrayed," which confines the meaning to the action of Judas; whereas the Father's surrender of the Son (John 19: 11) and Jesus' self-surrender (John 10: 17, 18) are also included.] Paul mentions the sad solemnity of the occasion in contrast to the irreverent revelry of the Corinthians, to

had given thanks, he brake it, and said, This is my body, which ⁹is for you: this do in remembrance of me. 25 In like manner also the cup, after supper, saying, This cup is the new covenant in my blood: this do, as often as ye

⁹Many ancient authorities read *is broken for you.*

---

show how they perverted the Supper.

took bread;—The bread used was the unleavened bread of the Passover week. (See Ex. 12: 15; 13: 3, 7; Deut. 16: 3.)

24 and when he had given thanks,—In Matt. 26: 26 and Mark 14: 22, it is "blessed." In Luke 22: 19, it is "had given thanks." The two expressions, being used interchangeably, mean the same thing. Both express the act of consecration, by a grateful acknowledgment of God's mercy and a prayer that God will make it a means of blessing to those who partake. (See note on 10: 16.)

he brake it, and said, This is my body, which is for you:— [That we may understand what the Lord meant when he spoke these words, we should place ourselves in the position of the apostles to whom they were first addressed. If, as Jesus spoke these words, he had suddenly disappeared, and they had seen nothing but the bread, they would have understood that the body had been miraculously transformed into the bread. But when his body was still there; and the bread which he held in his hand was also there; and as his body still remained there after the bread had been broken and eaten, it is impossible that the apostles could have understood him as meaning that the bread was literally his body, and impossible that he could have intended to be so understood. They could not, therefore, have understood it otherwise than as a representation or symbol of his body to them.]

this do in remembrance of me.—This solemn sacrifice and thanksgiving was so little in harmony with their selfish greed and lightness that to report it was to reprove them. To do it in remembrance of his sacrifice for them was to do it in a wholly different spirit from the way in which they acted.

25 In like manner also the cup, after supper, saying, This cup is the new covenant in my blood.—The covenant referred to was the one mentioned by Jeremiah (31: 31-34),

drink *it*, in remembrance of me. 26 For as often as ye eat this bread, and

and quoted with comments in Hebrews (8: 7-13). It was the new covenant or will of God set forth in his blood, shown in shedding it for the sins of the world. God, through Jesus Christ, made a new covenant, as that made through Moses is called the old covenant. This is the memorial of that blood to seal and confirm this new covenant. The old covenant was sealed with the blood of animals; this was sealed with the blood of Jesus Christ shed for the remission of sins.

this do, as often as ye drink it,—That it was the common custom of the disciples to meet together upon the first day of the week to break bread is clearly indicated by the following: "And upon the first day of the week, when we were gathered together to break bread, Paul discoursed with them, intending to depart on the morrow." (Acts 20: 7.) [In the original institution of the Supper nothing is said of the frequency with which it was to be observed. Had nothing more been said, every congregation of believers would have been left to its own judgment as to the frequency of the observance. But the apostles were guided by the Holy Spirit in this, and their example is our guide. Here it is represented as furnishing the purpose of the meeting on the first day of the week. Such being the purpose of the meeting, as surely as the disciples met every Lord's day, they broke bread on that day.]

in remembrance of me.—It was to be done in memory of him, to commemorate the shedding of his blood for the sins of the world, not as a feast to gratify the appetite.

26 For as often as ye eat this bread, and drink the cup, ye proclaim the Lord's death till he come.—From this we learn that it was a memorial institution to keep in memory the heroic deeds of Jesus in dying to redeem man. Monuments are designed to commemorate the worthy deeds of those in whose memory they were built, with the hope that future generations, when they learn the deeds commemorated by the monument, will be inspired with the same spirit, and be led to emulate those worthy deeds. Just so this memorial institution was ordained to perpetuate the memory of the self-denying

drink the cup, ye proclaim the Lord's death till he come. 27 Wherefore
whosoever shall eat the bread or drink the cup of the Lord in an unworthy
manner, shall be guilty of the body and the blood of the Lord. 28 But let a

---

spirit and heroic deeds of Jesus Christ for the good of man.
It is done with the view that those who see these memorials
of the deeds and death of Jesus will drink into the same spirit,
and be led to emulate his life and deeds of self-sacrifice for the
good of others. Man builds monuments of marble and gran-
ite; he seeks the imperishable; but despite all his precautions
they molder and crumble. God, through Jesus, selected the
perishable bread and volatile fruit of the vine as the material
out of which he would build a monument that would endure
with perennial freshness through all time. No mortal would
ever seek to build an imperishable monument out of material
so perishable as bread and the fruit of the vine. God only
could breathe into it a spirit that would render it immortal,
that would cause it to continue in its freshness till Jesus
comes again.

27 **Wherefore whosoever shall eat the bread or drink the
cup of the Lord in an unworthy manner,**—[To eat or drink in
an unworthy manner is in general to come to the Lord's table
in a careless, irreverent spirit, without the intention or desire
to commemorate the death of Christ as the sacrifice for sins,
and without the purpose of complying with the obligations
thereby assumed. The way in which the Corinthians ate unworthily was that they treated the Lord's table as though it
were their own; making no distinction between it and an ordinary meal; coming together to satisfy their hunger, and not to
feed on the blessings of the body and blood of Christ.]

shall be guilty of the body and the blood of the Lord.—Inasmuch as the eating and drinking were intended to proclaim
and keep in memory the death of Jesus Christ, whoever should
eat of this memorial in a light and frivolous manner, in forgetfulness of the spirit of sacrifice that led to the death of Christ,
is guilty of profaning the body and blood of Christ. He in-
curs the guilt of treating lightly the slain body of the Lord
Jesus.

man prove himself, and so let him eat of the bread, and drink of the cup. 29
For he that eateth and drinketh, eateth and drinketh judgment unto himself,
if he [10]discern not the body. 30 For this cause many among you are weak

[10]Gr. *discriminate.*

28 **But let a man prove himself, and so let him eat of the
bread, and drink of the cup.**—[Let him ascertain by earnest
consideration whether he is in a proper state of mind for com-
memorating and proclaiming the Lord's death; whether he
feels a suitable gratitude for the sacrifice it commemorates, and
is firmly resolved to observe the injunction of its founders.]
On this verse Macknight says: "First, whether he comes to this
service to keep up the memory of Christ; secondly, whether
he is moved to do so by a grateful sense of Christ's love in
dying for man; thirdly, whether he comes with a firm purpose
of doing honor to Christ, by living in all respects conformably
to his precepts and example." To this I add, whether he
comes in a submissive and worthy manner, drinking into the
same spirit of self-sacrifice for others that Christ manifested.
[Such examination of one's motive would have made impossible the shameful scenes here described.]

29 **For he that eateth and drinketh, eateth and drinketh
judgment unto himself, if he discern not the body.**—He who
comes to it not remembering the Lord's crucified body and
shed blood, not drinking into the true spirit of Christ, not
striving to walk worthy of his goodness and love, as shown in
his sufferings and death, eateth unto condemnation rather
than justification. Observing the body of Christ as a pledge
of sanctification and justification and redemption to him who
comes to it in a proper spirit, but of wrath and condemnation
to him who comes not observing this spirit.

30 **For this cause many among you are weak and sickly,—**
Because so many come to it unworthily, not discerning his
body and blood, not in the true spirit of Christ, many among
them were weak and sickly as Christians.

and not a few sleep.—Many are spiritually asleep—dead.
Some commentators have applied the expression to physical
disease and death; but spiritual neglect must bring spiritual

and sickly, and not a few sleep. 31 But if we [11]discerned ourselves, we should not be judged. 32 But [12]when we are judged, we are chastened of the Lord, that we may not be condemned with the world. 33 Wherefore, my brethren, when ye come together to eat, wait one for another. 34 If any man

---

[11]Gr. *discriminated.*
[12]Or, *when we are judged of the Lord, we are chastened*

---

penalties. Many had grown indifferent and some had lost interest in Christ and their duties to him.

31 But if we discerned ourselves, we should not be judged. —If they watched themselves to see that they waited upon the Lord in the proper spirit, with a true sense of their obligations to him, and kept themselves in a condition to be blessed in his service, then they would not be condemned by the Lord.

32 But when we are judged, we are chastened of the Lord, that we may not be condemned with the world.—When God judged and chastened them, as he did when they began to neglect their duties to him, he afflicted them to cause them to turn away from their ways, that they might be saved and not be condemned with the world that forgets God.

33 Wherefore, my brethren, when ye come together to eat, —[The eating referred to is, of course, the Lord's Supper, and he enjoins perfect order, respect, and sobriety. The table is common for the rich and poor, and the rich have no claim of priority over the poor.]

wait one for another.—By their indecent haste, each eating his own meal without waiting for the rest, they had turned the Supper from the memorial purpose into an ordinary and insignificant meal, a mere eating and drinking. He therefore exhorts them to wait for one another, and make their coming together a joint service in commemoration of the Lord's suffering and death.]

Every congregation should have a definite time for meeting and should never begin the service before that time without due notice. While the apostle says, "Wait one for another," he also says, "In diligence not slothful; fervent in spirit; serving the Lord." (Rom. 12: 11.) No man can be diligent and fervent in spirit and be lazy and laggard in assembling for religious service. Not only does he who is slow lack diligence

is hungry, let him eat at home; that your coming together be not unto judgment. And the rest will I set in order whensoever I come.

---

and fervor in spirit, but there is nothing that destroys the zeal
and fervor of others like having to sit and wear out their patience, waiting for the slothful and indifferent.

34 **If any man is hungry, let him eat at home;**—He should
take that in his own house which is necessary for the support
of the body before he comes to the assembly, where he should
have the feeding of the spiritual man alone in view.

that your coming together be not unto judgment.—[That
they may avoid the curse that must fall on such worthless
communicants as those mentioned; and that they may get
that special blessing which every one who discerns the Lord's
body and blood must receive.]

And the rest will I set in order whensoever I come.—
[There were other irregularities which the apostle leaves to be
corrected until he should again visit Corinth, but when that
would be was certainly regarded by him as uncertain.]

SECTION SEVEN

THE NATURE AND UTILITY OF SPIRITUAL GIFTS
12: 1 to 14: 40

1. TEST OF THE SPIRIT'S PRESENCE AS THE SOURCE OF ITS VARIOUS GIFTS
12: 1-3

1 Now concerning spiritual *gifts*, brethren, I would not have you igno-

1 **Now concerning spiritual gifts, brethren,**—When Jesus told his apostles that he was going away to prepare a place for them, he told them also that if he went away he would send them another Comforter to guide them into all the truth and prepare and fit them for the place he would make ready for them—that the Spirit would guide them into all the truth and call to their remembrance all things whatsoever he had commanded them. (John 14: 26; 16: 13.) The Holy Spirit came upon the apostles on the day of Pentecost; took up his abode in them to guide them in teaching to others the things Jesus had taught them.

The Holy Spirit in the apostles bestowed gifts upon disciples qualifying them for the performance of the different duties arising in their Christian life. These gifts were to remain and make known the will of. God, and continue until the perfect will was come. In speaking of these partial gifts, Paul says: "For we know in part, and we prophesy in part; but when that which is perfect is come, that which is in part shall be done away." (13: 9, 10.) The gifts which bestowed the partial knowledge were to be done away when the perfect will of God was made known. (Eph. 4: 11-16.) The different gifts are enumerated in the order of their importance and the measure of the Holy Spirit bestowed. (Verse 28.)

These gifts carried with them ability to know and to make known the will of God, and to confirm it by signs and wonders. These gifts were to serve until the full and perfect will of God was made known and confirmed to the world. The will of God was made known and confirmed through these gifts; then they passed away and left men to be governed by the word of God, to be led by the Spirit in that word. The

rant. 2 Ye know that when ye were Gentiles *ye were* led away unto those dumb idols, howsoever ye might be led. 3 Wherefore I make known unto you, that no man speaking in the Spirit of God saith, Jesus is anathema ; and no man can say, Jesus is Lord, but in the Holy Spirit.

Corinthians had been bountifully supplied with these gifts, but difficulties concerning their use had arisen.

I would not have you ignorant.—They had no doubt inquired of Paul concerning the use of these gifts and the privileges of those possessing them.

2 Ye know that when ye were Gentiles ye were led away unto those dumb idols, howsoever ye might be led.—[He contrasts their former miserable condition as idolaters with their present state in order to make them sensible of their advantages as Christians and that they might be led more highly to appreciate their present condition.]

3 Wherefore I make known unto you, that no man speaking in the Spirit of God saith, Jesus is anathema ;—Because of their former ignorance and evil life, he would have them know that the Spirit of God instructs, teaches, leads out of this idolatry into the knowledge of the Son of God. So that one led by the Spirit cannot say that Jesus is anathema, or that he is the source of evil.

and no man can say, Jesus is Lord, but in the Holy Spirit. —No one can truly believe and say that Jesus is the Son of God, save as he is taught by the Holy Spirit. The Spirit came to testify concerning Jesus, and all the testimony we have of him comes through the teaching of the Holy Spirit. The word of God is the teaching given by the Spirit, and in it is contained all that man knows concerning Jesus. No man can believe that Jesus is the Christ save upon the testimony given in the word of God by the Holy Spirit.

2. MANIFOLD OPERATIONS OF THE SPIRIT WITH ONENESS OF PURPOSE AND AIM
12 : 4-11

4 Now there are diversities of gifts, but the same Spirit. 5 And there are

4 Now there are diversities of gifts, but the same Spirit.— The Holy Spirit came to the apostles, and through them bestowed a number of gifts or powers on others. The gifts dif-

diversities of ministrations, and the same Lord. 6 And there are diversities
of workings, but the same God, who worketh all things in all. 7 But to each
one is given the manifestation of the Spirit to profit withal. 8 For to one is

fered in the work they enabled each to perform, and the degree of spiritual power they bestowed; but the same Spirit is
the giver; it is he who is the immediate and proximate author
of all these various endowments.

5 **And there are diversities of ministrations, and the same
Lord.**—There are different services, such as rendered by apostles, prophets, teachers, discerners of spirits; but they are all
from the same Lord in whose service and by whose authority
these various gifts are exercised.

6 **And there are diversities of workings, but the same God,
who worketh all things in all.**—It is the same God, who having exalted the Lord Jesus, and "put all things in subjection
under his feet, and gave him to be head over all things to the
church, which is his body, the fulness of him that filleth all in
all" (Eph. 1: 22, 23), and having sent the Holy Spirit, works
all these things.

7 **But to each one is given the manifestation of the Spirit to
profit withal.**—But whatever gifts or manifestations of the
Spirit are given to any one, are given for the instruction and
profit of all. No gift was bestowed by the Spirit for the personal good of him alone on whom it was bestowed. These
gifts were never so used. The most highly gifted suffered
persecution, hunger, and sickness; but no one used the gifts
for personal relief or help. Nor did the possession of the gift
bestow moral strength or spiritual power to free from or resist
temptation, save as it gave them knowledge of the will of God
and left them to contend with the temptations the same as
those not gifted. Hence Peter dissembled and did wrong
(Gal. 2: 11, 12), and Paul prayed that he might not, after having preached to others, be rejected (9: 27). The gift bestowed
on each one was for the instruction and help of all the church,
and not for the private benefit of the gifted. The apostle now
gives the separate gifts bestowed by the Spirit. It is difficult
to define the scope, as they have all disappeared in the appearance of the completed word of God contained in the New Testament.

given through the Spirit the word of wisdom; and to another the word of knowledge, according to the same Spirit: 9 to another faith, in the same Spirit; and to another gifts of healings, in the one Spirit; 10 and to another workings of ¹miracles; and to another prophecy; and to another discernings

¹Gr. *powers.*

---

8 **For to one is given through the Spirit the word of wisdom;**—The word of wisdom is generally construed to mean the gospel, which is the power of God to save. It is God's wisdom. [This was the gift which enabled its recipients to reveal the whole plan of salvation. It stands first in the list of spiritual gifts as the most important, as the characteristic gift of the apostles, and was peculiar to them, having been promised to them by Christ, as the effect of the constant indwelling of the Spirit. (John 14: 17; 15: 26, 27; 16: 13-15.) And of Paul an apostle has said: "Account that the longsuffering of our Lord is salvation; even as our beloved brother Paul also, according to the wisdom given to him, wrote unto you." (2 Pet. 3: 15.) And besides this, Paul says: "We have the mind of Christ." (2: 16.)]

and to another the word of knowledge,—The word of knowledge enabled the gifted to understand and teach the truths revealed by the apostles.

according to the same Spirit:—[The Spirit governs these manifestations giving the law of them. The fact, that in the same Spirit in all these manifestations, is emphasized throughout the paragraph, in order to show the unity as well as purpose of these gifts.]

9 **to another faith, in the same Spirit;**—A faith that enabled one to remove mountains, of which Jesus speaks. It enabled one to exert power.

and to another gifts of healings, in the one Spirit;—The gift of healing diseases is one of the powers bestowed by the Holy Spirit.

10 **and to another workings of miracles;**—All the gifts here enumerated enabled them to work miracles as we use the term. To know all things without learning, to heal diseases, to speak with tongues, to discern spirits are all miracles. Why, then, among these should one special gift be called the

working of miracles? The word here translated "working" literally means the "inworking" of powers. That is, the bestowing on persons the ability to impart the power of working miracles to others. Simon Magus offered Peter money for this power. (Acts 8: 18, 19.)

Macknight says: "The word *energius* does not signify *to work* simply, but *to work in another*. Thus verse 11: 'All these (*gifts*) the one and the same Spirit (*energei*) inworketh,' namely, in the spiritual men." One and the same Spirit inworks all the different powers into the gifted persons, distributing to each severally as he will. It is generally contended that none save the apostles could impart the power to work miracles. That they possessed it in common with all Spiritual powers is not doubted. The apostles were endowed with all the power and gifts of the Spirit. But to others these gifts were distributed. All other gifts of the Spirit were distributed to one or another person, why not this also? Ananias, having been instructed by the Lord to go to the house where Saul abode, "departed, and entered into the house; and laying his hands on him said, Brother Saul, the Lord, even Jesus, who appeared unto thee in the way which thou camest, hath sent me, that thou mayest receive thy sight, and be filled with the Holy Spirit." (Acts 9: 17, 18.) While it is not said that the Holy Spirit was imparted by the imposition of his hands, it is certain that he was to be filled with the Holy Spirit by the coming of Ananias, and that Ananias laid his hands on him, and he did receive his sight and a gift of the Spirit that enabled him at once to proclaim Jesus, "that he is the Son of God."

And when Simon the sorcerer proposed to purchase the power to bestow miracle working power on others, Peter did not tell him that no one but an apostle could have such power. But he said to him: "Thou hast neither part nor lot in this matter." (Acts 8: 21). This implies that it might have been possible for him to have part or lot in the matter had his heart been right in the sight of God.

Once more, I quote from Macknight: "Though *the inworking of powers* be the spiritual gift which most forcibly struck

of spirits; to another *divers* kinds of tongues; and to another the interpreta-

the minds of mankind, and raised the apostles highest in their estimation, *the word of wisdom, the word of knowledge,* and *faith,* are placed before it in the catalogue. The reason is, by these gifts the gospel was communicated to the world; whereas it was only confirmed by the inworking of powers." Those placed before the inworking are greater than this. If the apostles bestowed the greater gifts, why not this less one?

and to another prophecy;—[This was the speaking of the message of God under the guidance of the Holy Spirit, whether with reference to the past, the present, or future. The purpose of this ministry was to edify, to comfort, and to encourage the believers (14: 3), while its effect upon unbelievers was to show that the secrets of man's heart are known to God, to convict of sin, and constrain to the worship of God (14: 24, 25). With the completion of the canon of Scripture this gift passed away. (13: 8, 9.) In his measure the teacher has taken the place of the prophet. The difference is that, whereas the message of the prophet was a direct revelation of the mind of God for the occasion, the message of the teacher is gathered from the completed revelation contained in the Scriptures.]

and to another discernings of spirits:—The power bestowed on certain persons by the Spirit to discern the secret dispositions of men. It was one of the gifts peculiar to that age, and was especially necessary at a time when God's revelation was not fully established or generally understood, and when many deceivers were abroad. (2 John 7.) This seemed to have been exercised chiefly upon those who came forward as teachers of others, and whose real designs it was important that the church should know.

to another divers kinds of tongues; and to another the interpretation of tongues:—The ability to speak different tongues. Some spoke in tongues they did not understand and could not interpret, and so Paul commanded them to be silent, unless they or some one else present could interpret. (14: 28.)

11 but all these worketh the one and the same Spirit, divid-

tion of tongues: 11 but all these worketh the one and the same Spirit, dividing to each one severally even as he will.

---

ing to each one severally even as he will.—This unity of the source of all spiritual gifts, in the midst of their variety, he presses as against those who valued some and undervalued others, or who deprecated them all.

3. CORRESPONDENCE BETWEEN THE UNITY OF THE SPIRIT IN THE VARIETY OF ITS GIFTS AND THE UNITY IN THE VARIETY OF ITS MEMBERS
12: 12-30

12 For as the body is one, and hath many members, and all the members of the body, being many, are one body; so also is Christ. 13 For in one Spirit were we all baptized into one body, whether Jews or Greeks, whether

---

12 For as the body is one, and hath many members, and all the members of the body, being many, are one body; so also is Christ.—He now introduces the human body with the different members performing different offices, yet altogether composing the one body, to illustrate the body of Christ or the church with its different members, and these different gifts performing the different offices needful to the well-being of the body.

13 For in one Spirit were we all baptized into one body, whether Jews or Greeks, whether bond or free;—As the body is animated by one spirit and under the guidance of one spirit, the different members of the body act, so guided or ruled by the one Spirit, all the members of the church, the body of Christ, were baptized into the one body, whether Jews or Greeks or bond or free.

The baptism is that commanded by Christ and the Holy Spirit, but inasmuch as it is done by the disciples under the direction of the Holy Spirit, it is said that the Spirit baptizes. God sent his Son, his Son sent the Holy Spirit as the abiding guest of the church of God, and he is ever present to guide and help every one walking under the guidance of the word of God. If we could realize that in deed and in truth Jesus baptizes every one that is baptized according to his will, that we are baptized by the directions of the Spirit, that this is God's

bond or free; and were all made to drink of one Spirit. 14 For the body is
not one member, but many. 15 If the foot shall say, Because I am not the
hand, I am not of the body; it is not therefore not of the body. 16 And if the
ear shall say, Because I am not the eye, I am not of the body; it is not

work, it would be a security and safety to us, and would help
us to walk with him that he might be our God and dwell in
and with us.

Some expositors think that being baptized in one Spirit refers to the baptism in the Holy Spirit. The example of the
body led by one Spirit does not bear this interpretation. For
it could not be said that they were all made to drink of one
Spirit if they had all been baptized or overwhelmed by the
Holy Spirit as the apostles had been on the day of Pentecost.
Beside this, there is no evidence that all the disciples at Corinth had been baptized in the Holy Spirit. There is no evidence whatever that any of them had been.

and were all made to drink of one Spirit.—The drinking
into one Spirit is gradually imbibing the Spirit of Christ that
we may be animated and led by it and become like him in
character.

14 For the body is not one member, but many.—The human
body, like the church, is not all one member, but is composed
of many different members. [The word members means a
constituent part having a function of its own.]

**15 If the foot shall say, Because I am not the hand, I am
not of the body; it is not therefore not of the body.**—There
seems to have been some strife between the spiritually endowed as to the standing of each. Some seemed to contend
that because they did not have certain of the more important
gifts, they were not essential to the body. He corrects this by
saying that each of the members of the human body constitutes an important part of it.

**16 And if the ear shall say, Because I am not the eye, I am
not of the body; it is not therefore not of the body.**—All the
members are essential to the performance of all the functions
of the body. [The point is that the humble members as well
as the more honored are all members of the body. Each, be-

therefore not of the body. 17 If the whole body were an eye, where were
the hearing? If the whole were hearing, where were the smelling? 18 But
now hath God set the members each one of them in the body, even as it
pleased him. 19 And if they were all one member, where were the body?
20 But now they are many members, but one body. 21 And the eye cannot
say to the hand, I have no need of thee: or again the head to the feet, I have

---

cause of this fact, must perform his function to the best of his
ability.]

17 **If the whole body were an eye, where were the hearing?
If the whole were hearing, where were the smelling?**—[The
very existence of the body as an organism depends on the
union of the members of the body endowed with different
functions, and it would be absurd to require or expect all the
members to perform the same function; and the application to
the church is equally plain. It, like the human body, requires
a diversity of gifts and offices; all, therefore, are to be satisfied with their allotment; all are to be honored in their proper
place.]

18 **But now hath God set the members each one of them in
the body, even as it pleased him.**—God set each in its proper
place in the body, to perform a needed office as God saw was
good, and if they were all one member, even the most important or honorable, they could not constitute the body.

19 **And if they were all one member, where were the body?**
—The different members, with their distinct functions and
offices, are each needful to the completion of the body.

20 **But now they are many members, but one body.**—[He
here repeats this truth, for on it everything which he desires
to indicate turns. From the oneness of the whole the mutual
dependence of the parts follows of necessity.]

21 **And the eye cannot say to the hand, I have no need of
thee: or again the head to the feet, I have no need of you.**—
One member of the body cannot do without another. The eye
needs the foot, the hand, the head. The eye is a member of the
body, and depends upon the health and life of the body for its
own good and vigor. The body could not maintain its life
without the offices of the hands and feet. So the eye depends
on the hands and feet for ability to perform its office. So of

no need of you. 22 Nay, much rather, those members of the body which
seem to be more feeble are necessary: 23 and those *parts* of the body, which
we think to be less honorable, upon these we ²bestow more abundant honor;
and our uncomely *parts* have more abundant comeliness; 24 whereas our
comely *parts* have no need: but God tempered the body together, giving

²Or, *put on*

---

the ear. So of all the members. They depend one upon the
other as members of the body.

22 **Nay, much rather, those members of the body which
seem to be more feeble are necessary:**—The vital organs, as
we call them, are the more weak and helpless, and must be
carried, protected, supplied by the other members, yet the
body is more dependent upon these members for life and
strength than upon others. The body can lose the hand, the
foot, the eye, and live; but it cannot lose any of those dependent organs and live.

23 **and those parts of the body, which we think to be less
honorable, upon these we bestow more abundant honor;**—
[Naturally no member of the body is dishonorable or uncomely, since God has made each and all to subserve the purposes for which the whole frame of members is put together;
but we esteem some members less honorable than others.]
The honor which seems to be comparatively wanting to the
parts themselves we clothe, giving them in the clothing we
put on them and the body a more comely appearance.

and our uncomely parts have more abundant comeliness;—
[The parts referred to, that in themselves are unseemly and
immodest, have for that very reason more pains bestowed on
them to give them seemliness.]

24 **whereas our comely parts have no need:**—The comely
parts of the body—the ear, the eye, the nose, the mouth—add
of themselves comeliness to the body, so do not need to be or-
namented or covered up.

**but God tempered the body together, giving more abundant
honor to that part which lacked;**—God has put the members
of the body in such relation to each other that the stronger
and the more beautiful are compelled, for their own good and

more abundant honor to that *part* which lacked; 25 that there should be no schism in the body; but *that* the members should have the same care one for another. 26 And whether one member suffereth, all the members suffer with it; or *one* member is [3]honored, all the members rejoice with it. 27 Now ye are the body of Christ, and [4]severally members thereof. 28 And God hath

[3]Or, *glorified*
[4]Or, *members each in his part*

indeed for their existence, to defend and care for, and thus to honor, the weaker members.

25 that there should be no schism in the body;—That there should be no divisions in the body, and that all the members mutually depending one upon the other for its own good would look to the common good of all.

but that the members should have the same care one for another.—[Each member should be moved by anxious care for the well-being of all. And it was in order to evoke this harmony and mutual care that God so joined the members together that we are compelled to treat them not according to their beauty but their need; and has done this that [here may be complete harmony in the body, and that each member may put forth its peculiar powers for the general good, thus securing for veery part of the body the benefit of all the various powers with which its various members are endowed.]

26 And whether one member suffereth, all the members suffer with it;—[So wonderfully is the nervous system diffused through the body that every part sympathizes with every other part, and the whole with any part. They are not only physically joined together, but they are so united as to feel together.]

or one member is honored, all the members rejoice with it. —[All the members partake of the benefit. If one member is sound and healthy, the benefit extends to all. If the hands, the feet, the heart, the lungs, the brain be in a healthy condition, the advantage is felt by all the members, and all derive advantage from it.]

27 Now ye are the body of Christ,—The ye referred to the membership at Corinth as a whole. They constituted the body of Christ. Not a part of it, but the body complete and entire, within itself a complete body of Christ. To another church Paul says: "In whom ye also are builded together for a habitation of God in the Spirit." (Eph. 2: 22.) The Bible clearly recognizes each separate congregation as the body of Christ, as builded together for a dwelling place in the Spirit. So that God in his Spirit dwells in each distinct and separate church. The church is the body of Christ in the community in which it is situated. It is not a foot in Corinth, an arm in Colosse, an eye in Ephesus, and an ear in Thessalonica; but each was a complete integral body of Christ composed of all the different members needed to make up his body. Take the church at Jerusalem, it was in existence before any other church. Was it not the body of Christ when it was the only church on earth? Did the planting of another and another church take from it any of its parts, and of its functions, despoil it of its integralism and completeness as a body of Christ? Certainly not.

What about the eunuch? My conviction is that he possessed within himself all the elements of a church of Christ when no other churches were in reach of him, and the multiplication of the seed or the word of God in him would produce a church of God wherever he went, and the same is true of every child of God. A child of God in a strange land has only to worship God himself, multiply the word of God in the hearts of others and the result is a church of the living God, complete in itself without reference to any other organism in the world.

and severally members thereof.—That is, each has his own place and function in the body of Christ. All the members constitute the one body as the human body is composed of the separate and distinct members and is dependent upon the others for happiness, and should have the same care one of another as the members of the fleshly body. One cannot suffer but all must suffer with it. The members that are most lacking in Christian graces, that are most helpless, need our care. And those most helpless are necessary for the good of all. This may seem strange at first, but the object of church service is to discipline the members into characters that please God and make the persons like unto Jesus Christ in character.

The poor, the sickly, the helpless, the wayward, and sinning are needful to school the more comely members. Without the patience and self-denial developed in looking after and helping the poor, the sick, and the wayward, the members of the church could never be fitted in character to dwell with God.

As the church, the body of Christ, is here compared to the human body, an apologist for the innovations that are being introduced into the churches makes the following argument: "The human body is composed of different organs and members. Some of these organs or members are vital, necessary to the life of the body—such as the heart, the liver, the lungs, and the stomach. Without these the body cannot live or exist. Then there are other members—as the hands, the feet, and the eyes—that are not vital organs; they are not necessary to the life or existence of the body. The body may exist and live without these. So the church, as the body of Christ, is composed of parts or organs. Some of these are vital, necessary to the existence of the church—such as faith, repentance, and baptism. Others are not vital or necessary to the life or sustenance of the church—such as instrumental music, societies, etc."

The illustration is an apt one if properly applied. In the first place, every organ or member set in the human body by God is vital or necessary to the performance of the work God appointed it to perform. The foot is essential to walking; the eye, to seeing; and the hand, to doing the work of the hand.

That work of God ceases when the member God appointed to do it is destroyed. Sometimes when the member God appointed is destroyed, an artificial or man-made member is supplied, but fails to do the work the natural or God-made member performs. An artificial foot or hand is a poor substitute for a God-given one. An artificial eye may deceive the people, but can never see. What this man calls the organs not vital to a church are not organs or members of the church, or body of Christ. They are artificial, man-made members. The organs God gave to do the work are the churches themselves, with the members for the work and the human voices for the worship. These, like the hands and feet of the human body,

set some in the church, first apostles, secondly prophets, thirdly teachers, then ¹miracles, then gifts of healings, helps, ⁵governments, *divers* kinds of

⁵Or, *wise counsels*

may not be necessary to the bare life or existence of the body, but are vital and necessary to the work and vigor of the body.

Sometimes the church fails to use its natural members to do the service God ordained them to do, and then substitutes artificial members or man-made substitutes to do the work the real organs or members fail to do. The whole thing is a miserable makeshift and a failure. No life or warmth or vigor can ever dwell in or pass through these artificial limbs; no spiritual life or warmth or vigor can ever dwell in or pass through these artificial additions to the church of God. The whole work of substituting these man-made or artificial organs, or works, to do the work of the church of God destroys the true work of God, drives out the Spirit and life of God. The whole business of mending the body of Christ, or patching up or changing the church of God, drives out the Spirit, and is an insult to God.

28 **And God hath set some in the church,**—This is the order in which these gifts bestowed by the Spirit are set in the church.

first apostles,—The apostles were the first and highest, endowed with the fullness of the Spiritual gifts and knowledge. They were sent as ambassadors of Christ, to be witnesses of what he did and taught. Jesus said to his apostles: "Ye are witnesses of these things." (Luke 24: 48.) "And ye also bear witness, because ye have been with me from the beginning." (John 15: 27.) When one was to be chosen to take the place of Judas, Peter said that he must be one that had been "with us all the time that the Lord Jesus went in and went out among us, beginning from the baptism of John, unto the day that he was received up from us, of these must one become a witness with us of his resurrection." (Acts 1: 21, 22.) So, too, Paul had to see Jesus after his resurrection and in his glorified state before he could be an apostle. Ananias said to him: "The God of our fathers hath appointed thee to know his will, and to see the Righteous One, and to hear a voice from

tongues. 29 Are all apostles? are all prophets? are all teachers? are all *workers* of ¹miracles? 30 have all gifts of healings? do all speak with tongues? do all interpret?

---

his mouth. For thou shalt be a witness for him unto all men of what thou hast seen and heard" (Acts 22: 14, 15); and Jesus said: "I have appeared unto thee, to appoint thee a minister and a witness both of the things wherein thou hast seen me, and of the things wherein I will appear unto thee." (Acts 26: 16.) No one could be an apostle unless he had seen Jesus after his resurrection from the dead.

secondly prophets,—The prophets were inspired to make known the will of God after it had been revealed through the apostles.

thirdly teachers,—Those endowed to feed and teach those already Christians the duties and obligations resting on them as the children of God.

then miracles,—The inworking of powers. (See note on 12: 10.)

then gifts of healings,—The power which enabled them to heal diseases.

helps,—This denotes the various kinds of relief which it was sought to procure for all sufferers, widows, orphans, and others in need.

governments,—Wise counselors, and advisors of the weak and erring.

divers kinds of tongues.—This was to speak in tongues they had never learned. It was the least and lowest of all gifts. The New Testament enumerations all begin with the greatest and end with the least. In the beginning of the church, men were enabled by the Holy Spirit to do what they were afterward trained to do by the word of God.

29, 30 Are all apostles? are all prophets? are all teachers? are all workers of miracles? have all gifts of healings? do all speak with tongues? do all interpet?—These questions were in answer to the complaint that they all did not have the higher gifts. As in other things, the fewest number attained to them, and these questions were to impress on them this truth; and yet, all were required to make one body.

4. CONTRAST OF THE MOST EXCELLENT WAY WITH THE USE OF SPIRITUAL GIFTS
12: 31 to 13: 13

31 But desire earnestly the greater gifts. And moreover a most excellent way show I unto you.
1 If I speak with the tongues of men and of angels, but have not love, I

---

31 **But desire earnestly the greater gifts.**—If they desired the greater gifts, they must fit themselves to use them. God bestows honors and privileges as men are fitted to use them. While he admonishes them to seek the greater gifts, he tells them there is a better way than seeking or using any gifts. The gifts were temporary and would soon pass away.

And moreover a most excellent way show I unto you.—The more excellent way is doing the will of God to all "out of a pure heart and a good conscience and faith unfeigned."

13:1 **If I speak with the tongues of men and of angels,**—The apostle in this chapter presents the most excellent way. He shows that one may possess spiritual gifts and not be in this way. Though he should be able to speak all the tongues known to men or angels, that would not insure his salvation without he possessed love. Judas Iscariot possessed the power to work miracles in common with the other apostles. (Matt. 10: 1.) He did not possess love, betrayed the Lord, and went to his own place. (Acts 1: 25.) Paul himself, endowed with the apostolic measure of the Holy Spirit, said: "I buffet my body, and bring it into bondage: lest by any means, after that I have preached to others, I myself should be rejected." (9: 27.) There is no doubt that some of those who were endowed with the spiritual gifts turned aside into sin and were lost. When they turned from the Lord, it is certain that they lost their gifts.

but have not love,—The possession of love is the essential requirement. What is love? Passion is often mistaken for love. They differ widely, yet resemble in some points. Love denies self for the good of object. Passion seeks its own gratification. The test and measure of love is how much of his own pleasure he is willing to forego for the well-being of the object of his love. The test of a mother's love for her child is how much of her selfish pleasure she will forego for the good of the child; the test of a husband's love is how much of his selfish pleasure he will deny himself to make his wife happy; the test of a child's love for its parents is how much of its pleasure it will forego to please the parent.

Man's love to God is measured by his willingness to sacrifice his own pleasure and his own ways to please God. "This is the love of God, that we keep his commandments." (1 John 5: 3.) Christ's love to men was shown by his willingness to give up the glory of heaven and die to save man. Love looks to the good of the person loved. "Love worketh no ill to his neighbor: love therefore is the fulfilment of the law." (Rom. 13: 10.) The greatest good any one can do to another is to fulfil the requirements of the law of God to him. To do what the law of God requires to a wife, a child, a husband, a parent, a neighbor, or an enemy is to do the greatest good to them possible. Then the highest and truest love is shown in fulfilling the law of God toward them. "And hereby we know that we know him, if we keep his commandments . . . whoso keepeth his word, in him verily hath the love of God been perfected" (1 John 2: 3-5)—that is, the love that God has toward us is transformed to our hearts by the Holy Spirit, and is perfected in us by our keeping his commandments.

These Scriptures show plainly that love as used in the Bible is not a mere sentiment nor an excitement of the passions nor a feeling of magnetic attraction, but is an active desire to do good. In a believer in Jesus Christ it can be manifested only by doing to God, to man, in all the relations in which one stands to him, what God's law directs, this will bring the highest and only true good, and so is the manifestation of love.

I am become sounding brass, or a clanging cymbal.—To be able to speak with tongues, while refusing to do their duty to

am become sounding brass, or a clanging cymbal. 2 And if I have *the gift
of* prophecy, and know all mysteries and all knowledge; and if I have all
faith, so as to remove mountains, but have not love, I am nothing. 3 And if
I bestow all my goods to feed *the poor,* and if I give my body [6]to be burned,
but have not love, it profiteth me nothing. 4 Love suffereth long, *and* is kind;

[6]Many ancient authorities read *that I may glory.*

God and man was like sounding brass or a clanging cymbal,
an empty pretense without sense or good.

**2 And if I have the gift of prophecy, and know all mysteries
and all knowledge; and if I have all faith, so as to remove
mountains, but have not love, I am nothing.**—Though he
should have all these greater gifts and have not love, or fail to
perform the commands of God toward God and man, he would
be a spiritual bankrupt before heaven and earth.

3 And if I bestow all my goods to feed the poor,—The giving of goods to feed the poor is considered by many to be the
very essence of love. When done from a proper motive, it is a
fruit of love, but if it is done for any other motive than to
honor God, and to bless man in the name of God, it is not
love.

**and if I give my body to be burned, but have not love, it
profiteth me nothing.**—[A willingness to suffer for one's faith
is not in every case a guarantee of the existence of a heart
transformed from selfishness to love. Gifts and conduct
which bring men prominently before the eyes of men are often
no index to the character; and if they be not rooted in and
guided by love to God and man, their possessor has but little
reason to congratulate himself. Too often it is a snare to
judge himself by what he does rather than by what he is. At
one period martyrdom became fashionable, and Christian
teachers were compelled to remonstrate with those who fanat-
ically rushed to the stake and the arena. It is possible that
many suffered through vainglory rather than the love of
Christ.]

4 Love suffereth long,—This long-suffering is the pro-
tracted endurance of wrong, such as is fitted to provoke re-
sentment. [It is that command over natural impulse which
keeps just displeasure from breaking forth into action. Moses
had more of this than any other in his day, yet to his cost he

love envieth not; love vaunteth not itself, is not puffed up, 5 doth not behave
itself unseemly, seeketh not its own, is not provoked, taketh not account of

once failed in it. Indeed, Jesus Christ was the only one who
possessed it in the fullest sense: "Who, when he was reviled,
reviled not again." (1 Pet. 2: 23; see also Col. 3: 12, 13.)

and is kind;—It is kind to those who do evil. [It is good-
natured, gentle, tender, affectionate. It is not sour, harsh,
morose, ill-natured. It is active in doing good things to as
many as possible, moved by the conviction: "I shall pass
through this world but once, any good thing, therefore, that I
can do, or any kindness that I can show to any human being,
let me do it now, let me not defer it, for I shall not pass this
way again."]

love envieth not;—[Envy is chagrin, mortification, discon-
tent, or uneasiness at the sight of another's excellence or good
fortune, accompanied with some degree of hatred and a desire
to possess equal advantages; malicious grudging. Love does
not envy the happiness and prosperity others enjoy; but de-
lights in their welfare, and as their happiness is increased by
their endowments, their reputation, their health, their domestic
comforts, and their learning, it rejoices in it all and would not
diminish it, and would not detract from that happiness.]

love vaunteth not itself,—It does not thrust itself forward,
nor take the highest seats in the synagogue. [Does not osten-
tatiously parade its superiority to others, whether real or supposed, priding itself on it. This quality is the exact opposite
of envy; the one envying in another what is not possessed by
ourselves, the other looking down on another for the want of
something which we possess.]

is not puffed up,—[It does not indulge in inflated opinions
of itself; the words imply an instinctive aversion from all false
glitter, pompous bluster, strutting in borrowed plumes, from
extravagant words, looks, tones, styles, in short, a deep hatred
of seeming to be more than one is.]

5 doth not behave itself unseemly,—It behaves not haugh-
tily; but is kind, gentle, loving in character, defers to the
wishes and rights of others, and in honor prefers others. [It

seeks that which is proper or becoming in the circumstances
in which we are placed. It prompts to that which is becoming
in life; it saves from all that is unfit and unbecoming. It
prompts to due respect for superiors; to a proper regard for
inferiors, not despising their poverty, their dress, their dwell-
ings; it prompts to the due performance of all the duties
growing out of the relations of life, as those of husband, wife,
parent, child, brother, sister, and procures proper deportment
in all these relations.]

seeketh not its own,—Seeks not its own selfish desires and
ends, but looks to the good and happiness of all. [And who
so eminent in this as Paul himself—next to "our Lord Jesus
Christ, that, though he was rich, yet for your sakes he became
poor, that ye through his poverty might become rich"—who
so often inculcated this grace. (9: 22, 23; 10: 33; 2 Cor. 7: 3;
Rom. 15: 2.) And yet, even then, rarely found noticeably
among Christians. (Phil. 2: 21.) The love here commended
will prompt us to seek the welfare of others with self-denial,
personal sacrifice, and toil. If all Christians would make it
their grand object not to seek their own but the good of others; then true love would occupy its appropriate place in the
heart, of every professed child of God; then there would be no
lack of funds to carry forward the glorious gospel; then there
would be no lack of men willing to devote their lives to the
glorious work; then there would be no lack of prayer to implore aid from God to live up to the fullest measure of duty.]

is not provoked,—It does not readily take offense, nor is it
easily excited to anger, or provoked to resent evils. [The one
who is under the influence of love is not prone to violent
anger or exasperation; it is not his character to be hasty, excited, or passionate. He is serious, calm, and patient. He
looks soberly at things; and though he may be injured, yet he
governs his temper, restrains and subdues his feelings.]

taketh not account of evil;—It does not surmise evil and
put the worst construction on the acts of others. [It makes
no memorandum of evil done to itself, but allows it to pass
unnoticed. It does not attribute evil motives to others, neither is it suspicious. It desires to think well of those whom it

evil; 6 rejoiceth not in unrighteousness, but rejoiceth with the truth; 7
¹beareth all things, believeth all things, hopeth all things, endureth all things.
8 Love never faileth: but whether *there be* prophecies, they shall be done

¹Or, *covereth* Comp. 1 Pet. 4. 8.

loves, and will not think ill of their motives, or conduct until
it is compelled to do so by the most irrefragable evidence.]

6 **rejoiceth not in unrighteousness,**—It does not rejoice in
the wrongdoing committed by others. (Rom. 1: 32.) It cannot sympathize with what is evil, neither can it share the glee
of the successful transgressor.

but rejoiceth with the truth;—Rejoices when the truth rejoices; sympathizes with it in its triumphs: "I rejoice greatly
that I have found certain of thy children walking in truth, even
as we received commandment from the Father." (2 John 4.)
The truth is the gospel truth, the inseparable ally of love.
(Eph. 4: 15; 3 John 12.) The false love which compromises
the truth by glossing over iniquity or unrighteousness is thus
tacitly condemned. (Prov. 17: 15.)

7 **beareth all things,**—"Love covereth a multitude of sins."
(1 Pet. 4: 8.) It does not lay bare and expose to public gaze
the infirmities and wrongs of the erring and those led into sin.
It covers them up and tries to deliver from them.

believeth all things,—It believes all the good which it can
of any one as long as it is possible to do so without betraying
the truth of God.

hopeth all things,—Works for all, even the worst, hoping
they will repent.

endureth all things.—It suffers, endures, bears all evils, and
is not driven from the true course by the wrongs and injuries
of the wicked. These qualities seem to be successive steps in
the treatment of the erring. They manifest true Christian fortitude.

8 **Love never faileth:**—He now shows that spiritual gifts
were temporary, and must pass away; while love, the doing of
God's will to all, as a principle of action and a means of justification, would never pass away. Love is the ruling principle
in heaven, and is eternal.

away; whether *there be* tongues, they shall cease; whether *there be* knowledge, it shall be done away. 9 For we know in part, and we prophesy in part; 10 but when that which is perfect is come, that which is in part shall

but whether there be prophecies, they shall be done away; —Prophecy, the foretelling of future events and the teaching by inspiration the will of God after it had been given by the apostles, would be done away.

whether there be tongues, they shall cease;—The speaking with tongues they had never learned would cease.

whether there be knowledge, it shall be done away.—The time would come when miraculously bestowed knowledge would be known no more. All those spiritual gifts pertained to the introductory age of the church. These powers were given to help men do what they could not do without the power, as the New Testament had not been completed.

9 For we know in part, and we prophesy in part;—At the time this was written, some things were unknown, had not been revealed. For the knowledge of God's will they were dependent upon those possessing the gift of prophecy. Most expositors think this refers to the partial knowledge of divine things we possess in this world, compared with the clear vision we shall possess when we shall have passed into the future; but this is wholly outside the scope of the apostle's writing here. He is contrasting the spiritual gifts, their teachings and blessings, with the service of love under the completed and perfect law.

10 but when that which is perfect is come, that which is in part shall be done away.—These gifts were to continue in the church to guide and instruct it until the completed will of God was made known. They were to serve a temporary purpose; then when their office was fulfilled, they were to pass away and give place to it.

That perfection was completed, so far as God's work of the revealing work of the Spirit is concerned, when the full will of God should be revealed, or made known, and his provisions for saving men should be set in operation, as is set forth in the following: "And he gave some to be apostles; and some, prophets; and some, evangelists; and some, pastors and teachers;

for the perfecting of the saints, unto the work of ministering, unto the building up of the body of Christ: till we all attain unto the unity of the faith, and of the knowledge of the Son of God, unto a fullgrown man, unto the measure of the stature of the fulness of Christ: that we may be no longer children, tossed to and fro and carried about with every wind of doctrine, by the sleight of men in craftiness, after the wiles of error; but speaking truth in love, may grow up in all things into him, who is the head, even Christ." (Eph. 4: 11-15.) In this passage Paul explains the whole matter; showing that these miraculous gifts were to serve till the full knowledge was received to make them one in faith and to bring them to the fullness of men and women in Christ. That knowledge is given in the New Testament.

There are two reasons why the gifts of the Spirit are not now imparted. These gifts were miraculous powers. First, there are no apostles now to impart gifts. The apostles were inspired men; so they knew all truth through inspiration, and they had seen and heard Jesus. Secondly, having revealed all truth needed to make men perfect, and thoroughly furnish them to all good works, having put in operation all the provisions of God for instructing and blessing men, there is no further need for miraculous revelations. Men can now learn all truth needed for present and eternal well-being from his will revealed and recorded in the Bible, and it will lead him into all the blessings of God in this world and in that to come, if he will study it to know and do the will of God. What man can learn himself, God will not work miracles to make known to him.

Again, to all creations and orders of God there have been creative and procreative ages. The creative age is that in which new creatures and a new order of things are brought into being; the procreative age is that in which these beings are multiplied and developed and the order is continued. In the creative age, the age of miracles, things are miraculously formed and created, afterwards they multiply and grow through the workings of law. Life was imparted to Adam and Eve by miracle; life, the same life that was given to them, has been passed on to their children through all the genera-

be done away. 11 When I was a child, I spake as a child, I felt as a child, I thought as a child: now that I am become a man, I have put away childish things. 12 For now we see in a mirror, ²darkly; but then face to face: now I know in part; but then shall I know fully even as also I was fully known.

²Gr. *in a riddle.*

tions from them to us by law. No miracle has been needed to impart physical life since they were made alive. A miracle giving physical life would be a violation of the order of God. The same is true in the spiritual world. In the beginning spiritual life was imparted miraculously. Jesus Christ came into the world; through his teaching in precept and example; his suffering, death, burial; his struggle in the grave with the power of death and hell (in the grave the battle for man was fought and the victory won); his resurrection and ascension to his Father's throne, he created the material for the new spiritual kingdom. The apostles and their fellow disciples constituted the nucleus. Christ completed his work and left them with the words ringing in their ears: "Behold, I send forth the promise of my Father upon you: but tarry ye in the city, until ye be clothed with power from on high." (Luke 24: 49.) The Holy Spirit came, imparted unto them spiritual life miraculously, organized them, gave laws to guide in the operation and development in the spiritual realm. The same spiritual life bestowed on them through miracle has been perpetuated and multiplied through "the law of the Spirit of life in Christ Jesus" (Rom. 8: 2), so that all Christians now enjoy that life without miracle. It was given by miracle; it is perpetuated by law.

11 **When I was a child, I spake as a child, I felt as a child, I thought as a child:**—He compares this time of partial gifts in the church to childhood; that, when the perfect law is completed, to manhood. While the gifts last, he would use and speak by them as he spoke when a child.

now that I am become a man, I have put away childish things.—When the perfect law is come, he will put away these partial gifts bestowed as helps for the childhood of the church and use the perfect law given to guide its manhood.

12 **For now we see in a mirror, darkly; but then face to face: now I know in part; but then shall I know fully even as**

13 But now abideth faith, hope, love, these three; and the ³greatest of these is love.

³Gr. *greater.* Comp. Mt. 18. 1, 4; 23. 11.

---

also I was fully known.—While in the state of childhood, with only the partial knowledge made known through the spiritually gifted, they saw as in a mirror darkly; but when the perfect revelation should be made known, they would know the things revealed through all. So that the knowledge we possess through the completed will of God is greatly more than any one of the gifted or inspired ones possessed, since the revelations made to and through all are given in the Scriptures.

13 **But now abideth faith, hope, love, these three;**—While these miraculous gifts must pass away, faith, hope, and love remain as the permanent and abiding fruits of the word of God. Without these no one can be a child of God; with them and the perfect law of liberty, gifts are no longer needed. The word of God as the seed of the kingdom received into the heart produces faith. Faith, in the promises contained in the word of God, produces hope. The end of faith and hope is to bring man into perfect harmony with the will of God. Complete harmony with the will of God is perfect love to every being in the universe.

and the greatest of these is love.—Love is the filling of all requirements, duties, and obligations contained in the law of God toward God and to all the creatures of heaven and earth. Love is the great underlying and all-pervading principle of the universe. God is love, and the laws of the universe are the manifestations and outgrowth of his love; and to love is to conform to the laws of God, to bring ourselves into harmony with them, and through these to work good to every being in the universe. This love will only be perfected in the state of glory, when we shall see him as he is and be like him, and it will be eternal.

[Faith is not an end; it is faith in a Divine Deliverer and in his promise of salvation; it is the means toward eternal life. Hope is not an end; it is hope of final and eternal fellowship with God; it is the means to steadfastness and to heaven. But love is an end in itself. It is the bond of perfectness; beyond this even Christianity cannot carry us. As faith and hope realize their purpose when they produce love, it is obvious that the virtue which is their final purpose is greater than they. And this conviction is confirmed when we consider that, of all virtues, love is usually the most difficult and the last to be acquired. Love is the test and the crown of spiritual maturity. Society needs above all things to be penetrated with the spirit of love to God, sympathy and brotherly kindness to man. This is the radical cure for all its ills—this, and only this. Without it, all is disorder and chaos; with it, all is regularity and beauty. It represses hatred, malice, envy; and it cultivates considerateness, pity, gentleness, self-denial, and generous help.]

5. SUPERIORITY OF PROPHECY TO THE GIFT OF TONGUES AS EVINCED BY THEIR COMPARATIVE UTILITY
14: 1-19

1 Follow after love; yet desire earnestly spiritual *gifts,* but rather that ye may prophesy. 2 For he that speaketh in a tongue speaketh not unto men, but unto God; for no man [4]understandeth; but in the spirit he speaketh mys-

[4]Gr. *heareth.*

1 **Follow after love;**—With eager efforts they were to seek to realize this wonderful grace of love by resisting temptations to any course of conduct that would hinder it and by using every opportunity to further it.

yet desire earnestly spiritual gifts,—He now shows that there is no incompatibility between seeking after love and the help of spiritual gifts while they remained. Indeed, they were given to help forward the attainment of love.

but rather that ye may prophesy.—He exhorts them that they should earnestly desire these gifts of the Spirit, but rather that they might prophesy. Prophesying after the apostolic was the highest gift. It enabled them to foretell things to come, and to teach the word of God to the people. When they sought this gift, they qualified themselves to receive and practice its teachings.

2 For he that speaketh in a tongue speaketh not unto men, but unto God;—Speaking in unknown tongues was the most striking of these gifts, and from Paul's repeating its inferiority

teries. 3 But he that prophesieth speaketh unto men edification and [5]ex-
hortation, and consolation. 4 He that speaketh in a tongue [6]edifieth himself; but he that prophesieth [6]edifieth the church. 5 Now I would have you
all speak with tongues, but rather that ye should prophesy: and greater is he
that prophesieth than he that speaketh with tongues, except he interpret, that
the church may receive edifying. 6 But now, brethren, if I come unto you

[5]Or, *comfort*
[6]Gr. *buildeth up.*

to other gifts, it must have been sought after to the exclusion
of the higher and the more helpful gifts.

for no man understandeth;—He that speaks in a tongue unknown to his hearers does not speak to them, since they do
not understand him, but he speaks to God.

but in the spirit he speaketh mysteries.—He speaks mysteries, things unknown to the people who cannot understand
him.

**3 But he that prophesieth speaketh unto men edification,
and exhortation, and consolation.**—He who, by the gift of
prophecy, makes known the will of God instructs, strengthens,
builds up, and comforts Christians in their temptations, troubles, and distresses.

4 He that speaketh in a tongue edifieth himself;—He speaks
the truths of God that will build up and strengthen himself.

but he that prophesieth edifieth the church.—The church
can understand him, and he instructs and strengthens it.

5 Now I would have you all speak with tongues,—Since it
helps him who speaks in an unknown tongue, he would be
glad for all to do so.

but rather that ye should prophesy:—Prophesying helps
both the prophet and the church, and for that reason he would
rather they prophesied.

**and greater is he that prophesieth than he that speaketh
with tongues,**—He who prophesies is greater than he who
speaks with tongues, because he does more good than he who
speaks in tongues.

except he interpret, that the church may receive edifying.—
This is the only way to instruct and build up those who hear
those who speak in an unknown tongue.

speaking with tongues, what shall I profit you, unless I speak to you either
by way of revelation, or of knowledge, or of prophesying, or of teaching? 7
Even things without life, giving a voice, whether pipe or harp, if they give
not a distinction in the sounds, how shall it be known what is piped or
harped? 8 For if the trumpet give an uncertain voice, who shall prepare
himself for war? 9 So also ye, unless ye utter by the tongue speech easy to

---

6 **But now, brethren, if I come unto you speaking with
tongues, what shall I profit you, unless I speak to you either
by way of revelation,**—Paul now transfers the matter to himself—that if even he, though he was an apostle, came speaking
with a tongue, they would receive no profit unless he interpreted the words of the tongue as conveying some revelation
received from God.

or of knowledge, or of prophesying, or of teaching?—
Knowledge, as here conceived, is the matter ordinarily communicated by teaching. Some who spoke in tongues could
not interpret what they spoke.

7 **Even things without life, giving a voice, whether pipe or
harp, if they give not a distinction in the sounds, how shall it
be known what is piped or harped?**—[Even the lifeless instruments, if they are to speak in the language of music, and affect the feelings and passions of those who hear them, must
give a distinction in sounds. That is, be subject to the laws of
tone and rhythm, to the interval of scale and measure. This
illustration is to show the uselessness of making sounds which
are not understood. And it is plain from what follows, as
well as from the whole context, that the point of analogy is
that as we cannot know what is piped or harped, or be benefited by it unless we can discriminate the sounds emitted, so
we cannot be benefited by listening to one who speaks in a
language which we do not understand. The point is, not the
folly of the gift, but the use made of it.]

8 **For if the trumpet give an uncertain voice, who shall prepare himself for war?**—Since in all ages the advance and re-
treat of armies have been directed by the sound of a trumpet,
it is indispensable that the notes expressing each should be
sufficiently distinct, the one from the other, and easily understood. Otherwise they would never know when to make
ready for battle or for other duties.

be understood, how shall it be known what is spoken? for ye will be speaking into the air. 10 There are, it may be, so many kinds of voices in the world, and ⁷no *kind* is without signification. 11 If then I know not the meaning of the voice, I shall be to him that speaketh a barbarian, and he that speaketh will be a barbarian ⁸unto me. 12 So also ye, since ye are zeal-

⁷Or, *nothing is without voice*
⁸Or, *in my case*

9 **So also ye, unless ye utter by the tongue speech easy to be understood, how shall it be known what is spoken? for ye will be speaking into the air.**—So also unless the teachers spoke in words easy to be understood, the hearers cannot know what is said, such will be speaking into the air [without conveying any meaning to any person. There will be noise, but nothing else. Gifts of that kind, used without interpretation, are good for nothing. It may well be observed that there is much of this same kind of speaking now, where unintelligible terms are used, or words are employed that are above the comprehension of the people. All preaching should be plain, simple, and adapted to the capacity of the hearers.]

10 **There are, it may be, so many kinds of voices in the world, and no kind is without signification.**—[All languages are significant, so the languages used by those who spoke with tongues were significant. The difficulty was not in the language used, but the ignorance of the hearers. The argument is that as all the languages that are in the world are for utility, and none are used for the sake of mere display, so it should be with those who had the power of speaking them in the church. They should speak them only when they would be understood.]

11 **If then I know not the meaning of the voice, I shall be to him that speaketh a barbarian,**—If he who hears does not know the meaning of the language spoken, the hearer will be a barbarian to the speaker.

and he that speaketh will be a barbarian unto me.—The speaker will be a barbarian to the hearer. Neither will be profited by the other in speaking or hearing the language that is not understood. The Greeks used the word barbarian of any foreigner ignorant of the Greek language and the Greek culture.

ous of ⁹spiritual *gifts,* seek that ye may abound unto the edifying of the church. 13 Wherefore let him that speaketh in a tongue pray that he may interpret. 14 For if I pray in a tongue, my spirit prayeth, but my understanding is unfruitful. 15 What is it then? I will pray with the spirit, and I will pray with the understanding also: I will sing with the spirit, and I

---

⁹Gr. *spirits.*

---

12 **So also ye, since ye are zealous of spiritual gifts, seek that ye may abound unto the edifying of the church.**—Since they were zealous of spiritual things, let them seek above all else those who would abound to the edification of the church.

13 **Wherefore let him that speaketh in a tongue pray that he may interpret.**—Let him pray that he may have the gift of interpreting what he says in the tongue, else he will not profit those who hear.

14 **For if I pray in a tongue, my spirit prayeth, but my understanding is unfruitful.**—[If he uses words in a tongue unknown to the congregation in a prayer to God, he realizes in his own spirit what he says to God, but his understanding is not fruitful because he has not the benefit which he ought to have from every spiritual exercise.]

15 **What is it then?**—What shall I do then?

I will pray with the spirit, and I will pray with the understanding also: I will sing with the spirit, and I will sing with the understanding also.—Here the same thought is presented and the idioms of the Greek and the English languages require a change of expression to bring out the thought. Neither the Authorized Version nor the American Revised Version does this as the connections show. The thought evidently is: "I will sing as the Spirit directs or inspires, and I will sing in a language that those who hear can understand." This expression is often quoted in connection with song service in a sense in which it was not used. The following verse shows clearly that Paul's meaning is: "I will pray and sing by the inspiration of the Spirit, and in a language that they will understand to their profit."

16 **Else if thou bless with the spirit, how shall he that filleth**

will sing with the understanding also. 16 Else if thou bless with the spirit, how shall he that filleth the place of [10]the unlearned say the Amen at thy giving of thanks, seeing he knoweth not what thou sayest? 17 For thou verily givest thanks well, but the other is not [11]edified. 18 I thank God, I speak with tongues more than you all: 19 howbeit in the church I had rather speak five words with my understanding, that I might instruct others also, than ten thousand words in a tongue.

[10]Or, *him that is without gifts:* and so in ver. 23, 24.
[11]Gr. *builded up.*

---

the place of the unlearned say the Amen at thy giving of thanks,—It was customary in prayer and thanksgiving for the hearer to approve and adopt the spoken prayer as his own, by saying, Amen.

seeing he knoweth not what thou sayest?—But if it is not spoken in language that he can understand, how could he say, Amen?

17 For thou verily givest thanks well, but the other is not edified.—As it was expressed in a tongue which he did not understand, he was not edified. [It is impossible to join in prayers uttered in an unknown tongue. This proves that the speaker must have understood what he said. For if the unintelligible is useless, it must be so to the speaker as well as to the hearers. If it was necessary that they should understand in order to be edified, it was no less necessary that he should understand what he said in order to be benefited.]

18 I thank God, I speak with tongues more than you all:—Paul as an apostle spoke more languages than all the Corinthians. His travels and labors among so many different peoples made this necessary, and it was with him a subject of thanksgiving that this power had been bestowed upon him.

19 howbeit in the church I had rather speak five words with my understanding, that I might instruct others also, than ten thousand words in a tongue.—In the assembly of the church Paul would not speak in foreign languages, where its only use would have been display; but he chose to speak in such a way as to convey instruction that would benefit others. As the object of public worship is the edification of the church, five words spoken so as to edify were of far greater value than ten thousand, not being understood, which could convey none. No higher estimate than this was ever put on practical wisdom. The best and profoundest utilitarian is the man who advocates utility on this high ground. Paul argued so warmly in behalf of the understanding because he felt so deeply the importance of benefiting others.

6. COMPARISON OF PROPHECY AND THE GIFT OF TONGUES IN THE LIGHT OF THE SPECIFIC OBJECT OF EACH
14: 20-25

20 Brethren, be not children in mind: yet in malice be ye babes, but in mind be [12]men. 21 In the law it is written, [13]By men of strange tongues and by

[12]Gr. *of full age.* Comp. ch. 2. 6.
[13]Is. xxxviii. 11 f.

20 **Brethren,**—It seems that strife had arisen over these gifts, as to which was the greater and the more honorable. He pleads with them as brethren, insisting that it was the part of wisdom to desire to so speak that others would be profited, and that there should be no strife or bitterness over these questions. So he turns aside to reprove them.

be not children in mind:—Be not weak and attracted by the sound and show of tongues like children who are pleased with anything that will amuse, and at little things that afford them play and pastime. The Corinthians had displayed a childish disposition in estimating the gift of tongues above the more useful and important gifts, and in using it when it could answer no good purpose.

yet in malice be ye babes,—In malice and bitterness, be free from all malicious thoughts and actions as little children who cannot cherish such.

but in mind be men.—[As to judgment in approving those things which are excellent, be full-grown persons, by attaining of the maturity of the calling in Christ Jesus.]

21 **In the law it is written,**—The whole of the Old Testament Scripture is called the law, because it was written during the reign of the law, and was intended to uphold and enforce it. [This we might naturally expect from Paul's manner of regarding the whole Mosaic dispensation as a progressive order of things having its completion in Christ (Rom. 3: 19;

the lips of strangers will I speak unto this people; and not even thus will
they hear me, saith the Lord. 22 Wherefore tongues are for a sign, not to
them that believe, but to the unbelieving: but prophesying *is for a sign,* not

Gal. 3: 23, 24.) John uses the word in the same manner.
(10: 34; 12: 34; 15: 25.)]

**By men of strange tongues and by the lips of strangers will
I speak unto this people;**—Here Paul shows that the gift of
tongues had little or no value except as an evidence of unbelievers, and illustrates it by this quotation from Isaiah (28: 11,
12.) In that passage Isaiah tells the drunken priests, who
scornfully imitated his style, that since they derided God's
message so delivered to them, God would address them in a
very different way by the Assyrians, whose language they did
not understand.

and not even thus will they hear me, saith the Lord.—Since
the Jews had refused to hear the prophets speaking their own
language, God threatened to bring upon them a people whose
language they could not undertand. This was a mark of displeasure designed as a punishment, and not for their conversion. [From this it was intended to teach the Corinthians
that it was no mark of the divine favor for them to have
teachers whose language they could not understand. They
were turning a blessing into a curse. The gift of tongues was
designed, among other things, to aid Christians in proclaiming
the gospel to the various peoples in their own language.
When used for this purpose it was a blessing; but to employ
it for the sake of vain display, in addressing those who could
not understand the language employed, was to make it a
curse.]

**22 Wherefore tongues are for a sign, not to them that be-
lieve, but to the unbelieving:**—Speaking in unknown languages was to reach the unbelieving nations and thus teach
them the gospel. For people to hear strangers speak in their
own tongue, never having learned it, as was done on Pentecost, attracted attention, convinced the people that the power
of God was with them, and prepared them to hear and believe
the truth.

to the unbelieving, but to them that believe. 23 If therefore the whole
church be assembled together and all speak with tongues, and there come in
men unlearned or unbelieving, will they not say that ye are mad? 24 But if
all prophesy, and there come in one unbelieving or unlearned, he is ¹reproved
by all, he is judged by all; 25 the secrets of his heart are made manifest;

¹Or, *convicted*

**but prophesying is for a sign, not to the unbelieving, but to
them that believe.**—This was instructing them in the truths of
the gospel, in a language they understood, which would help
and profit the believers; but would not profit those who believed not.

**23 If therefore the whole church be assembled together and
all speak with tongues, and there come in men unlearned or
unbelieving, will they not say that ye are mad?**—If unbelievers who do not understand the languages come into the assembly, it will seem like senseless jargon. They will be as
barbarians to each other (verse 11). The difference between
these and those in the preceding verse is that the unbelievers
understood the language spoken, in this they do not.

**24 But if all prophesy, and there come in one unbelieving or
unlearned, he is reproved by all,**—If all prophesy or teach by
the Spirit and use the gift in a language all understand, and
one comes in that understands, but believes not, and by the
spiritual gift his thoughts are laid bare, he is convinced that
God is with them, he is convicted or condemned as a sinner.

he is judged by all;—Some think this means that he was examined by those who discerned spirits and that the things he
needed were taught him; but it is more in harmony with the
context and scope of the passage to say that he was made to
know his true condition.

25 the secrets of his heart are made manifest;—As he heard
the prophets, one by one, he would be reproved by all, and his
real character and moral state would be made known to him.
His conscience would be awakened, and he would see that it
was evil. And it is possible that he would suppose that the
speakers were aiming directly at him, and revealing his
feelings to others; for such an effect is often produced.
Prophetic preaching must have had great power to make men

and so he will fall down on his face and worship God, declaring that God is
²among you indeed.
_____
²Or, *in*
_____

feel that they stood face to face with God, for even faithful
preaching today lays bare the sinner's heart, and often causes
him to feel that the preacher particularly intends him, and
wonders that he has such acquaintance with his feelings and
his life.]

**and so he will fall down on his face and worship God, de-
claring that God is among you indeed.**—Being thus smitten
with their divine knowledge and mission, he would fall down
and worship God, and report that God was in them enabling
them to know the secrets of the heart. [This description of
the effect of prophecy upon the unbeliever is in no way contrary to the assertion in verse 22. There the apostle is speaking of a sign to attract the attention of the unbeliever; here
his attention is already attracted. He has come to the assembly of the church, and is listening to the words spoken there
in the name of Jesus Christ. And as faith comes by hearing
there will be no need of signs to induce him to become a believer.]

7. REGULATIONS RESPECTING THE USE OF SPIRITUAL
     GIFTS AND THE CONDUCT OF PUBLIC WORSHIP
                        14: 26-40

26 What is it then, brethren? When ye come together, each one hath a
psalm, hath a teaching, hath a revelation, hath a tongue, hath an interpreta-
_____

26 What is it then, brethren? When ye come together,—
[How are these gifts to be exercised? The principle governing
their exercise is edification. This principle is now applied to
the orderly exercise, particularly of the gift of tongues and
prophecy. A graphic picture is given of the assembled
church, eager to contribute, each his part, to the services.]

**each one hath a psalm, hath a teaching, hath a revelation,
hath a tongue, hath an interpretation.**—The directions which
follow, with the statements made in verses 32, 33, indicate
that they attempted all these things at once and created discord and confusion in the services.

tion. Let all things be done unto edifying. 27 If any man speaketh in a tongue, *let it be* by two, or at the most three, and *that* in turn; and let one interpret: 28 but if there be no interpreter, let him keep silence in the church; and let him speak to himself, and to God. 29 And let the prophets speak *by* two or three, and let the others ³discern. 30 But if a revelation be made to another sitting by, let the first keep silence. 31 For ye all can

³Gr. *discriminate.*

Let all things be done unto edifying.—The edification of the church should be the object aimed at in the exercise of these gifts. It was not enough that a man felt himself a subject of spiritual influence; or that acting under it would be agreeable or even profitable to himself, he must remain silent unless the exercise of his gift would benefit the church as a worshiping assembly.

27 If any man speaketh in a tongue, let it be by two, or at the most three, and that in turn; and let one interpret:—To correct this confusion, he gives directions that if any should speak in an unknown tongue, that not more than two or three should speak at one meeting; these one at a time, and one should interpret.

28 but if there be no interpreter, let him keep silence in the church; and let him speak to himself, and to God.—If there were none present who could interpret, those who spoke in tongues were to keep silent. It is useless to speak in an assembly in a language unknown to all. The profit of what is spoken depends on its being understood. He and God could understand, and so he might be profited to speak to God, not to others.

29 And let the prophets speak by two or three, and let the others discern.—The prophets or teachers likewise should speak not more than two or three at a meeting and the other inspired men including him who speaks in a tongue judge of what is spoken.

30 But if a revelation be made to another sitting by, let the first keep silence.—If while one is speaking an important truth is revealed to another, let him make it known, and let him that was speaking conclude his discourse, so that there be no confusion arising from two persons speaking at the same time.

prophesy one by one, that all may learn, and all may be *exhorted; 32 and the
spirits of the prophets are subject to the prophets; 33 for God is not *a God*
of confusion, but of peace.

*Or, *comforted*

---

31 **For ye all can prophesy one by one, that all may learn,
and all may be exhorted;**—All having gifts may prophesy, one
at a time, so that all might know what had been revealed to
each and all. The same things were not revealed to the different prophets. This was true of the apostles. Some things
were revealed to one, other things revealed to another. A
conference of all was needful that the full revelation of God
might be known. So of these prophets or gifted persons, each
should hear what was revealed to the others. So that each
would learn all that was revealed to all and to be comforted
thereby.

32 **and the spirits of the prophets are subject to the prophets;**—This no doubt was said in view of the claim frequently made that, as they were under the guidance of the
Spirit, they could not restrain themselves; but the influence
was not of such a nature as to destroy the self-control of those
who were its subjects. The prophets of God were calm and
self-possessed. This being the case there was no necessity
why one should interrupt another, or why more than one
should speak at the same time. The one speaking could stop
when he pleased; and the one who had received the revelation
could wait as long as he pleased.

33 **for God is not a God of confusion, but of peace.**—God
does not give the gifts of the Spirit to produce confusion, but
peace. Any feeling, impluse, or desire of the heart, however
religious in its character, that leads man to disregard a command of God, is another spirit than the Spirit of God.

As in all the churches of the saints.—The majority of the
best critics, including the distinguished scholars who prepared
the American Revised Version, decide that according to the
sense, this clause should stand connected with verse 34. So it
reads: "As in all the churches of the saints, let the women
keep silence in the churches." It is therefore evident that at
the time Paul wrote the propriety of the prohibition was recognized and practiced by all the churches.

As in all the churches of the saints, 34 let the women keep silence in the churches: for it is not permitted unto them to speak; but let them be in

34 let the women keep silence in the churches; for it is not permitted unto them to speak;—[No instruction in the New Testament is more positive than this; it is positive, explicit, and universal; and however plausible may be the reasons which are urged for disregarding it, and for suffering women to take an active part in conducting public worship, yet the authority of the inspired apostle remains positive and his meaning cannot be misunderstood. He looks at it from every viewpoint, forbids it altogether, and shows that from every consideration it was to be regarded as improper for them to take any active part in conducting the public service.]

but let them be in subjection, as also saith the law.—This was ordained by God in the beginning when he said unto the woman: "Thy desire shall be to thy husband, and he shall rule over thee." (Gen. 3: 16.) It was required all through the Patriarchal and Jewish dispensations. Sarah was subject to Abraham calling him lord. (1 Pet. 3: 5, 6.) Rebekah veiled her face when she approached Isaac, and during the whole ministry of Christ and the apostles, no record is given of a woman leading in public service, although some of them were spiritually endowed and required to teach in private. (Tit. 2: 3, 4.)

The following command to Timothy was given to guide him in setting in order the churches of Christ: "Let a woman learn in quietness with all subjection. But I permit not a woman to teach, nor to have dominion over a man, but to be in quietness. For Adam was first formed, then Eve; and Adam was not beguiled, but the woman being beguiled hath fallen into transgression." (1 Tim. 2: 11-14.) Here are two reasons given: (1) Adam was first created, and the precedence, the right to rule and lead, was given him; (2) the woman was deceived and led into the transgression. Both reasons are universal in their bearing, showing clearly that the rule is universal. I do not see how God could have made it clearer and more certain than he has done. The reasons given for this command apply to every woman in the world

subjection, as also ⁵saith the law. 35 And if they would learn anything, let them ask their own husbands at home: for it is shameful for a woman to

⁵Gen. iii. 16?

alike. There is not the least difficulty in explaining all the passages in harmony with these, if we will recognize what is true—that God intended the great burden of praying, teaching, exhorting, and admonishing to be done in private, not in public. Woman has free access to this great field. We have perverted this; we do our preaching, teaching, exhorting, and, I fear, praying often in public; so interpret the Scriptures by our practices, and not by the will of God.

The truth of the whole matter is that many of the churches are infected more or less with a spirit of modernistic infidelity that does not hesitate to set aside any order of God when it stands in the way of their fancies. The habit of women preaching originated in the same hotbed with easy divorce, free love, birth control, repugnance to childbearing and child rearing.

35 **And if they would learn anything, let them ask their own husbands at home:**—She should not ask questions as leading to the teaching. She should ask her own husband concerning the things she would learn.

for it is shameful for a woman to speak in the church.—It is shameful because it does not comport with propriety and her womanly modesty, which in all nations is her shield and power. It is contended that, since there is no specific law forbidding women taking public part in the service under the law of Moses, Paul is wrong in forbidding her doing so in the church. But to assign all duties to men and none to women is to prohibit their performing such duties. It shows that such a thing as their taking active part was never considered. This epistle was not addressed to the Corinthians exclusively, but "unto the church of God which is at Corinth, even them that are sanctified in Christ Jesus, called to be saints, with all that call upon the name of our Lord Jesus Christ in every place, their Lord and ours" (1: 2), showing clearly that it was written for the guidance of all Christians in every place and for all time.

speak in the church. 36 What? was it from you that the word of God went forth? or came it unto you alone?

37 If any man thinketh himself to be a prophet, or spiritual, let him take knowledge of the things which I write unto you, that they are the commandment of the Lord. 38 ⁶But if any man is ignorant, let him be ignorant.

⁶Many ancient authorities read *But if any man knoweth not, he is not known.* Comp. ch. 8. 3.

This cannot be interpreted as meaning that it is improper for women to speak or to pray in meetings of their own sex, assembled for prayer or Bible study.

36 What? was it from you that the word of God went forth? or came it unto you alone?—[They had acted in the matter of allowing women to preach as if they were the authors of Christianity—as if, because of their manifold spiritual gifts, the word of God had gone forth from Corinth, instead of from Jerusalem. He reminds them that instead of such being the case the word of God was brought to them by himself. They had received all from him.]

37 If any man thinketh himself to be a prophet, or spiritual, let him take knowledge of the things which I write unto you, that they are the commandment of the Lord.—Having given these rules regulating the use of the spiritual gifts showing that they were liable to be misused and abused, he lays down this rule by which all claims to prophetic or spiritual powers were to be tested. Doing this he will, of course, be regulated by these rules. If he refused to do this he might know, and others too, that he had no gift of the Spirit.

To accept and obey the commandments of God as revealed in the Scriptures is the rule for all at this day by which to test their claims to spirituality. Men are probably more liable to deceive themselves as to whether they are spiritual in the sense of being led by the Spirit than they were in reference to miraculous gifts of the Spirit. The rule is good for all ages.

38 But if any man is ignorant, let him be ignorant.—Since Paul wrote under the direction of the Spirit, any one filled with the Spirit would be guided to recognize his words as of divine authority, for the Spirit would not say one thing to Paul and a different thing to another. Therefore if any one

39 Wherefore, my brethren, desire earnestly to prophesy, and forbid not to speak with tongues. 40 But let all things be done decently and in order.

---

denies Paul's claims to inspiration, he does it willfully and let him remain in his ignorance and suffer the consequences.

39 **Wherefore, my brethren, desire earnestly to prophesy, and forbid not to speak with tongues.**—In consideration of all the matters written, let all earnestly desire to prophesy—teach, exhort, strengthen, and comfort one another. While recognizing this as the highest and best gift, do not despise the lower and humble gifts.

40 **But let all things be done decently and in order.**—Let all things be done in an appropriate and becoming manner; regularly, without confusion, discord, or tumult as becomes the worship of God.

SECTION EIGHT

THE RESURRECTION OF THE DEAD

15 : 1-58

1. GROUND OF THE ARGUMENT
15: 1-11

1 Now I make known unto you, brethren, the [7]gospel which I [8]preached unto you, which also ye received, wherein also ye stand, 2 by which also ye are saved, if ye hold fast the [9]word which I [8]preached unto you, except ye

---

[7]See marginal note on ch. 4. 15.
[8]See marginal note on ch. 1. 17.
[9]Gr. *with what word.*

---

1 **Now I make known unto you, brethren, the gospel which I preached unto you,**—Paul now states the fundamentals of the gospel which he preached as a basis of the argument contained in this chapter. In the gospel the chief fact was the resurrection of Christ from the dead. On it Christ's claim to be the Son of God turns, and on it the resurrection of man and his eternal hopes rest. It was proper that he should state what he had taught them at first of the great elementary truths on which the church had been established, but from which their minds had been diverted.

which also ye received,—[They had embraced it as true—that Christ rose from the dead, and that the saints would rise.]

wherein also ye stand,—[On this truth the church was founded, and on it their hope rested. This doctrine was vital and fundamental.]

2 **by which also ye are saved,**—By it they were brought into a saved state.

if ye hold fast the word which I preached unto you,—If they held fast or were steadfast to the end.

except ye believed in vain.—To believe in vain is to believe and not act on the faith. Faith is intended to lead to obedience to God; and when it fails to do this, it is vain faith. Every one who claims to believe God, and does not continue faithful to the end, makes faith vain.

When a man adds the inventions of men to the appointments of God, he makes faith vain.

believed in [10]in vain. 3 For I delivered unto you first of all that which also I received: that Christ died for our sins according to the scriptures; 4 and that he was buried; and that he hath been raised on the third day according

[10]Or, *without cause*

---

3 **For I delivered unto you first of all**—First in importance, not in time; the doctrine of the resurrection is primary and cardinal, central and indispensable.

that which also I received:—He received that which he had preached to them by direct revelation. (11: 23; Gal. 1: 11, 12; 2: 6.) He could therefore speak with infallible confidence, both as to what the gospel is and as to its truth.

that Christ died for our sins according to the scriptures;— [Christ's death was a propitiatory sacrifice for sin; and the occurrence of such a statement in this place proves that Christ's death constituted an essential part of the gospel.] Man was under sentence of death, an outlaw in the court of heaven; but Jesus Christ purchased him "with his own blood." (Acts 20: 28.) "The Son of man came not to be ministered unto, but to minister, and to give his life a ransom for many." (Matt. 20: 28.) "Who gave himself for us, that he might redeem us from all iniquity, and purify unto himself a people for his own possession, zealous of good works." (Tit. 2: 14.) "Who his own self bare our sins in his body upon the tree, that we, having died unto sins, might live unto righteousness; by whose stripes ye were healed." (1 Pet. 2: 24.) "He is the propitiation for our sins; and not for ours only, but also for the whole world." (1 John 2: 2.) "For ye were bought with a price: glorify God therefore in your body." (6: 20.) The idea of Jesus redeeming, purchasing man from under the sentence of condemnation is so interwoven with the whole of the Scriptures that it cannot be rejected without rejecting the truth of the Bible. He is the Redeemer and Savior of man.

4 **and that he was buried;**—[The inclusion of this detail in so brief a statement of facts is remarkable. But the burial is carefully recorded in all four Gospels, and was evidently regarded of great importance. The importance here and there is that the burial was the evidence of a bodily resurrection.

to the scriptures; 5 and that he appeared to Cephas; then to the twelve; 6

The death of Jesus having been certified by the centurion (Mark 15: 44, 45), his body was committed to Joseph of Arimathea, who took it down from the cross, and laid it in a tomb that was hewn in stone (Luke 23: 53), and rolled a great stone before the door of the tomb, and departed (Matt. 27: 60). Then the chief priests and the Pharisees came before Pilate, saying: "Sir, we remember that that deceiver said while he was yet alive, After three days I rise again. Command therefore that the sepulchre be made sure until the third day, lest haply his disciples come and steal him away, and say unto the people, He is risen from the dead: and the last error will be worse than the first. Pilate said unto them, Ye have a guard: go, make it as sure as ye can. So they went, and made the sepulchre sure, sealing the stone, the guard being with them." (Matt. 27: 63-66.)]

and that he hath been raised on the third day—[Since the death and burial of Christ are historic facts, the effect of the resurrection is abiding. It is not said that Christ arose, but that he was raised. His resurrection is the work of God (verse 15), the divine seal upon the work of Christ.]

according to the scriptures;—These prophecies and their fulfillment are given to prove that the death and resurrection of Jesus were in accord with them. [The double appeal to Scripture in so brief a statement is deliberate and important; and the divine prediction of what would take place is appropriately placed before the apostolic testimony as to what did take place. The agreement of what did take place with what was foretold in Scripture is pointed out with special frequency in the New Testament. (Luke 22: 37; 24: 25-27, 44-46; Acts 2: 25-32; 3: 24-26, 34-37; 17: 3; 18: 28; 26: 22, 23.)]

5 and that he appeared to Cephas;—Having presented the prophecies, he introduces as witnesses those to whom he appeared after his resurrection. [The resurrection of Christ was a fact to be proved, like other facts, by competent witnesses. Paul, therefore, appeals to the witnesses who attested the truth of the resurrection of the Lord Jesus, and shows that it

then he appeared to above five hundred brethren at once, of whom the greater part remain until now, but some are fallen asleep; 7 then he ap-

was not possible that so many witnesses should have been deceived. The appearance to Peter is nowhere directly mentioned in the Gospels, but is implied in the exclamation of the apostles on the return of the disciples from Emmaus, "Saying, The Lord is risen indeed, and hath appeared to Simon." (Luke 24: 34.)]

then to the twelve;—[The apostles were called "The Twelve" by a figure of speech common to all languages, where any body of persons who act as colleagues are called by the number of which the body is properly composed though it may not be completed. It is most likely that Paul refers to the appearance mentioned by Luke (24: 36-43), and John (20: 19, 24), when Thomas was absent.]

6 **then he appeared to above five hundred brethren at once,** —[The place of this appearance is not designated, but there are two circumstances mentioned which throw light on the subject. Just before his death he told his disciples: "After I am raised up, I will go before you into Galilee" (Matt. 26: 32); and after his resurrection, the angel said to the women who had gone to the sepulchre: "Go quickly, and tell his disciples, He is risen from the dead; and lo, he goeth before you into Galilee; there shall ye see him: lo, I have told you. And they departed quickly from the tomb with fear and great joy, and ran to bring his disciples word. And behold, Jesus met them, saying, . . . Fear not: go tell my brethren that they depart into Galilee, and there shall they see me," and "the eleven disciples went into Galilee, unto the mountain where Jesus had appointed them." (Matt. 28: 7-16.) Jesus had spent most of his public life in Galilee, and made most of his disciples there. It was proper, therefore, that those disciples, who would hear of his death, should have some public confirmation of the fact that he had risen.]

of whom the greater part remain until now,—[The strength of this witness lies in the fact that the majority of them were still living when Paul wrote this epistle, making it possible still to get full evidence at first hand. What more conclusive

peared to [11]James; then to all the apostles; 8 and last of all, as to the *child untimely born*, he appeared to me also. 9 For I am the least of the apostles,

[11]Or, *Jacob*

argument for the truth of his resurrection could there be than that five hundred had seen him, who had been intimately acquainted with him in his life, and who had become his followers.]

but some are fallen asleep;—This is the usual expression employed in the Scripture to describe the death of the saints.

7 then he appeared to James;—Of this appearance we have no other mention. [There can be little doubt that this James was "the Lord's brother" (Gal. 1: 19), who became so prominent in the church in Jerusalem (Gal. 2: 9), and is placed here among the chief witnesses because of his prominent position. He was not a believer during the Lord's personal ministry (John 7: 5); but he was united with the apostles, and with "the women, and Mary the mother of Jesus" in "the upper chamber," immediately after the ascension (Acts 1: 14.)]

then to all the apostles;—This appearance was on the day of the ascension. (Acts 1: 4-11; Luke 24: 44-51.) [From the expressions—"being assembled together with them," and "they therefore, when they were come together"—it is evident that this gathering was the result of a convocation on the part of Jesus. It was to be his final appearance to the apostles. They must all be present, and Jesus had provided that none of them should be wanting.]

8 and last of all, as to the child untimely born, he appeared to me also.—This last appearance was after his ascension as Paul was on his way to Damascus. (Acts 9: 5; 22: 14; 26: 16.) Because of his late appearance to him, he was as "the child untimely born." [This denotes the violent and unnatural mode of his call to the apostleship, especially at the moment when he was recalling the appearing of the Lord on the way to Damascus. The other apostles were called when they were already believers; and which the Lord's hands gathered without effort, whereas Paul was torn, as by a violent operation, from that Phariseeism to which he was yet clinging with all the fibers of his heart and will.]

that am not meet to be called an apostle, because I persecuted the church of God. 10 But by the grace of God I am what I am: and his grace which was bestowed upon me was not found [12]vain, but I labored more abundantly than they all: yet not I, but the grace of God which was with me. 11 Whether then *it be* I or they, so we preach, and so ye believed.

[12]Or, *void*

9 **For I am the least of the apostles, that am not meet to be called an apostle,**—Paul keenly felt his guilt in persecuting the church, often spoke of it, always confessing his sinfulness, and on account of it he felt that he was the least of all the apostles, and was not worthy to be called an apostle.

because I persecuted the church of God.—This sense of wrong done the church of God became a spur to increased sacrifice for Christ.

10 **But by the grace of God I am what I am:**—While Paul was sinful, God's grace opened the way for his forgiveness and made him what he was. The Lord saw his earnestness, zeal, self-sacrificing spirit, fidelity to his convictions, and his fitness to preach the gospel, so appeared unto him, brought him to believe, and started him upon his work of self-sacrificing service.

and his grace which was bestowed upon me was not found vain; but I labored more abundantly than they all:—The favor bestowed on him was not fruitless, for he labored more abundantly than all the apostles.

yet not I, but the grace of God which was with me.—God's goodness and mercy to him constrained him to labor and suffer as he had done more than all the other apostles.

11 **Whether then it be I or they, so we preach, and so ye believed.**—He and the other apostles preached the same gospel of the resurrection and the Corinthians became Christians by accepting Christ's resurrection as the fundamental truth of the gospel which they received.

[The resurrection of Christ was attested by a plurality of occasions, a plurality of witnesses, and a plurality of the senses. Hence the apostles gave their testimony to the world without a shadow of doubt upon their souls as to its truthfulness and encountered every form of persecution in its behalf with unfaltering confidence and the utmost composure. They were not credulous dupes blindly led by "cunningly devised fables."]

2. THE ESSENTIAL CONNECTION BETWEEN CHRIST'S RESURRECTION AND THE RESURRECTION OF THE DEAD IN GENERAL
15: 12-19

12 Now if Christ is preached that he hath been raised from the dead, how say some among you that there is no resurrection of the dead? 13 But if there is no resurrection of the dead, neither hath Christ been raised: 14 and

12 **Now if Christ is preached that he hath been raised from the dead,**—The resurrection of Christ was the vital truth in their faith. It had been preached and believed by all Christians. On it their acceptance of Christ turned. It was the foundation stone of their faith. To deny this was to deny the faith and become an infidel.

how say some among you that there is no resurrection of the dead?—Since all admit that Christ was raised from the dead, how can it be that there can be no resurrection? It was probably held by some that resurrection was impossible. To which Paul answered by demonstrating a fact, and showing that such an event had occurred, and that consequently all the difficulties were met. Facts are unanswerable demonstrations; and when a fact is established, all obstacles and difficulties in the way must be admitted to be overcome. He had established the fact that one had been raised, and thus met at once all the objections which could be arrayed against the doctrine.

13 **But if there is no resurrection of the dead, neither hath Christ been raised:**—The two stand or fall together. The resurrection of Christ is only the beginning of the general resurrection. Jesus said to the Jews: "Marvel not at this: for the hour cometh, in which all that are in the tombs shall hear his voice, and shall come forth; they that have done good, unto the resurrection of life; and they that have done evil, unto the resurrection of judgment." (John 5: 28, 29.) When Jesus died on the cross: "The earth did quake; and the rocks

if Christ hath not been raised, then is our preaching ¹²vain, ¹³your faith also
¹³Some ancient authorities read *our.*

were rent; and the tombs were opened; and many bodies of
the saints that had fallen asleep were raised; and coming forth
out of the tombs after his resurrection they entered into the
holy city and appeared unto many." (Matt. 27: 51-53.) That
was the beginning of the resurrection, to be completed only
when "the Lord himself shall descend from heaven, with a
shout, with the voice of the archangel, and with the trump of
God: and the dead in Christ shall rise first; then we that are
alive, that are left, shall together with them be caught up in
the clouds, to meet the Lord in the air: and so shall we ever
be with the Lord." (1 Thess. 4: 16, 17.)

14 **and if Christ hath not been raised, then is our preaching
vain,**—The central truth and fundamental fact of their preaching was that Christ was raised from the dead; but if he had
not been raised, their preaching was false.

your faith also is vain.—Their faith in Christ as the Son of
God was based on the belief that God raised him from the
dead. When the Jews asked a sign of Jesus he said unto them:
"An evil and adulterous generation seeketh after a sign; and
there shall no sign be given to it but the sign of Jonah the
prophet; for as Jonah was three days and three nights in the
belly of the whale; so shall the Son of man be three days and
three nights in the heart of the earth." (Matt. 12: 39, 40.) That
is, he should be buried and rise again; and Paul says he "was
declared to be the Son of God with power, according to the
spirit of holiness, by the resurrection from the dead." (Rom.
1: 4.) His resurrection was the foundation on which their
faith rested, and if that was not true their faith was vain.
The system could not be true unless Christ had been raised
from the dead, as he said he would be; and to believe a falsehood could be of no use to any man.

15 **Yea, and we are found false witnesses of God; because
we witnessed of God that he raised up Christ: whom he raised**

is [12]vain. 15 Yea, and we are found false witnesses of God; because we witnessed of God that he raised up [1]Christ: whom he raised not up, if so be that the dead are not raised. 16 For if the dead are not raised, neither hath Christ been raised: 17 and if Christ hath not been raised, your faith is vain; ye are yet in your sins. 18 Then they also that are fallen asleep in Christ

[1]Gr. *the Christ.*

---

not up, if so be that the dead are not raised.—If there be no resurrection, then Christ was not raised; and if Christ was not raised, the apostles bore false witness when they claimed to have seen him alive after his burial. They told a falsehood when it could bring no present good, but bring much suffering, and finally death; and if false, there could be no hope of anything but infamy and shame. Yet if Christ was not raised the apostles bore false witness of God. To bear witness of God, or his words and deeds, so as to mislead men in their faith in and duty to God is a more heinous offense than to bear false witness of men. It is a grievous sin to bear false witness of men. It is a terrible sin against God and man to bear false witness of what God does and says, for it misleads men where eternal interests are at stake. Peter said to Ananias: "Thou hast not lied unto men, but unto God" (Acts 5: 4), showing that it is a greater crime to lie to and of God than of man.

16 For if the dead are not raised, neither hath Christ been raised:—[This verse is repetition of verse 13, to emphasize the argument that faith in the resurrection rests on historic fact.] He insists that unless the dead do rise, then Christ did not rise. To raise him when no others would arise would be meaningless. If he did rise, then the dead must rise.

17 and if Christ hath not been raised, your faith is vain;—If Christ had not been raised from the dead, their faith in a risen Lord was false and vain.

ye are yet in your sins.—Without the resurrection of Christ, there is no forgiveness of sins. The resurrection is interwoven with the whole scheme of redemption. It lies at the foundation of faith and forgiveness of sins, and without it a confession of faith in Christ is meaningless.

have perished. 19 ²If we have only hoped in Christ in this life, we are of all men most pitiable.

²Or, *If in this life only we have hope in Christ &c.*

---

18 Then they also that are fallen asleep in Christ have perished.—Many had suffered and died with a living faith in Christ. Many had yielded up their life in testimony of their faith in Christ Jesus. All these had perished, suffered, and died, and are without hope or reward in the world to come; indeed, there is no world to come if Christ be not raised. His resurrection is the guarantee and hope of the future life.

19 If we have only hoped in Christ in this life, we are of all men most pitiable.—If all we have done is merely having hoped in Christ in this life, if it is there to end, we are of all men most pitiable. We may gain an idea of what Paul suffered for Christ from his own account: "Are they ministers of Christ? (I speak as one beside himself) I more; in labors more abundantly, in prisons more abundantly, in stripes above measure, in deaths oft. Of the Jews five times received I forty stripes save one. Thrice was I beaten with rods, once was I stoned, thrice I suffered shipwreck, a night and a day have I been in the deep; in journeyings often, in perils of rivers, in perils of robbers, in perils from my countrymen, in perils from the Gentiles, in perils in the city, in perils in the wilderness, in perils in the sea, in perils among false brethren; in labor and travail, in watchings often, in hunger and thirst, in fastings often, in cold and nakedness. Besides those things that are without, there is that which presseth upon me daily, anxiety for all the churches." (2 Cor. 11 : 23-28.)

[It is not the fulfillment of the moral law which is here in question; no natural duty imposed on Paul a life of labors, privations, and sufferings of all kinds such as he accepted, and which should be accepted by all Christians in the service of Christ. The free choice of such a life can only be justified by the hope of the most excellent blessings and these blessings consist by no means of certain external pleasures granted by way of reward, but in the satisfaction of the noblest and most elevated wants of human nature, of the aspiration after holiness and life eternal. To see these blessings escape, where all

inferior ones have been sacrificed to gain them—to have re-
nounced earth for heaven, and instead of heaven to find perdi-
tion, like sinners—would not this still be a sadder condition
than that of worldly men who at least allow themselves on
earth a comfortable life and the lawful pleasures which were
in their reach? To the sufferings accumulated during this
life there would come to be added the most cruel disappointment after this life—no eternal life.]

3. BLISSFUL RESULTS OF CHRIST'S RESURRECTION IN CONTRAST WITH THE CONSEQUENCES OF UNBELIEF
15: 20-28

20 But now hath Christ been raised from the dead, the firstfruits of them
that are asleep. 21 For since by man *came* death, by man *came* also the

20 **But now hath Christ been raised from the dead,**—None
really denied the resurrection of Christ, but how meaningless
and fruitless his resurrection would be without the resurrection of others. His resurrection is not a solitary occurrence
affecting only himself. [It is the resurrection of the head of a
new humanity and pledge, therefore, of the resurrection of all
the dead.]

the firstfruits of them that are asleep.—First fruits denotes
the beginning of anything, regarded as a pledge of the rest;
and so Christ's resurrection is the beginning, and the pledge
of all the rest. [There is marked suggestiveness in the term
first fruits. It is taken from the ancient ceremony in Israel of
waving the sheaf of first fruits of the ripening grain before
the Lord. (Lev. 23: 9-11.) The sheaf was at once the pledge
and the sample of the entire harvest; it was a part of the harvest to be gathered. Christ is the first fruits of all the sleep-
ing saints in his resurrection. As certainly as he is risen,
so certainly shall they rise, for he is the pledge and assured part of their resurrection. Our faith in the resurrection
rests on the proved fact of Christ's resurrection.]

21 **For since by man came death, by man came also the resurrection of the dead.**—The resurrection of all as naturally
follows the resurrection of Jesus Christ as the death of all follows the sin and death of Adam. By Adam's sin death came

resurrection of the dead. 22 For as in Adam all die, so also in ¹Christ shall all be made alive. 23 But each in his own order: Christ the firstfruits; then they that are Christ's, at his ²coming. 24 Then *cometh* the end, when he shall deliver up the kingdom to ⁴God, even the Father; when he shall

³Gr. *presence.*
⁴Gr. *the God and Father.*

upon him; so all inherited his mortal, dying body. So as Christ by his obedience triumphed over death and was raised from the dead to die no more, so all the world through Christ will be raised from the dead. The world of mankind will be raised, no more to live a fleshly life or to die a fleshly death—"they that have done good, unto the resurrection of life; and they that have done evil, unto the resurrection of judgment." (John 5: 28.)

22 For as in Adam all die, so also in Christ shall all be made alive.—What man lost through the disobedience of Adam he gained through the obedience of Jesus Christ. He lost the fleshly or physical life in Adam. That life is restored to all men through Christ.

23 But each in his own order: Christ the firstfruits; then they that are Christ's, at his coming.—They will not all be raised at one time. Christ came forth as the first fruits. When Christ died on the cross, many of the graves were opened, and "many bodies of the saints that had fallen asleep were raised; and coming forth out of the tombs after his resurrection they entered into the holy city and appeared unto many." (Matt. 27: 52.) Those who accept Christ, put him on, live in him, "shall rise first; then we that are alive, that are left, shall together with them be caught up in the clouds, to meet the Lord in the air: and so shall we ever be with the Lord." (1 Thess. 4: 16, 17.) The wicked shall afterward be raised: "Many of them that sleep in the dust of the earth shall awake, some to everlasting life, and some to shame and everlasting contempt." (Dan. 12: 2.) "And death and Hades were cast into the lake of fire. This is the second death, even the lake of fire. And if any was not found written in the book of life, he was cast into the lake of fire." (Rev. 20: 14, 15.)

24 Then cometh the end,—The consummation of the gospel

have abolished all rule and all authority and power.   25 For he must reign,
till he hath put all his enemies under his feet.   26 The last enemy that shall

dispensation or state of things, which will open the new and
eternal period.

**when he shall deliver up the kingdom to God, even the
Father;**—The mission of Jesus Christ on earth was to redeem
and rescue the world from the rule of the evil one, to whom it
had been surrendered by the first Adam, and deliver it up to
God, even the Father.

**when he shall have abolished all rule and all authority and
power.**—Everything that is in the world, that exercises rule,
authority, or power, save as it comes directly from God, and is
used under his direction, to promote his rule and dominion, is
an enemy of God and of his Son Jesus Christ, and must be destroyed by the rule and dominion of the Son before the kingdom and dominion of the world can be delivered up to the
Father.   Jesus Christ came into the world to rescue it from
the evil one, and to destroy everything that exerts power or
authority or dominion on the earth, and to establish the kingdom of God on earth.   When that work is done every one will
render homage and obedience to God.   Then, and only then,
will peace and harmony and good will dwell among men, and
every being in the universe will realize that his happiness will
be promoted, by promoting the happiness of every other
being, and all guided by one law will work in unison and harmony to the promotion of the glory of God and the good of
men.   Before the consummation can come every plant not
planted of God shall be rooted up.   (Matt. 15: 13.)   Every institution or organization of earth that exerts rule or authority
or power must be destroyed.   This earth in the material,
moral and spiritual world must become again a garden of
God's own planting.   Not a brier, or thistle, or thorn can grow
in the material, moral, or spiritual world.   Only those plants
planted by the Father's hand and nurtured by his love will
grow in that redeemed and rescued Eden of God.

**25 For he must reign, till he hath put all his enemies under
his feet.**—Jesus Christ must rule and reign here on earth till
he has put down and destroyed all powers and dominions of

be abolished is death. 27 For, He put all things in subjection under his feet.
⁵But when he saith, ⁶All things are put in subjection, it is evident that he is

⁵Or, *But when he shall have said, All things are put in subjection (evidently ex-*
cepting him that did subject all things unto him), when, I say, all things &c.
⁶Ps. viii. 6.

---

earth. Everything exercising rule and authority and dominion
under the evil one is an enemy of God, and Jesus Christ must
reign until all have been destroyed. He reigns in his church;
and his church is his kingdom established by God, which
"shall break in pieces and consume all these kingdoms, and it
shall stand for ever." (Dan. 2: 44.) All the kingdoms, and
institutions on earth shall be broken in pieces and destroyed,
then shall he deliver up to God his redeemed kingdom, out of
which everything built up under the dominion of the devil has
been destroyed.

Since Christ's mission—the mission of his kingdom—is to
put down and destroy all these kingdoms, and to destroy everything that exercises rule, authority, or power on earth, how
can the servants of Christ and the subjects of his kingdom
enter into, strengthen, and build up that which Christ and his
kingdom are commissioned to destroy?

26 **The last enemy that shall be abolished is death.**—Death
came as a result of sin and is an enemy of God and man.
While resulting from sin, it serves as a boundary line for sin,
beyond which no active rebellion can go. So long as man sins
he must die; but when all sin and rebellion shall have been
destroyed, then death as the last enemy shall be abolished.
While Jesus conquered death, he still permits it to reign as a
punishment and restrainer of sin. But when sin and rebellion
shall have ceased, and all the institutions that have grown up
out of the rebellion of man shall have been destroyed, then
death itself, the last surviving enemy, will be destroyed, and
the kingdom will be delivered up to the Father, with no
enemy to oppose his rule and reign.

27 **For, He put all things in subjection under his feet.**—
These words are found in Psalm 8: 6, and relate to man in
general at the time of his creation (Gen. 1: 28-30) ; but as the
destiny of man thus declared is not realized, because of his
fall, in any one save in the person of the Son of man, it is here

excepted who did subject all things unto him. 28 And when all things have
been subjected unto him, then shall the Son also himself be subjected to him
that did subject all things unto him, that God may be all in all.

applied to him as representative of man in his highest state.
(See also Eph. 1: 22; Heb. 2: 5-9.)

But when he saith, All things are put in subjection, it is evident that he is excepted who did subject all things unto him.
—God did not place himself under Jesus. He is excepted
when he said he put all things under him.

28 And when all things have been subjected unto him, then
shall the Son also himself be subjected to him that did subject
all things unto him, that God may be all in all.—Jesus came to
bring all things under subjection to himself. He established a
kingdom and put in operation forces that will break down all
rebellion against God and will bring all things into subjection
unto himself as ruler. This he is doing through his kingdom.
When the work of bringing them into subjection has been
completed, he will be subject to God who put all things under
his feet, that God may be the only ruler in the universe. All
things in all places will honor and obey him.

4. COMPLETION OF THE ARGUMENT BY SHOWING THE
CONDUCT OF CHRIST'S WITNESSES TO BE INEX-
PLICABLE, IF THERE IS NO RESURRECTION
15: 29-34

29 Else what shall they do that are baptized for the dead? If the dead
are not raised at all, why then are they baptized for them? 30 why do we

29 Else what shall they do that are baptized for the dead?—
As is apparent to every thoughtful person, this is an earnest
argument to prove that Christians will rise from the dead.
The purpose, scope, and connection will admit of but one
meaning—If the dead rise not, what shall they do who are
baptized in the hope of the resurrection? Men are "baptized
into Christ," that they may live in him, die in him, and finally
be justified and saved in him.

If the dead are not raised at all, why then are they baptized
for them?—In view of their dying they are baptized in order
to their well-being after death. If they are not to be raised
from the dead, why are they baptized to fit them for the res-

also stand in jeopardy every hour? 31 I protest by [7]that glorying in you, brethren, which I have in Christ Jesus our Lord, I die daily. 32 If after the manner of men I fought with beasts at Ephesus, [8]what doth it profit me? If

[7]Or, *your glorying*
[8]Or, *what doth it profit me, if the dead are not raised? Let us eat &c.*

urrection? [There is no doubt that the allusion is to some act performed in expectation of future benefit to themselves, which would be lost if the dead did not rise. And the view given here suits the argument and agrees with the context. Foreseeing that faith would cost them the loss of all things, perhaps of life itself, not a few persons, in being baptized, did so, virtually saying with the apostle, "We who live are always delivered unto death for Jesus' sake." (2 Cor. 4: 11.) The meaning then is: What is to become of those who on being baptized do so knowing that it may prove their death warrant, if the dead rise not?]

30 **why do we also stand in jeopardy every hour?**—It was in view of this condition after death that made Paul stand in jeopardy of life every hour. [He had no other object in encountering so many dangers than to make known the gospel which looked forward to the glorious future state; but if there is no resurrection, and therefore no life beyond death, his exposure of himself to so great danger in proclaiming it was infinite folly. For he thus risked at the same moment both the present life and the life to come. The best comment on this passage is found in 2 Cor. 11: 23-28.]

31 **I protest by that glorying in you, brethren, which I have in Christ Jesus our Lord,**—He gloried in them as his children in Christ, and, in spite of their many defects, they were very precious to him. The very joy and gratitude worked by his thought of them recalls the peril he had endured for their salvation.

I die daily.—To die daily incurred the danger of death. [This is a vivid picture of his constant danger. Not that each day he actually dies, but that the process of death is ever going on; as though the executioner was already at work putting him to death.]

32 **If after the manner of men I fought with beasts at Ephesus,**—[These words describe the deadly enemies encountered

the dead are not raised, let us eat and drink, for to-morrow we die. 33 Be
not deceived: Evil companionships corrupt good morals.

---

by Paul during his long sojourn in Ephesus. They are a terrible picture of the perils which culminated not only in Ephesus
but in every place where he proclaimed the gospel. He was
surrounded by men thirsty for his blood, men against whose
fury he was as powerless to defend himself as were the cap-
tives thrown to the wild beasts in the amphitheatre. (Acts
13: 50; 14: 19; 16: 22; 17: 5; 18: 23; 2 Tim. 4: 17.)]

what doth it profit me?—If this voluntary exposure to
deadly peril be from worldly motives common to men, what is
the worldly gain to be derived from it? No such gain can be
conceived. Consequently, his self-exposure was because he
believed in a life beyond death.

**If the dead are not raised, let us eat and drink, for to-mor-
row we die.**—[The conclusion given here is a quotation from
Isaiah 22: 13, where it is given as the sensualistic cry of the
people of Jerusalem under the judgment of Jehovah, which
moved them to recklessness instead of repentance. These
words are not quoted as having any original reference to the
subject of the resurrection, but as language appropriately expressing the idea that, if there is no future state, it is vain and
foolish to subject ourselves to trials and privations here. We
should the rather make the most of this life; enjoy all the
comforts we can; and make pleasure our chief good rather
than look for happiness in the future state. This is the language of the great mass of mankind today. They look to no
future state; they, therefore, give themselves up to unre-
stained enjoyment in this life.]

33 **Be not deceived:**—[Do not be led astray by such spe-
cious maxims. They can only arise from that too great familiarity with the heathen against whom he had already put
them on guard.]

Evil companionships corrupt good morals.—It is contact,
association with evil, that is declared to be corrupting. This
is a fact of common experience. [It is only when Christians
associate with the wicked with the express desire and purpose

34 Awake to soberness righteously, and sin not; for some have no knowledge of God: I speak *this* to move you to shame.

to do them good that they can rely on the protection of God to preserve them from contamination.]

34 **Awake to soberness righteously,**—These words imply that the denial of the resurrection was already producing immoral results; and the appeal is to arouse them, as from a state of drunkenness, to prompt action to shake off the delusion under which they were lying as to their security. [The denial of such a doctrine as the resurrection was in Christians not only a matter of opinion but of unrighteousness. Righteousness embraces not only our duty to men but to God; and since he has revealed to us certain unspeakably great benefits which he intends to confer upon us, it is our duty to meet his loving offers with grateful acknowledgment. If we do not we are ungrateful and unrighteous.]

and sin not;—[The awakening to righteousness must be followed up by a continous effort to live a righteous life.]

for some have no knowledge of God: I speak this to move you to shame.—[Their culpable ignorance of Paul was at the root of their disbelief of the resurrection; and Paul assigns this as the strongest reason for awakening out of spiritual lethargy which led them to associate with those who denied that God would raise the dead. And the object of all that he was saying was to excite them to shame for having some in their fellowship who denied the resurrection.]

5. CONSIDERATION OF OBJECTIONS SUGGESTED BY THE DISSOLUTION OF THE BODY

35 But some one will say, How are the dead raised? and with what

35 **But some one will say, How are the dead raised?**—Some troubled themselves to know how the dead are raised. [The objection was urged that, though the historical testimony and natural fitness are in favor of believing that Christ rose from the dead as an earnest that we shall be raised, is our bodily resurrection possible, can we conceive such a thing? We can-

not be expected to believe what is impossible and inconceivable.]

and with what manner of body do they come?—Are they raised up in the same bodies as those in which they lived here, or, if not, what are the properties of the bodies in which they are raised?

36 **Thou foolish one,**—The one who involves himself in such needless difficulties he calls a foolish one.

that which thou thyself sowest is not quickened except it die:—He illustrates the resurrection by the analogy of the grain. As long as the grain remains in the bin, it is a dead thing—there is a germ of life in it, but that is to all appearance as if it did not exist. It can only start into life by being buried in the earth, and the whole body of the seed thus buried decays and becomes food for the life germ which cannot be seen till it has attained some size by having received nourishment from the decayed seed, and by this principle of life gathers the matter in a body as suits its wants; so that here is the great mystery of nature, patent on all sides of us, and the beginning of a new life from a dead seed.

[This, of course, is only an analogy, and an analogy is not a proof; for the proof of the resurrection is historical. It is the resurrection of Jesus Christ, who during his life displayed supernatural power and wisdom, and whose resurrection was proclaimed by men who lost every worldly advantage and exposed themselves to death daily, because they asserted its truth. This, in the apostle's view, was the proof of the resurrection, but when men asked, How are the dead raised up? as if it were an impossible thing, then he used the analogy of the seed and the plant. How the plant is actually developed from the seed is as great a mystery as the resurrection—not, of course, as great a thing—but as great a mystery, as inexplicable, as unsearchable. And the unbeliever who says that it is produced by a law of nature only introduces a still greater mystery—the mystery of laws not imposed by any intelligent being, but acting no one knows how—blindly, unintelligently,

sowest is not quickened except it die: 37 and that which thou sowest, thou
sowest not the body that shall be, but a bare grain, it may chance of wheat,
or of some other kind; 38 but God giveth it a body even as it pleased him,
and to each seed a body of its own. 39 All flesh is not the same flesh: but
there is one *flesh* of men, and another flesh of beasts, and another flesh of

---

though they require the brightest intellects of the human family to describe or measure their action.]

37 and that which thou sowest, thou sowest not the body
that shall be, but a bare grain, it may chance of wheat, or of
some other kind;—The naked grain is sown, not the body that
shall be.

38 but God giveth it a body even as it pleased him, and to
each seed a body of its own.—Neither the seed itself, nor the
sower, provides the new body; but it is God who gives it a
body as it pleases him. He does not deal with each case sepa-
rately, just as he pleases at the moment, but according to
fixed laws, just as it pleased him when the world was created
and regulated. (Gen. 1: 11, 12.) [The development of any
plant from a seed is a deep mystery, and still more mysterious
is that uniform action of God, by which each seed develops
not into any plant, but into the plant which God has appointed from the first; so that, as far as we can see, not only is
there an infinite variety of seeds, but an infinite variety of principles of life. There is a particular character of life in the
grain of wheat, and a different one in the grain of barley, and
they never interchange. This is introduced because he meant
not merely life out of the dead seed, but a particular form of
life from each seed. Therefore to every human being God
will give a proper resurrection body. There shall be a fitness
or appropriateness of the new body of the character of him
who is raised.]

39 All flesh is not the same flesh: but there is one flesh of
men, and another flesh of beasts, and another flesh of birds,
and another of fishes.—All flesh is no more the same flesh
than all grains are the same grain. Man, beasts, birds, and
fish are all different kinds of flesh. [The beast has a body
which fits it for life on the earth, the bird for life in the air,
and the fish for life in the water. If God from animal tissue

birds, and another of fishes. 40 There are also celestial bodies, and bodies terrestrial: but the glory of the celestial is one, and the *glory* of the terrestrial another. 41 There is one glory of the sun, and another glory of the moon, and another glory of the stars; for one star differeth from another star in glory. 42 So also is the resurrection of the dead. It is sown in corruption; it is raised in incorruption: 43 it is sown in dishonor; it is raised

can produce such a variety of forms of life, he certainly can, with his wisdom and inexhaustible resources, raise a body for the saints, perfectly adapted to the faculties of their minds, and to the new world in which they are to live.]

40 There are also celestial bodies, and bodies terrestrial:— [The principle is now further extended to the heavenly bodies, and another argument is thus drawn from the close analogy which subsists between the kingdom of nature and kingdom of grace.]

but the glory of the celestial is one, and the glory of the terrestrial is another.—Earthly and heavenly bodies have different glories. [The words "one" and "another" here denote difference, as well as distinction. This statement carries the thought farther in the analogy and completes it, showing that there is a difference, not only in character, but in glory between bodies on earth and bodies in heaven.]

41 There is one glory of the sun, and another glory of the moon, and another glory of the stars; for one star differeth from another star in glory.—There is no reference here to the different degrees of glory among the saints in heaven. It is the amazing variety observable in the heavens above us, suggesting the reasonableness of expecting that the resurrection body will differ greatly from the mortal body, consistent with essential identity.

42 So also is the resurrection of the dead.—He applies the truths illustrated in verses 36-38, where the seed is sown to die, and is laid in the earth, in order that it may spring up a plant wholly different in form and beauty from the seed sown, to the resurrection.

It is sown in corruption;—It is now a corruptible body, constantly tending to decay, subject to disease and death, and destined to entire dissolution. "Dust thou art, and unto dust shalt thou return." (Gen. 3 : 19.)

in glory: it is sown in weakness; it is raised in power: 44 it is sown a
⁹natural body; it is raised a spiritual body. If there is a ⁹natural body, there
is also a spiritual *body*. 45 So also it is written, ¹⁰The first man Adam be-

⁹Gr. *psychical.*
¹⁰Gen. ii. 7.

it is raised in incorruption:—The resurrection body will not
be subjected to earthly conditions; it will be imperishable,
free from all impurity, and incapable of decay.

43 it is sown in dishonor;—The body here is dishonored
with sin, with weakness, with suffering; it goes down to the
grave because of its weak, perishing, and sinful state. [A
dead body becomes so repulsive that one would say, with
Abraham, of the dearest object of this life, "that I should bury
my dead out of my sight." (Gen. 23: 8.)]

it is raised in glory:—The Lord said that those who attain
to this glory "are equal unto the angels; and are sons of God,
being sons of the resurrection." (Luke 20: 36.)   Paul said:
"For our citizenship is in heaven; whence also we wait for a
Saviour, the Lord Jesus Christ: who shall fashion anew the
body of our humiliation, that it may be conformed to the body
of his glory." (Phil. 3: 20, 21.)   And Daniel said: "They that
are wise shall shine as the brightness of the firmament; and
they that turn many to righteousness as the stars for ever and
ever." (Dan. 12: 3.)

it is sown in weakness; it is raised in power:—Weakness is
the characteristic of the lifeless body, which is relaxed and
powerless. [The resurrection body is ever fresh and fair and
strong. Not only can it never be subject to the same weakness again, but it will be endowed with new facilities superior
to the former body.]

44 it is sown a natural body;—A natural body is a body of
which animal life is the animating principle. It consists of
flesh and blood; is susceptible of pain and decay; and needs
air, food, and rest. It is adapted to the conditions of an
earthly existence.

it is raised a spiritual body.—[What a spiritual body is, we
know from Paul's description, and from the manifestation of
Christ in his glorified body. It is incorruptible, glorious, and

came a living soul. The last Adam *became* a life-giving spirit. 46 Howbeit

powerful, adapted to the high state of existence in heaven, and therefore not adapted to an earthly condition.]

If there is a natural body, there is also a spiritual body.— [If it is right to speak of a body adapted to the principle of animal life, it is right to speak of a body adapted to the spirit. Just as certainly as we have a body adapted to our lower nature, we shall have one adapted to our higher nature.]

45 **So also it is written,**—[It is only the first part of the verse (Gen. 2: 7) that is quoted. The words "First" and "Adam" are added by Paul as an inspired comment to give prominence to the fact that Adam was the beginning of the human race.]

The first man Adam became a living soul.—[The Scriptures teach that Adam was created with an animal nature, and that therefore he had an animal body. The proof with regard to the nature of Adam does not rest exclusively on the words quoted, but on the whole account of his creation, of which these words form a part. It is evident from the entire history that Adam was formed for an existence on this earth, and therefore with a body adapted to the present state of being; in its essential attributes not differing from those which we have inherited from him. But God personally inbreathing the principle of life into a lifeless, but organized body, the man, who before was only a lifeless body, became a living soul. The soul was the result of the entrance of the life principle into a mortal body.]

The last Adam became a life-giving spirit.—The second Adam gives spiritual and immortal life to those who are his. [Christ is called the last Adam in reference to the first Adam, whose antitype he is as the head of the new humanity, justified and redeemed through him. Hence it is said: "Wherefore if any man is in Christ, he is a new creature: the old things are passed away; behold, they are become new." (2 Cor. 5: 17.) But at the same time in reference also to the fact that after him no other is to follow as the head of the new race.]

that is not first which is spiritual, but that which is ⁹natural; then that which is spiritual. 47 The first man is of the earth, earthy: the second man is of heaven. 48 As is the earthy, such are they also that are earthy: and as is the heavenly, such are they also that are heavenly. 49 And as we have borne the image of the earthy, ¹we shall also bear the image of the heavenly.

¹Many ancient authorities read *let us also bear.*

46 **Howbeit that is not first which is spiritual, but that which is natural; then that which is spiritual.**—Adam, as an inhabitant of earth, came before Jesus; so the earthly body comes to all before the spiritual body. [This does not mean perfection in general, but one kind only of perfection, that which has been revealed in Christ as the second head of humanity.]

47 **The first man is of the earth, earthy:**—Our first body, or the man in his first body, is of the earth; like Adam, earthly.

the second man is of heaven.—The second, or resurrection body, will be spiritual like the body of Christ after his resurrection.

48 **As is the earthy, such are they also that are earthy:**—All bodies in the mortal state are like Adam subject to corruption and decay.

and as is the heavenly, such are they also that are heavenly. —All the spiritual bodies of Christians are like the second Adam, Jesus Christ, in his ascended state. (1 Thess. 4: 16; 2 Thess. 1: 7; Phil. 3: 20, 21.)

49 **And as we have borne the image of the earthy, we shall also bear the image of the heavenly.**—All men born into the world bear the image, the nature of Adam's body, so all counted worthy of the resurrection of the just shall bear the image of the heavenly, of Jesus Christ in his heavenly state. The apostle says: "Beloved, now are we children of God, and it is not yet made manifest what we shall be. We know that, if he shall be manifested, we shall be like him; for we shall see him even as he is." (1 John 3: 2.)

6. FURTHER ELUCIDATION OF FUTURE GLORIFICATION BY THE CHANGE TO BE EFFECTED IN THE BODIES OF THE LIVING SAINTS AT THE END OF TIME
15: 50-58

50 Now this I say, brethren, that flesh and blood cannot inherit the kingdom of God; neither doth corruption inherit incorruption. 51 Behold, I tell you a mystery: [2]We all shall not sleep, but we shall all be changed, 52 in a moment, in the twinkling of an eye, at the last trump: for the trumpet shall

[2]Or, *We shall not all &c.*

50 **Now this I say, brethren, that flesh and blood cannot inherit the kingdom of God;**—Our fleshly, mortal bodies cannot inherit the immortal kingdom; neither doth the fleshly body, subject to decay and corruption, inherit the incorruptible state in heaven.

neither doth corruption inherit incorruption.—The natural body must undergo a change and become incorruptible before it can enter the immortal state.

51 **Behold, I tell you a mystery:**—The mystery is how this change is to take place, for it had not hitherto been made known. The disclosure to which reference was made, and the corresponding one in 1 Thess. 4: 15, was made through Paul.

We all shall not sleep,—[This refers to the death of the body, but only of such as are Christ's; yet never of Christ himself, though he is said to be "the firstfruits of them that are asleep." (15: 20.) It is used of saints who departed before Christ came (Matt. 27: 52; Acts 13: 26); of Lazarus while Christ was yet upon the earth (John 11: 11); and of believers since the ascension (1 Thess. 4: 14, 15; Acts 7: 60; 2 Pet. 3: 4.)]

but we shall all be changed,—Those who die before the coming of the Lord will not fail of the blessings of Christ's eternal kingdom, and those who are alive when he comes again will not be left in their corruptible bodies. Both shall be changed, and thus prepared for the heavenly state.

52 **in a moment, in the twinkling of an eye, at the last trump:**—This change will be instantaneous and at that solemn final moment when the last trump shall sound and the dead Christians shall be raised incorruptible and those who are alive shall be changed.

sound, and the dead shall be raised incorruptible, and we shall be changed.
53 For this corruptible must put on incorruption, and this mortal must put
on immortality. 54 But when [a]this corruptible shall have put on incorruption, and this mortal shall have put on immortality, then shall come to pass

[a]Many ancient authorities omit *this corruptible shall have put on incorruption, and.*

**for the trumpet shall sound, and the dead shall be raised in-
corruptible, and we shall be changed.**—[These words were
likely added to give the order in which the three great acts of
the last day will follow one another. The first will be the sud-
den signal of the Lord's presence. Then the dead in Christ
will rise in immortal bodies. Last of all, the living will be
changed. He declares: "For this we say unto you by the
word of the Lord, that we that are alive, that are left unto the
coming of the Lord, shall in no wise precede them that are
fallen asleep. For the Lord himself shall descend from
heaven, with a shout, with the voice of the archangel, and
with the trump of God: and the dead in Christ shall rise first;
then we that are alive, that are left, shall together with them
be caught up in the clouds, to meet the Lord in the air: and so
shall we ever be with the Lord." (1 Thess. 4: 15-17.)]

**53 For this corruptible must put on incorruption, and this
mortal must put on immortality.**—The fleshly, mortal, must
be immortalized. [This confirms the preceding statement in
regard to the raising of the dead, and the change of the living
by showing the necessity of putting off the mortality common
to them both. If the present bodies are to become incorruptible and immortal they must indeed be changed, so that that
decay which is inherent in all nature must be done away, and
they will then become as incapable of dying as they are now
incapable of living beyond their alloted time.]

54 But when this corruptible shall have put on incorruption,
—When this is done death loses its power. [The striking
parallelism of the two propositions marks the ascending
movement of the thought as well as the growing exultation of
feeling. Perhaps this applies to the resurrection of the bodies
which have already passed through the dissolution of death.]

and this mortal shall have put on immortality,—The immortal will be no longer subject to death. Death will be swal-

the saying that is written, ⁴Death is swallowed up ⁵in victory. 55 ⁶O death, where is thy victory? O death, where is thy sting? 56 The sting of death is sin; and the power of sin is the law: 57 but thanks be to God, who giveth us the victory through our Lord Jesus Christ. 58 Wherefore, my beloved brethren, be ye stedfast, unmovable, always abounding in the work of the

⁴Is. xxv. 8.
⁵Or, *victoriously*
⁶Hos. xiii. 14.

lowed up and destroyed. [This refers most likely to the transformation of bodies constantly threatened with death during their earthly life.]

then shall come to pass the saying that is written,—This is added to denote the certainty of the fulfillment. God cannot lie.

Death is swallowed up in victory.—[The state of perfect inward vigor which excludes all possibility of outward decay. Such a life is victory gained forever over death its enemy. The deathless change is called a swallowing up, an absorption, of the mortal by the principle of life in Christ.]

55 O death, where is thy victory? O death, where is thy sting?—These are the different forms of expressing the fact that death has been completely conquered.

56 The sting of death is sin;—Sin inflicts on the sinner a wound that is mortal, "For the wages of sin is death." (Rom. 6: 23.)

and the power of sin is the law:—Sin exerts its power to bring about death through the law when it is violated. [The best comment on this expression is found in Rom. 5: 12-15; 7: 7-12. Paul was confronted with the horror of a broken law, which reminds him of a being infinitely holy, and of his own self-condemnation.]

57 but thanks be to God, who giveth us the victory through our Lord Jesus Christ.—For this blessed consummation of victory over sin and death, he breaks out into thanksgiving to God who has so wonderfully provided the great salvation through our Lord Jesus Christ.

58 Wherefore, my beloved brethren, be ye stedfast, unmovable,—In view of these riches and glories, he admonishes his

Lord, forasmuch as ye know that your labor is not ⁷vain in the Lord.

⁷Or, *void*

---

brethren to be firm, steadfast, unmovable in the faith of the gospel.

always abounding in the work of the Lord,—The work of the Lord is the work in which God has ordained that his children shall walk. Their labor, doing his work in Christ's name, as his servants, ransomed and redeemed by the precious blood of Christ, is not in vain. God watches over, guards, and preserves that work as the work of his own Son whose redeemed servants we are. "It is God who worketh in you both to will and to work, for his good pleasure." (Phil. 2: 13.) God's servants do the work of God. All work not in the Lord is vain and fruitless and must perish. If not in the Lord, it will go down to ruin.

forasmuch as ye know that your labor is not vain in the Lord.—This applies to the whole sentence and its several clauses. They knew by this time, from the apostle's argument, that the living and the dead will appear before Christ, and that faithfulness will be rewarded with participation in Christ's glory; for every man's work will be tested. (3: 13; 4: 5.) Paul began the discussion by declaring that, if there is no resurrection of the dead, his preaching and their faith are equally vain. He closes this argument with an appeal to their conviction that, because there will be a resurrection, their humble toil (3: 8), from day to day in the work of the Lord, will be no more in vain than their faith in Christ, no more in vain than the ministry of the apostles, no more vain than Christ's death and resurrection.

[Thus, with beautiful calmness and ease, does the apostle come down, in this closing verse, from the height to which he had risen in the verses immediately preceding, to the everyday work and warfare of life. Nor is this wonderful; for the spring of all Christian activity, energy, and progress lies in such soul-stirring themes as are handled in this chapter, whose practical outcome is expressed in this closing verse.]

SECTION NINE

CONCLUSION OF THE EPISTLE WITH VARIOUS
DIRECTIONS, AND ADMONITIONS, AND
SALUTATIONS
16: 1-24

1. INSTRUCTION CONCERNING THE COLLECTION FOR THE
POOR SAINTS IN JUDEA
16: 1-4

1 Now concerning the collection for the saints, as I gave order to the

---

1 **Now concerning the collection**—The occasion of this collection was the "great famine over all the world," predicted by
Agabus, "which came to pass in the days of Claudius." (Acts
11: 27, 28.) This fell with great severity upon Judea and Jerusalem, and the poor Christians who were despised by their
Jewish brethren as traitors to the faith, so that their lot was
especially hard. In prospect of the coming calamity, the Gentile Christians of Antioch at once "determined to send relief
unto the brethren that dwelt in Judaea: which also they did,
sending it to the elders by the hand of Barnabas and Saul."
(Acts 11: 29, 30.) Paul, intent on soothing the prejudices of
his Jewish brethren against the Gentile Christians seems to
have resolved on utilizing the example of the Antioch Christians by gathering funds from other Gentile churches for the
relief of the Christians in Judea. It is likely that he broached
the proposal first at Corinth where it was taken up with great
zeal. (2 Cor. 9: 1, 2; 8: 10.) He then laid the matter before
Macedonia and Achaia (Rom. 15: 26), and the churches of
Galatia. The great object in view, over and above the temporal relief which the contribution would give, being to soften
the prejudices of the Jewish Christians against their Gentile
brethren.

for the saints,—The saints were the poor Christians in
Judea. (Rom. 15: 26.) This would remind the Corinthians
that, in giving, it was to the Lord's people, their own brethren
in the Lord.

churches of Galatia, so also do ye. 2 Upon the first day of the week let each
one of you lay by him in store, as he may prosper, that no collections be

---

as I gave order to the churches of Galatia, so also do ye.—
This no doubt points to the detailed and explicit character of
the directions given to the churches of Galatia as to the manner of raising the contribution. And the order is pointed out
in the following verse. This order seems to have been universal.

2 **Upon the first day of the week**—Unto the apostles and
early disciples the first day of the week was very significant
and important. Christ was raised from the dead on the first
day of the week. He met with his disciples on three succeeding first days of the week after his resurrection, and there is
no evidence that he met with them at any other time. The
Holy Spirit descended on Pentecost, the first day of the week,
The disciples met together on the first day of the week, under
apostolic teaching, "to break bread." (Acts 20: 7.) Paul
said: "Not forsaking our own assembling together, as the custom of some is." (Heb. 10: 25.) That the assembly on the
first day of the week was to engage in "the apostles' teaching
and fellowship, in the breaking of bread and the prayers"
(Acts 2: 42), is clearly set forth. It is the only regular service
for which there is precept or example in the New Testament.

let each one of you lay by him in store,—On the first day of
the week, each should separate or lay by itself something,
casting it into the treasury. Some contend that the storing
was to be at home, but that would be incompatible with the
idea "that no collections be made when I come," for if stored
at home, it would have to be gathered when he came. It was
to be separated at home from the amount not given, then cast
into the treasury. [The collection was directed to be made
weekly, because it is easier to contribute in small amounts than
all at once; and on the Lord's day when the thought of the
Lord's resurrection should touch every man's heart to peculiar
gratitude. Each one was to esteem it his duty and privilege to
give to the Lord's work. It was not to be confined to the rich
only, but was the common duty of all.]

made when I come. 3 And when I arrive, ⁸whomsoever ye shall approve, them will I send with letters to carry your bounty unto Jerusalem: 4 and if

⁸Or, *whomsoever ye shall approve by letters, them will I send &c.*

as he may prosper,—[The amount is to be fixed by each one in proportion to his weekly gains, remembering that "he that soweth sparingly shall reap also sparingly; and he that soweth bountifully shall reap also bountifully. Let each man do according as he hath purposed in his heart: not grudgingly, or of necessity: for God loveth a cheerful giver." (2 Cor. 9: 6, 7.) The words do not imply that only in case of exceptional prosperity was a man to contribute, but every one was to give out of whatever fruits he had from his labors.]

that no collections be made when I come.—[The object of this measure is that the collection may be ready when Paul comes, and that there may be nothing to do except to lift it, which will be done quickly and easily, and will give an ampler sum than if the gift were all bestowed at one time.]

3 And when I arrive, whomsoever ye shall approve, them will I send with letters to carry your bounty unto Jerusalem: —Paul was not to receive the money himself. It was to be given to men selected and approved by the church, whom Paul would send, furnished with letters from himself, to the church in Jerusalem. There were no facilities for commercial exchange, the money was bulky and heavy, and a company would be a protection against robbers. So a number was selected to carry this fund to Jerusalem. A list of those who accompanied Paul to Jerusalem is given in Acts 20: 4. He went through Asia where it is likely that this number was increased, as there were contributions from Asia for the same purpose, and some brethren from Asia were with him after he reached Jerusalem.

[If Paul deemed it wise to place himself above suspicion, and to avoid giving even the most malicious the opportunity of calling his integrity and honesty in question, as is intimated here, and expressly stated in 2 Cor. 8: 19-21, it must be wise for other men to act with equal caution. If called upon

it be meet for me to go also, they shall go with me. 5 But I will come unto

to disburse the money of others, or of the church, let that
money, if possible, be disbursed in cooperation with others,
that they may know that it is handled honestly and used as
directed.]

4 and if it be meet for me to go also, they shall go with me.
—He wrote the church that, if it was best, he would accompany their messengers. This was to be determined after he
reached Corinth and consulted with them. He went, and it
was his last trip to Jerusalem. In his defense before Felix, he
said: "Now after some years I came to bring alms to my nation, and offerings." (Acts 24: 17.)

2. REFERENCE TO A VISIT TO THE CORINTHIANS SOON TO BE MADE BY THE APOSTLE
16: 5-9

you, when I shall have passed through Macedonia; for I pass through Macedonia; 6 but with you it may be that I shall abide, or even winter, that ye

**5 But I will come unto you, when I shall have passed
through Macedonia; for I pass through Macedonia;**—His previous intention was to go direct to Corinth (2 Cor. 1: 15, 16),
and proceed from there to Macedonia, then return from Macedonia to Corinth, and thence on to Jerusalem. This plan,
however, he had altered. (2 Cor. 1: 15, 23.) [He now intends to journey first through Macedonia and then to Corinth.
In the Second Epistle we see him actually engaged on this
journey in Macedonia (2: 13; 8: 1; 9: 2-4); and upon the way
to Corinth (2: 1; 12: 14; 13: 1). The account given in Acts
(20: 1, 2) agrees with this. This change was made in order to
spare them. (2 Cor. 1: 23.) He wishes to give them time,
while he would be in Macedonia, to heal their divisions, to deliver to Satan the incestuous man, and amend their conduct in
the assemblies of the church.]

6 but with you it may be that I shall abide, or even winter,
—He expresses the probability of remaining with them
through the winter. From Acts (20: 2, 3) we learn that he

may set me forward on my journey whithersoever I go. 7 For I do not
wish to see you now by the way; for I hope to tarry a while with you, if the

came into Greece (Corinth), and abode there three months,
[which were winter months. The summer months of that year
he had spent in Macedonia, and he "was hastening, if it were
possible for him, to be at Jerusalem the day of Pentecost"
(Acts 20: 16) ; but as the Aegean Sea was not favorable for
navigation till spring, he spent the intervening winter at Corinth.]

that ye may set me forward on my journey—Whether this
means help forward with money, conveyance, or merely encourage him with their company, is not certain. [This accom-
panying forward the teachers of the gospel was an established
custom in the early days of the church. (Acts 15: 3; 20: 38;
21: 5; Rom. 15: 24; 2 Cor. 1: 16; Tit. 3: 13; 3 John 6.)]

whithersoever I go.—[Paul well knew that some uncer-
tainty must attach to his plans. As it was, he had to change
his plans at the last moment. His intention was to sail from
Corinth, but, owing to a plot to assassinate him, he changed
his plan and went the overland route through Macedonia.
(Acts 20: 3.)]

7 For I do not wish to see you now by the way;—He did
not expect to see them on his trip to Macedonia, but would
see them as he returned. [It seems that the information
which Paul received in Ephesus concerning the disorders in
the Corinthian church caused him to write this letter, instead
of making them a passing visit, and to defer his visit for some
months in order that this letter might have time to produce its
effect. The same reason caused him, when he did go to Corinth, to remain there some time, that he might correct the
abuses which had sprung up in his absence. The Second Epistle shows how anxious he was about the effects of this letter,
and how overjoyed he was when Titus brought him word that
it had brought them to repentance.]

for I hope to tarry a while with you,—[As things were between them and him time was necessary to make everything

Lord permit. 8 But I will tarry at Ephesus until Pentecost; 9 for a great
door and effectual is opened unto me, and there are many adversaries.

clear, and consequently he defers his future visit until he shall
be able to prolong the visit as much as necessary.]

if the Lord permit.—[Paul regarded the entering on a journey as dependent on the will of the Lord, and felt that he had
all in his hands. Christians ought to follow up all their plans
and deliberations with this thought in mind; for it is rashness
to undertake and determine things of the future while we
have not even a moment in our power. The main thing indeed is that, in the affection of the heart, we submit to the
Lord and his providence in everything that we undertake and
resolve upon—that whenever we have to do with what is future we should make everything dependent upon the divine
will.]

8 But I will tarry at Ephesus until Pentecost;—This was before the Pentecost in the year preceding his last journey to Jerusalem. Pentecost was fifty days after the Passover. The
Passover of the next year, he was in Jerusalem. This letter
was written between the Passover and Pentecost the year previous to this last trip to Jerusalem.

9 for a great door and effectual is opened unto me,—The
reason given for remaining was that there was a good opening
for preaching the gospel, and many ready to hear and obey.
[The metaphor of an open door to represent the access of the
preacher to the hearts of the people was a favorite with Paul.
When he and Barnabas returned to Antioch from the first
mission ever sent to the heathen world, "they rehearsed all
things that God had done with them, and that he had opened
a door of faith unto the Gentiles" (Acts 14: 27); reporting the
favorable outlook at Troas, he said: "When I came to Troas
for the gospel of Christ, and when a door was opened unto me
in the Lord, I had no relief for my spirit" (2 Cor. 2: 12, 13);
unto the Colossians he said "Continue steadfastly in prayer,
watching therein with thanksgiving; withal praying for us
also, that God may open unto us a door for the word, to speak
the mystery of Christ, for which I am also in bonds" (Col. 4:

2, 3) ; and of the Thessalonians he requested: "Finally, brethren, pray for us, that the word of the Lord may run and be
glorified" (2 Thess. 3: 1). The account of the great and effectual opening for the gospel, and the virulence of the adversaries, is given in Acts 19: 8-20.]

and there are many adversaries.—It was necessary for him
to stay and refute them. The much opposition made him
leave a place when none would obey; but when many obeyed,
it was needful that he should stay and reap the harvest and
meet the adversaries. [But Satan would not suffer the great
success of the gospel without great opposition. There was no
small stir which ended in the dangerous riot in the theatre,
and Paul's departure to Macedonia.]

3. PERSONAL ALLUSION TO TIMOTHY AND APOLLOS
16: 10-12

10 Now if Timothy come, see that he be with you without fear; for he

10 **Now if Timothy come,**—[We learn from Acts 19: 22)
that Paul had dispatched Timothy, accompanied by Erastus, to
Macedonia, and desired him to continue his journey to Corinth; but as his time was limited, he did not feel sure that he
would reach there. His route took him through the churches
which he had assisted in founding. It is probable that, after
accomplishing the special work assigned to him, he was inter-
cepted by Titus who prevented his reaching Corinth, and this
seems to have happened, for Titus and Timothy returning,
met Paul, possibly at Thessalonica where Paul wrote the Second Epistle to the Corinthians, and join him in the greeting to
the church; but only Titus is spoken of as having brought any
report from Corinth. (2 Cor. 7: 6, 7, 13.)]

see that he be with you without fear;—Timothy was young
and an ardent friend of Paul, who had some strong enemies in
Corinth. These were liable to mistreat Timothy.

for he worketh the work of the Lord, as I also do:—If they
put difficulties in Timothy's way, they will be hindering the
work which God has given Paul to do. (4: 17; Phile. 19-21.)]

worketh the work of the Lord, as I also do: 11 let no man therefore despise
him. But set him forward on his journey in peace, that he may come unto
me: for I expect him with the brethren. 12 But as touching Apollos the
brother, I besought him much to come unto you with the brethren: and it

---

11 let no man therefore despise him.—Paul exhorted Timothy
to "let no man despise thy youth; but be thou an ensample
to them that believe, in word, in manner of life, in love, in
faith, in purity." (1 Tim. 4: 12.) The admonition here is
that the Corinthians should not despise him or lightly esteem
him on account of his youth, or hinder his work.

**But set him forward on his journey in peace, that he may
come unto me:**—Set him on his way with every mark of respect, and with whatever he needs.

for I expect him with the brethren.—[Erastus is mentioned
by Luke as being with Timothy (Acts 19: 22); but this by no
means excludes the possibility of others having gone with
them, or of expecting that Timothy be joined by Titus and
others on his return fulfilling his mission.]

12 But as touching Apollos the brother,—Apollos is presented to us at Ephesus as a man, mighty in the Old Testament Scriptures, knowing only John's baptism, whom
Priscilla and Aquila took to themselves, "and expounded unto
him the way of God more accurately. And when he was
minded to pass over into Achaia, the brethren encouraged
him, and wrote to the disciples to receive him: and when he
was come, he helped them much that had believed through
grace; for he powerfully confuted the Jews, and that publicly,
showing by the scriptures that Jesus was the Christ." (Acts
18: 24-28.) One of the parties at Corinth claimed him as their
leader. For this and some other reasons, it has been claimed
that he was the opponent of Paul at Corinth mentioned in this
letter. (1: 12; 3: 4-6.)

I besought him much to come unto you with the brethren:
—Paul besought Apollos to go to Corinth to use his influence
to correct the evils at work there, and this shows the close relation that existed between them and the unreasonableness of
regarding them as representatives of rival parties.

was not at all ⁹*his* will to come now; but he will come when he shall have opportunity.

⁹Or, God's *will that he should come now* Comp. Rom. 2. 18 marg.

and it was not at all his will to come now; but he will come when he shall have opportunity.—He declined going at that time, but promised that he would go at a convenient time. Paul always spoke of Apollos with brotherly love. There was no conflict between them.

4. GENERAL EXHORTATIONS
16: 13, 14

13 Watch ye, stand fast in the faith, quit you like men, be strong. 14 Let all that ye do be done in love.

13 Watch ye,—Be watchful and careful in deportment. [They were to watch or be vigilant, against the evils of which they had been admonished—of dissensions, of erroneous teaching, and of disorders. They were to watch lest their souls should be ruined, and their salvation endangered; lest the enemy of the truth and of holiness should steal silently upon them, and surprise them.]

stand fast in the faith,—["The faith" is a synonym for the gospel. They were to surrender themselves in mind and heart in obedience to the gospel, and abide in it in their daily life. So many are the impulses within, so many are the forces without, opposing the work, that nothing but an invincible determination could carry them through. They must be strong enough to bend and subordinate everything to the fruit. Paul said: "One thing I do, forgetting the things which are behind, and stretching forward to the things which are before, I press on toward the goal unto the prize of the high calling of God in Christ Jesus. Let us, therefore, as many as are perfect, be thus minded: . . . only, whereunto we have attained, by that same rule let us walk." (Phil. 3: 13-16.)]

quit you like men,—Discharge the duties like true men. [Be not cowards, or timid, or alarmed at enemies, but be bold and brave.]

be strong.—Trust God, and go forth doing his will, and his strength will be with you.

14 **Let all that ye do be done in love.**—All their affairs were to be conducted in a spirit of love to God and man.

5. SPECIAL ENTREATY CONCERNING STEPHANAS AND OTHERS
16: 15-18

15 Now I beseech you, brethren (ye know the house of Stephanas, that it is the firstfruits of Achaia, and that they have set themselves to minister unto the saints), 16 that ye also be in subjection unto such, and to every one that helpeth in the work and laboreth. 17 And I rejoice at the [10]coming of Stephanas and Fortunatus and Achaicus: for that which was lacking on your

[10]Gr. *presence*. 2 Cor. 10. 10.

---

15 **Now I beseech you, brethren (ye know the house of Stephanas, that it is the firstfruits**—The house of Stephanas was among the first who became Christians in Achaia. They were among the few baptized by the hands of Paul, probably before Silas and Timothy reached Corinth.

of Achaia,—[Originally Achaia was a state of Greece situated in the northern part of the Peloponnesus, and comprehended Corinth and its isthmus. After Greece had been conquered by the Romans, the emperor Augustus Caesar divided the country, with the adjacent regions into two regions, Macedonia and Achaia. The latter comprehended the whole of the Peloponnesus, with continental Greece south of Illyricum, Epirus, and Thessaly. Corinth was the capital, and was the residence of the proconsul by whom the province was ruled. It is in the second or comprehensive sense that the word Achaia is used in the New Testament. (Acts 18: 12, 27; 19: 21; Rom. 15: 26; 2 Cor. 1: 1; 9: 2; 1 Thess. 1: 7, 8.)]

and that they have set themselves to minister unto the saints),—They gave themselves to ministering to the poor, afflicted saints, and helping those who preached the gospel.

16 **that ye also be in subjection unto such,**—The church should pay deference to such as were the oldest of the members and who gave themselves to the service of the Lord as well as to all who were helpers and laborers with the apostles.

and to every one that helpeth in the work and laboreth.— Experience and association with the apostles made them able

part they supplied. 18 For they refreshed my spirit and yours: acknowledge
ye therefore them that are such.

---

to advise wisely. [To every faithful toiler for Christ the
Christian should give earnest and hearty support.]

**17 And I rejoice at the coming of Stephanas and Fortunatus
and Achaicus:**—Of Fortunatus and Achaicus nothing is
known further than that which is here given.

for that which was lacking on your part they supplied.—
The deficiency felt by Paul from the absence of the Corinthians, and the impossibility of communicating directly with
them, had been supplied by their messengers, because it
seemed to him as if in these three men he had the whole
church with him.

18 For they refreshed my spirit—They had refreshed him
by the help rendered. [They had dispelled the uneasiness
which filled Paul's heart in regard to them, by telling him of
the church, and perhaps, by showing him many things in a
less distressing light than he had supposed, they had given
him real comfort.]

and yours:—The information carried back to Corinth was
encouraging to the church, for it would be a great comfort to
them to learn what a comfort their messengers had been to
Paul.

acknowledge ye therefore them that are such.—They should
acknowledge and show the regard due them for their valuable
work.

6. CONCLUDING SALUTATIONS
16: 19-24

19 The churches of Asia salute you. Aquila and Prisca salute you much

---

19 The churches of Asia salute you.—The Roman province
of Asia embraced Mysia, Lydia, Phrygia, and Caria, with
Ephesus as its capital. In the New Testament, Asia always denotes the Roman province. To salute any one in the Lord is
to salute him as a Christian. The salutations were, "God be
with and bless you." It seems that the writing of this letter
was discussed in his meeting with the churches wherever he
was and they desired that their greetings should be sent to the
Corinthian church.

in the Lord, with the church that is in their house. 20 All the brethren
salute you. Salute one another with a holy kiss.

Aquila and Prisca salute you much in the Lord,—Aquila
and Prisca were born in Pontus, lived in Rome for a time, but
were compelled to leave that city when Emperor Claudius
commanded all its Jewish inhabitants to depart. He removed
to Corinth, where he worked at his craft of tentmaking. Paul,
who was of the same occupation, lodged with them, and
formed strong attachments to them. They were his fellow
passengers from Corinth as far as Ephesus, on his way to
Syria. At Ephesus they met Apollos, "and expounded unto
him the way of God more accurately." (Acts 18: 1-4, 18, 19,
26.) Now they have a church meeting in their house. Soon
after this they are in Rome again where they also have a
church in their house. Paul calls them his "fellow-workers in
Christ Jesus, who for my life laid down their own necks; unto
whom not only I give thanks, but also all the churches of the
Gentiles." (Rom. 16: 3-5.) They had rendered great service
in spreading the gospel among the Gentiles.

with the church that is in their house.—They, as old laborers at Corinth, with the church in their house, join in sending
salutations of love to the Corinthian brethren.

20 All the brethren salute you.—All the Christians with
whom Paul was connected in Ephesus. They felt deep interest in the Christians at Corinth, and sent to them Christian
salutations.

Salute one another with a holy kiss.—Some regard this as
ordaining a manner of salutation that was to be perpetual and
universal among the disciples; but no ordinance of God was
so treated. All the commands and ordinances were commanded by Jesus Christ, repeated by the apostles, and recorded in his life and teachings as part of his work; not left
simply to the salutations and greetings at the close of the
epistles to the churches. Take baptism: it was introduced by
John, approved by Jesus during his personal ministry, commanded in the commission (Matt. 28: 19; Mark 16: 16), and
in the first sermon by the Holy Spirit on Pentecost, is constantly presented in Acts of Apostles, then through the epis-

21 The salutation of me Paul with mine own hand. 22 If any man loveth
not the Lord, let him be anathema. ¹Maranatha. 23 The grace of the Lord

¹That is, O (or Our) Lord, come!

---

tles to the churches. Or, take the Lord's Supper: it was solemnly instituted by Jesus, with the command to the disciples
to do it in remembrance of him. Then the Holy Spirit presents it (Acts 2: 42); it is observed by the disciples, with
apostolic approval (Acts 20: 7); then it was commanded, in
the main body of the epistles, to be observed by the disciples.
On the other hand, Jesus did not practice or command kissing,
so far as recorded. We have no example of the apostles practicing it. It is mentioned only when the apostles were sending salutations to others, being thereby reminded of their
method of salutation. If it was intended as an ordinance of
God, I do not see why it was treated so differently from his
other ordinances and commands.

21 **The salutation of me Paul with mine own hand.**—Some
one wrote the body of the epistle for the apostle, but this closing salutation was done by his own hand, which was an en-
dorsement of the epistle as his own.

22 **If any man loveth not the Lord, let him be anathema.**—
The refusal to love Christ on the part of a professed Christian
deserves anathema, "for this is the love of God, that we keep
his commandments." (1 John 5: 3.) [The word anathema
solemnly pronounces that which the Lord at his coming will
confirm and ratify. This sentence is a stern epitome of the
whole epistle: If any one by profligacy, by contentiousness, by
covetousness, by idolatry, by arrogance, by heresy, evinces an
utter lack of the love of the Lord Jesus Christ, he must abide
the consequences of his moral status—there is no outlook in
the future for such a man, he "shall suffer punishment, even
eternal destruction from the face of the Lord and from the
glory of his might" (2 Thess. 1: 9), hence the words that follow.]

Maranatha.—[This is an Aramaic expression on which
scholars are not agreed as to whether it means "the Lord has
come," or "our Lord has come," or "our Lord cometh," or
"our Lord, come." With "our Lord cometh" compare James

Jesus Christ be with you. 24 My love be with you all in Christ Jesus. Amen.

5: 8; Rev. 1: 7; 3: 11; and this agrees with the context and the substance of the epistle. If this be right, the saying is admonitory. It warns them that at any moment they may have to answer for their shortcomings. Why this warning is given in Aramaic rather than in Greek is unknown.]

23 **The grace of the Lord Jesus Christ be with you.**—[Paul calmly passes to the closing prayer that the grace of Christ should abide with them. The risen Christ is the source of all spiritual blessings. (2 Cor. 12: 9.) The prayer is for the ever-abiding intercourse, which is the strongest possible contrast to the utter rejection implied in the anathema, and the anticipation by faith of the coming of the Lord. It is the grace of Jesus Christ, inasmuch as the love of God becomes an actual gift to man through Christ.]

24 **My love be with you all in Christ Jesus.**—He assures them of the continuance of his love towards them. [Though he had much occasion to rebuke, and even threaten, he sends his love to all, even to those who caused division, who called themselves by the names of men, who had abetted the fornicator, and who had denied the resurrection. They had none of them sinned so far as to be out of reach of the love of God, and so he sends to them his love. His love would be the love of one who had them ever in his heart, his prayers, and his sympathy. This is a suitable conclusion to an epistle containing so much reproof and ending with so tremendous a curse. For every word had been prompted by genuine love for every one of them. Thus Paul himself is an example of that which he prescribes for others (verse 14). His affection goes out after, and rests upon, and remains with, all of them. It is well to note that the epistle begins and ends with Jesus Christ.]

Amen.—[So be it, may it be as has been asked, said, promised, or threatened. (Deut. 27: 15-26; 2 Cor. 1: 20.) To render it more emphatic, it is sometimes repeated. (Num. 5: 22.) Jesus begins many of his sayings with this word, which is then translated "verily." This idiom is peculiar to him. The proper signification of it here is to confirm the words of this epistle and invoke the fulfillment of them.]

.

INDEX TO SUBJECTS

Fear and trembling, Paul was in, in Corinth, 39.

Feast, keep the, not with the old leaven, 77.

Fellowship, the, with Christ means partnership with him, 24; loss of, involves loss of recognition among Christians, 73; exclusion from the, is a serious matter, 75.

Fellow workers, we are God's, 49.

Filth, the apostles made as the, of the world, 67.

Fire, the, shall prove each man's work, 51; saved, yet through, 52.

First day of the week, 249.

First fruits, the, is regarded as the pledge of the rest, 230; Christ the, then they that are Christ's at his coming, 231.

Five hundred, the appearance to the, 223.

Five words, as the object of public worship is edification, understood is worth more than ten thousand not understood, 209.

Flesh, what is meant by the destruction of the? 75.

Flock, any man that feeds a, is entitled to the milk of the, 129.

Foolishness, the, of preaching, 32.

Fools, we are, for Christ's sake, 64.

Fornication, there is, among you as is not among the Gentiles, 71; the difference between, and adultery, 86; the body is not for, 90; takes the body as a whole and makes it an instrument of sin, 93; neither commit, 148.

Fornicators, keep no company with, 78.

Fortitude, true Christian, 199.

Fortunatus, 257.

Foundation, Paul aid the, of the church at Corinth, 50.

Freedman, the Lord's, is one set free from sin, 107.

Fullgrown, the, are those advanced in the Christian life, 40.

Future state, if there is no, why subject ourselves to trials and privations here? 236.

G

Gallio, Paul dragged before, **13**.

Gathered together, ye being, 74.

Gentiles, the, were not willing to obey God, and God left them without law, 136.

Gift, the, was so freely bestowed that they came behind in none, 23.

Gifts, the, he thanked God for, 22; spiritual, 179; diversity of, 180; the greater, 194; reasons why the, of the Spirit are not now imparted, 201; desire spiritual, 204; without interpretation are good for nothing, 207.

Give, each member is to, as he is prospered, 250.

Glory, let no man, in men, 57; all that Christians do should be to the, of God, 160.

Glorify, to, God is to exalt and honor him, 94.

Glorying, man has no room for, in himself, 37.

God, what is it to know? 32; the weakness of, stronger than men, 34; requires man to work through means unfitted to the end to be accomplished, 35; to love, is to so honor and serve him as to seek his will and to do it, 119; the one, 121; eating meat is not service to, 122; gives law to those willing to obey him, 135; all things are of, 167.

God's building, ye are, 50.

Gods, among the heathen there were many, 120.

Gospel, what is it to preach the, 30; the mighty effects of the, when first proclaimed are only slightly appreciated, 104; fundamentals of the, which Paul preached, 220.

Grace, the grace of the Lord be with you, 261.

Grecian games, enforcement of the duty of self-denial by reference to, 137.

H

Hair, long, is a glory of a woman, 168; nature teaches that it is a shame for man to have long, 168.

Harlot, when one who is a member of the body of Christ commits fornication, he makes the body of Christ one with a, 91.

Head, the, of the man is Christ, 162; the, of the woman is the man, 162; the, of the, of Christ is God, 163; woman must approach God with the tokens of her subjection on her, 164.

Helps, 193.

Holy Spirit, the body of the Christian a temple of the, 93; no man can say that Jesus is Lord but in the, 180.

Hope is not an end, 203.

Household, were there any infants in the, of Stephanas? 28.

Human, the folly of, leaders, 27; none could know or teach the will of God by, wisdom, 45.

Husband, let every woman have her own, 95; must render unto his wife her due, 95; that the, leave not the wife, 99; if the, be dead the widow is free to marry, 114.

Husbandry, ye are, 49.

I

Idolatrous sacrifice, meat sold in the market was wholly disassociated from the rites of, 159.

Idolatry, avoid, by fleeing from it, 153.

Idols, eating meats offered to, 117; all Christians know that, are nothing, 119.

Ill-prepared material tested by fire, 52.

Illustration, an apt, if rightly applied, 191.

Imitators, be, of me, 69.

Immorality, departures from the faith admits all types of, 72.

Immortalized, the fleshly mortal must be, 245.

In the name of the Lord, 74.

Incest, a case of, in the Corinthian church, 72.

Increase, God gave the, 49.

Infants, were any, baptized? 28.

Infidels, men become, by introducing their own opinions into the worship of God, 55.

Infidelity, many of the churches are infected with the spirit of modernistic, 217.

Inspired, those not, are not capable of determining whether the things taught by inspired men are of God, 43.

Instruction and learning, the conduct of the people under the law of God and his dealing with them were written for our, 143.

Intention, the, has everything to do with obedience to the command of God, 102.

J

James, the appearance to, 224.

Jeopardy, in, every hour, 235.

Jesus Christ, Paul's whole desire was to rivet the mind of the Corinthian church to the name of, 25; is the foundation of the church, 50; one, through whom are all things, 120; performs the same act of creating in the spiritual world he did in the material, 121; one Lord, 121; no man can say, is Lord but by the Holy Spirit, 180.

Jew, in what way did Paul become a, to the Jews? 134.

Judge, as the church they were to, those in the church, 80; how saints, the world? 82; the saints shall, angels, 83.

Judged, spiritually, 43.

Judgeth, he that, is the Lord, 61.

Judging, Paul had nothing to do with, those without, 79.

Judgment, Paul's, concerning virgins, 109.

K

Kindness, 197.

Kingdom, the, of God is not in word, 70; the unrighteous shall not inherit the, 86; Christ will deliver up the, to God, 232; Christ's kingdom will break down all rebellion against God, 234; fleshly, mortal bodies cannot inherit the immortal, 244.

Kiss, salute one another with a holy, 259.

Knowledge, the spiritual gifts that would bestow all, needful for sal-

is the duty of Christian parents to bring up their children in the, 115.

O

Occasion of writing the epistle, 15.

Opinion, the church must not be governed by viciated public, 76.

Opinions, two things are to be considered in all cases in the, and practices of others, 135.

Organ, every, set in the human body is vital and necessary; but the work of God ceases when the member God appointed is destroyed, 191.

Origin of the Corinthian church, 11.

Overthrown, as the Israelites were, in the wilderness, so are many who begin the Christian life, 147.

Ox, the, that treadeth out the corn shall not be muzzled, 130.

P

Part, that which is in, shall be done away, 200.

Parties, all grow out of the works of the flesh, 47; Paul and Apollos did not make the, 62; in the worship, 170.

Paul, why was, filled with fear and trembling at Corinth? 13, 39; dragged before Gallio, 13; I am of, 27, 47; was not elegant speaker, 38; false teachers were puffed up as though, would not come to them, 69; had seen Jesus after his resurrection, 126; did not use his right to a support, 131, 133; the appearance to, 224; and the other apostles preached the same gospel, 225.

Peace, the believer must make all efforts in his power to live in, 103.

Pentecost, I will tarry at Ephesus till, 253.

Perfection, that, was completed when the full revelation was made known, 200.

Persecutions, a holy life would bring on Christians, which the apostles endured, 68.

Peter, the appearance to, is nowhere mentioned in the Gsopels, but is implied, 223.

Pitiable, how of all men most? 229.

Place of writing the epistle to the Corinthians, 16.

Play, sat down to eat and drink and rose up to, 148.

Poor, giving goods to feed the, 196.

Praise, each man shall have, from God, 61.

Prayer, is impossible to join in prayer in an unknown tongue, 209.

Preach, the women are forbidden to, 216.

Pre-existent, Christ is represented as, 146.

Price, Christians bought with a, 94.

Privileges, the possession of great, is no safeguard, 143.

Procreative, the, age, 201.

Prophecies, 199.

Prophecy, to another, 184; the gift of, 184.

Prophesy, we, in part, 200; desire that you may, 204, 215.

Prophesies, he that, is greater than he that speaks in a tongue, 205; often lays bare the heart of the unbeliever, 122.

Prophesying is a sign to them that believe, 212.

Prophets, God set the, in the church, 193, 214; the spirit of the, subject to the prophets, 215.

Propitiatory, Christ's death was a, sacrifice, 221.

Prove himself, how can a man? 176.

Public opinion, a vitiated, 76.

Puffed up, I will know the power of them that are, 70; and ye are, 72; is not, 197.

Puffeth, knowledge, up, 118.

Purge out the old leaven, 76.

R

Raised, Christ was, from the dead, 222; if Christ was not, the apostles were false witnesses, 228; if Christ was not, there is no remission of sins, 228; if Christ be not, they that are fallen asleep have perished, 229; all will not be, at the same time, 231.